AFROCENTRIC
THOUGHT AND PRAXIS

AFROCENTRIC THOUGHT AND PRAXIS:

AN INTELLECTUAL HISTORY

CECIL CONTEEN GRAY

Africa World Press, Inc.

P.O. Box 1892　　　　　　　　　P.O. Box 48
Trenton, NJ 08607　　　　　　　Asmara, ERITREA

Africa World Press, Inc.

P.O. Box 1892
Trenton, NJ 08607

P.O. Box 48
Asmara, ERITREA

Cover design: Ashraful Haque
Book design: Wanjiku Ngugi

Library of Congress Cataloging-in-Publication Data

Gray, Cecil Conteen
    Afrocentric thought and praxis : an intellectual history / by Cecil Conteen Gray
    p. cm
    Includes bibliographical references and index
    ISBN 0-86543-825-0 --ISBN 0-86543-826-9 (pbk.)
    1. Afrocentrism. 2. Africa--History--Philosophy. 3. Blacks--Intellectual life. 4. Blacks--Race identity. I. Title.

DT4.G73 2000
909'.0496--dc21   99-059699

CONTENTS

ACKNOWLEDGMENTS

This document was prepared with the immeasurable assistance of THE AMON-AMUN-AMEN (The Hidden One)—The One Who Is and Who grants me Life; The Neters; my mother Victoria Jackson Gray Adams; my two fathers, Reuben E. Adams, Jr. and Tony W. Gray, Sr.; my wife Sonya Hunt, my sister Georgie Rosewitha Gray Henderson, my brothers Tony W. Gray, Jr. and Reuben E. Adams, III; Aunt Catherine Jackson, Uncle Glodies Jackson, Carolyn Preyor, Lillie Easton, LaNisha Shundale Perry, Hope Preyor, Keenan Preyor, Jartavis Easton, John Easton, and all of my Relatives; The Bennetts, The Rev. Jacquetta Parhams, The Rev. Ms. Thelma Price and Family, The Halls, Those of The University of Virginia—The MAAT-SANKOFA Group, Those of The Pennsylvania State University, Ms. Mary and Those of the Rites Of Pasage Shule Circle, The Circles of MAAFA-DAWN-MAAT,

Bishop Felton Edwin May—the one granted me time to do this work, Prof. Sonia Sanchez—my mentor, teacher, sister, and friend, Dr. Kariamu Welsh, Dr. Molefi Asante, Dr. Abu Abarry; all of my colleagues at Gettysburg College—and especially those who comprise the African and American Studies Advisory Council; Mitakuye Oyasin—"All My Relations of Every Kind," and the Ancestors, and the Beautiful Ones Coming.

Thank you all—for the opportunity, for your guidance, your caring, your presence, your vibes-prayers-chants-and-more. I have learned much and grown much. I hope I have extended to all of you some of the good that you have extended to me. I am grateful for and appreciative of The journey. I respect all of You. Dua (Thank You).

Finally, it is essential that I thank my editor—Mr. Damola Ifaturoti, and Mr. Kassahun Checole—the publisher, the one who considered this work worthy of publication and circulation. I thank you both for all of your consideration. I trust we will work together on other projects very soon.

PREFACE

The work in hand is a scholarly-and-practical history of Afrocentric thought *and* Afrocentric practice. This work attempts to do two things: (1)it attempts to offer a deeper understanding to those students, scholars, and people in local communities who have a basic understanding of Afrocentricity, yet desire more meticulous insight into, Afrocentric thought and praxis—its philosophical origins, its academic *and* practical possibilities; and (2)this work attempts to offer insight and assistance to students, scholars, and others who do not understand, or who misunderstand, or who lack empathy with Afrocentric thought and praxis.

Utilizing Africalogical method, this work examines the philosophical core of Afrocentric thought and praxis through the work of Molefi Asante, Maulana Karenga, and Kariamu Welsh. Thirteen major principles are extracted; and antecedent work of Aime Cesaire, Malcolm X, and Ayi Kwei Armah are assessed relative To the major principles. Assessment suggests their scholarship is important, anticipatory, pivotal, incipient Afrocentric work—pointing and leading to the necessary and welcome emergence of codified systematic, sophisticated Afrocentric thought and praxis.

This work was to be an offering explicating how the Afrocentric movement has come into being as a result of—and therefore should be linked to and should link itself to—The 1960s Civil Rights-Human Rights-Black Power-Black Arts Movement in the United States and The 1950s-1960s African Liberation Movement on the continent of Africa.

This work was to proceed from that point to explication of how The 1960s Movement has links to the Harlem and Chicago Renaissances in the United States of the 1920s-1940s and the Negritude Movement and other movements born in the Caribbean during the 1920s-1940s; and how those movements have links to African people's work during 1860s Reconstruction Period and the post-

Reconstruction Period from the 1875-1920s; and how those periods have links to African people's efforts to be free during the Enslavement Period; and how that period must be linked and examined with the long season when African people were free, self-defining, and self-determining, from humanity's birth in Africa, through the great ancient civilizations of Ethiopia-Nubia-Kemet/ Egypt, through the great free civilizations of Ghana, Mali, Monomotapa, and Songhai. This work wished to examine, analyze, and illustrate essential connections between important African movements, African persons and groups, African ideals, African ideas, and African documents—from continental Africa, the Caribbean and the Americas, the Middleast, Asia, Europe, and the South Pacific—from antiquity to the present. Of course, the aforementioned will be/is a monumental task and will result in a much larger text than the one in hand. This work, then, is not that offering; time did not allow it. At best, this work perhaps implies and begins to clear the path for the aforementioned tome to be written.

The work in hand is a scholarly-and-practical history of Afrocentric thought *and* Afrocentric practice. This work attempts to do two things: (1) it attempts to offer a deeper understanding to those students, scholars, and people in local communities who have a basic understanding of Afrocentricity, yet desire more meticulous insight into, Afrocentric thought and praxis—its philosophical origins, its academic *and* practical possibilities; (2) this work attempts to offer insight and assistance to students scholars, and others who do not understand, or who misunderstand, or who lack empathy with Afrocentric thought and praxis.

Utilizing Africalogical method, this work examines the philosophical core of Afrocentric thought and praxis through the work of Molefi Asante, Maulana Karenga, and Kariamu Welsh. Thirteen major principles are extracted; and antecedent work of Aime Cesaire, Malcolm X, and Ayi Kwei Armah are assessed relative to the major principles. Assessment suggests their scholarship is important, anticipatory, pivotal, incipient Afrocentric work—pointing and leading to the necessary and welcome emergence of codified systematic, sophisticated Afrocentric thought and praxis.

This work attempts (1) to offer a deeper understanding to those scholars and students who have a basic understanding of Afrocentricity and who desire a more meticulous insight into,

Afrocentric thought and praxis; and (2) to offer assistance to scholars and others who do not understand, or who misunderstand, or who lack empathy with Afrocentric thought and praxis. Utilizing Africalogical method, this work examines the philosophical core of Afrocentric thought and praxis through the work of Molefi Asante, Maulana Karenga, and Kariamu Welsh.

Thirteen major principles are extracted; and antecedent work of Cesaire, Malcolm X, and Ayi Kwei Armah are assessed relative to the major principles. Assessment suggests their scholarship is important, anticipatory, incipient Afrocentric work—pointing to the necessary and welcome emergence of codified systematic, sophisticated Afrocentric thought and praxis.

Chapter 1

INTRODUCTION

STATEMENT OF THE PROBLEM
In recent years, the Afrocentric project has been discussed and debated frequently, sometimes ferociously, within and beyond the Academy. Conceptually and philosophically, Afrocentricity has been applauded by some academicians and attacked by others.

Scholars, Molefi Asante, Barbara Sizemore, and Abu Abarry among them, seem to understand Afrocentricity and its positive intent. Such scholars support Afrocentricity's conception, growth, and constructive maturation.[1] Other scholars, Henry Louis Gates among them, seem to misunderstand the mission of Afrocentric thought and praxis, misinterpreting both content and intent.[2] Such misunderstanding and misinterpretation have resulted in some scholars, The University of Virginia's E. D. Hirsch and Columbia University's Diane Ravitch, for example, exerting substantial effort to discredit, divert, and/or deconstruct the good that Afrocentricity holds and heralds.[3] Indeed, it may be that some in the community of higher education are actually alarmed by the relatively recent emergence of the Afrocentric idea, coupled with its intrinsic power and meteoric rise.

PURPOSE
The purpose of this work is to set forth an intellectual history of Afrocentric thought and praxis, beginning with the writings of Aime Cesaire in 1939 through those of Molefi Asante and others in the 1990s.

First, this work will locate and anchor Afrocentricity historically, noting and discussing not only its birth and subsequent history, but also suggesting and discussing Afrocentricity's major defining contours and distinguishing characteristics. Further, this work will consider and critique contributions and expressions antecedent to Afrocentricity. As it concludes, this work will offer a vision of future forms of Afrocentric thought and praxis.

The significance of such a study is apparent when the significance of the Afrocentric project is considered. The Afrocentric project, or Afrocentric movement, has been a serious, recurring topic of discussion in the national press since 1988; and matters suggest that such reality will continue.[4] Therefore, an intellectual history is appropriate.

An *intellectual history of the sort presented here has not been attempted heretofore*. While similar studies are extant, their core concerns are different from this one. Consequently, this particular effort is fresh, evoking, it is hoped, substantial interest from within the academic community, and perhaps from among the broader community as well.

Further, this study is an Afrocentric effort. If this effort is successful, if and when similar discussions are attempted in the future, such discussions will have a precedent with which they will be measured and to which they will be accountable. Indeed this study will serve to check and/or challenge any similar efforts that are anti-African. If successful, this work can assist African people and the African intelligentsia in avoiding the disempowering reality of having to assume a defensive posture toward and having to *react* to hostile, hegemonic, non-African-based interpretations of African reality.

DEFINITIONS
To facilitate a clear understanding of this study's perspective and position, the following pivotal terms are defined:
- Afrocentric project
- Afrocentricity
- Afrocentric idea
- Afrocentric
- Africa centered
- Afrocentric thought and praxis
- Incipient Afrocentric thought and praxis
- Intellectual history

Specifically, the term "Afrocentric project/movement" refers to the various contributions of particular African American and African academicians from approximately 1980 to the present. It encompasses naming, defining, codifying, and disseminating an intellectual perspective and approach centered in and arising from the best of African people's history, culture, ideas, and ideals. The term "Afrocentric project" refers generally to the current efforts of many African people from various walks of life to place African people and African people's history-culture-and-well-being as the central concern and focus of all African people's lives.

The term "Afrocentricity" itself refers to Asante's broad, watershed, philosophical term:

> Afrocentricity is the belief in the centrality of Africans in post modern history. It is our history, our [unifying myths and values], our creative motif, and our ethos—s the same exemplify our collective will toward freedom and the humanizing of our own spirits, and the spirits of others.[5]

Asante notes further that Afrocentricity is a "critical perspective," consisting of "placing African ideals at the center of any analysis that involves African culture or behavior."[6]

Afrocentricity, then, can be understood as the pivotal referent term in this work. Essentially, all other words or phrases containing the root designation "Afrocentric" are derived from Afrocentricity; and all such words and phrases are best understood or clarified at any point by referencing the axis term"Afrocentricity."

The term "Afrocentric Idea" refers to an idea and a perspective which holds that African people can and should see study, interpret, and interact with people, life, and all reality from the vantage point of sane African people—rather than from the vantage point of European people, or Asian, or other non-African people, or from the vantage point of African people who are alienated from Africanness. The Afrocentric idea is explicated in detail in Asante's book by the same title.[7]

According to Asante, to "be Afrocentric is to place Africans and the interest of Africa at the center of our approach to problem solving."[8] Therefore, when utilizing the term "Afrocentric," this paper emphasizes the following: (1)being centered in or having a substantial understanding of the best—yet knowing the worst—aspects of classical African history and culture, especially of Kemet ("Land of the Black People"; known most popularly today as, "ancient Egypt"); and (2)moving in harmony with such understanding; making apparent, extensive, and constructive use of that understanding. Style, actions, attire, thought, analysis, research, written offerings, speech and oratorical offerings, various creative and artistic offerings, and so forth can be Afrocentric, or something other than Afrocentric.

C. T. Keto's term "Africa centered" has the same intent as the term "Afrocentric." While there is some nuanced variation in meaning for each, in this work, the terms are used interchangeably.[9]

The term "Afrocentric thought and praxis" refers to two related realities that sometime manifest as one reality. "Afrocentric thought" is used to refer to written offerings that are Afrocentric—for example, theory, history, poetry, prose, transcribed speeches and/or interviews, and more. "Afrocentric praxis" refers to thoughtful practical application of African-centered information, meeting the empirical and immediate needs of grassroots people and improving the quality of their lives; teaching, organizing, and empowering local and grassroots people for self-help projects; creating community-and-meta-community-based organizations which work to transform grassroots people's difficult lives into lives with purpose and promise. Other practical practices and actions also qualify as Afrocentric praxis.[10]

As implied above, Afrocentric thought and praxis sometimes proceed from the same source; and sometimes, a source offers only thought or only praxis. Ideally, offerings of Afrocentric thought and praxis are not antagonistic toward each other, nor do they compete with each other. At their best, such offerings and efforts are complementary and reinforcing.[11]

"Incipient Afrocentric thought and praxis" refers to thought and praxis that do not demonstrate all the major principles present in contributions that are classified as Afrocentric. Generally, incipient Afrocentric contributions lack the clarity, self-consciousness, and intentionality of Afrocentric contributions.[12]

In defining "intellectual history," first of all, it is necessary to set forth a number of presuppositions. (1)Ideas manifest within the minds of people as a result of life experiences, life observations, reading, dreams and related phenomena, and ultimately synthesis of and reflection upon all the preceding. (2) Individuals develop different or particular ideas. (3) People sometimes borrow and build upon ideas that pre-date and/or are contemporary with their own. (4) Some ideas can be infused with power and longevity. (5) Those particular ideas imbued with power and longevity influence and impact people, cultures, civilizations, and global society; such ideas demand historical, contextual, and content analysis.

Asante's idea of Afrocentricity—the Afrocentric idea—has anticipated, announced, inspired, and inspires various contributions of Afrocentric thought and praxis. Afrocentric thought and praxis must be linked to the Afrocentric idea. Clearly then, an intellectual history is appropriate and essential.

As intellectual history, this work intends to discuss the history, context, content, and intent of Afrocentric thought and praxis. In general, documents by particular Afrocentric scholars will be excavated, explicated, and critiqued.

As the first framer of the Afrocentric idea in its most crystallized form to date, Molefi Asante and his documents form the nucleus of this discussion. Some of Asante's peers and their documents are also discussed.[13] Interplay, direct as well as indirect, between particular personalities and documents is noted and discussed. Some of the professional exchange between contemporary proponents of Afrocentric thought and praxis is also noted and analyzed.

This intellectual history also attempts to identify, encircle, organize, and analyze some of the historical and historic human and conceptual antecedents contributing to the manifestation of Afrocentric thought and praxis. Finally, this intellectual history attempts to consider the future of Afrocentric thought and praxis.

REVIEW OF RELATED LITERATURE (DISSERTATIONS)

In researching previous works pertinent to this one, I have made an exhaustive manual search of the *Comprehensive Dissertation Index, 1861-1972*, Volumes 17, 18, 19, 20, 22, 28, and 32. I have also made an exhaustive, comprehensive computer search of the *UMI Dissertation Abstracts*, Compact Discs *1861-1980, 1981-1984, 1985-1988*, and *1989-1990*. The manual search considered all dissertations under the headings "anthropology," "education," "folklore," "history," "philosophy and religion," "psychology," and "sociology." The computer search consisted of looking at all dissertations, under every heading, utilizing any, some or all of the following terms: Afrocentric, Afrocentricity, Afrocentrism, Africentric, Africentricity, Africentrism, African-centered, and Africancenteredness.

Of course, the pertinence of the various dissertations' to this one varied. Some were and are quite pertinent, while others were and are less so.

One work appeared relatively pertinent in an inverted manner—a 1962 dissertation by Holm W. Neumann (Indiana University), entitled *The American Negro—His Origins and His Present Status as a Hybrid or Secondary Race*.[14] A number of works appeared somewhat pertinent peripherally; consider a 1967 dissertation entitled *The American Negro's Concept of Africa: A Study in the Ideology of Pride and Prejudice,* by Bernard Magubane (UCLA). Similarly, consider a 1970 work by Benson E. Penick (Kansas State University), *Knowledge of Black Culture as a Factor in Attitudes and Behaviours of Whites and Blacks*, and a 1970 work, *Two Views Of History: A Study Of The Relation Of European And African Culture*, by John J. Murungi (The Pennsylvania State University). Two other dissertations, both written in 1971, also appeared relatively pertinent in a peripheral manner: *Revival of Ideology: The Afro-American Society Movement*, by Ione Vargus (Brandeis University) and *Strategy for Teaching Afro-American Cultural Studies in the Humanities*, by Nathaniel Sims (University Of Massachusetts).[15]

A 1970 dissertation from Frederick W. Preston (The Ohio State University), entitled *Red, White, Black and Blue: The Concept of Race in American Sociology—An Exploration in the Sociology of Knowledge*,[16] was somewhat pertinent. While acknowledging the very important matter of the politics of knowledge indirectly, it dealt with the weighty matter of the sociology of knowledge directly.

Two documents from 1972 relate clearly to certain aspects of the work in hand. The concerns of William S. Sutton (Ohio University) in *The Evolution of the Black Studies Movement: With Spe-*

*cific Reference of The Establishment of the Black Studies Insti-
tute at Ohio State University* intersect noticeably with some of
the concerns in this work, i.e., intellectual evolution and certain
personalities from the 1960s. Further, in *Language and the Transformation of Consciousness: Foundations for a Hermeneutics
of Black Culture*, Lucius T. Outlaw (Boston College) traverses
some of the same terrain explored in this work, especially explication and critique of particular aspects of the Afrocentric idea.[17]

In the early 1980s, following the publication of and probably as
a relative outgrowth of Molefi Asante's 1980 book *Afrocentricity:
The Theory of Social Change*, along with Joseph A. Baldwin's
1980 manuscript *African (Black) Personality Theory: From an
Africentric Framework*, terms like "Afrocentric" and "Africentric"
began to appear in dissertations.[18]

In 1980, apparently having read Asante's work, Dorothy K.
Williamson (The Ohio State University) wrote *Rhetorical Analysis of Selected Modern Black American Spokespersons on the
Women's Liberation Movement*, utilizing Molefi Asante's
Afrocentric methodology for studying Black rhetors. Nineteen
eighty-two marked the first time the term "Afrocentric" appeared
within the title of a dissertation: *An Afrocentric View of the Rhetoric of Dick Gregory*; it was written by Ethel Patricia Harris. In
1983, Mark A. Fine's dissertation, *The Effects of World View on
Adaptatation to Single Parenthood,* concluded that holding an
Afrocentric belief system appeared to empower single mothers to
handle various stressors more successfully, enabling them to be
more fulfilled as mothers. Then in 1983, the term "Africentric"
appeared for the first time in a dissertation's title: *Traditional African Psychological Styles in Middle Income African-Americans:
An Africentric View of the Normal Black Personality as Measured by Rorschach Indices*; it was written by Garrett Laughton
Turke.[19]

Apparently, in 1984, 1985, and 1987, there were no dissertations
written dealing with the Afrocentric perspective. Two disserta-
tions written in 1986 utilized aspects of the Afrocentric perspective:
Ngwarsungu Chiwengo authored *Peter Abrahams in Perspective
(South Africa)*; and Pamela Joan Smith wrote *The Forest of the
Almighty: Being a Translation of D.O. Fagunwa's "Igbo
Olodumare" from Yoruba into English*.[20] Neither of the two

works, however, are pertinent to this book

Micheal Van Cubie's dissertation, *The Missing Link in the Afrocentric Model: Employment and the Role of the Black Father*, was written in 1988. It discussed the need for a model of psychopathology appropriate for African American people in general and the African American father in particular.[21] In 1989, aspects of Asante's "Afrocentric metatheory" were utilized by Janice Denise Hamlet in analyzing sermons in a dissertation entitled *Religious Discourse As Cultural Narrative: A Critical Analysis Of The Rhetoric Of African-American Sermons.* In that same year, Frenzella E. De Lancey fused Afrocentricity as explicated in Asante's *The Afrocentric Idea*, with womanism as explicated by Alice Walker in her 1983 book, *In Search of Our Mothers' Gardens.* In De Lancey's dissertation, entitled *Intertexuality and Willful Transformation as Narrative Strategies in African-American Women's Writing: From Whence the Imperative? (Jacobs, Hurston, Asante)*, "Afrocentric womanism" was posited as "activist praxis" and "a crucial part of the African American woman's experience." Also, in 1989, Ann Josephine Adams, utilizing an interdisciplinary approach in her dissertation *Sisters of the Light: The Importance of Spirituality in The Afra-American Novel*, stressed "the importance of spirituality...as defined by Afrocentric values and worldview."[22]

Finally, while a number of the aforementioned dissertations are related more or less peripherally to this writer's work, only one proved extremely pertinent: P. Oare Dozier's *The Politics Of Knowledge: Selected Black Critiques Of Western Education 1850-1933.* Written in 1985 at the University of Massachusetts, Dozier's document posits the following:

> . . . as an academic discipline, Black studies has as its historical antecedent more than a century of vigorous struggle for interpretive power and definitional control of the Black experience.[23]

Dozier holds that while Black students' demands for a relevant education during the middle and late 1960s "shook the foundations of the Academy," theirs was not the first serious offensive challenging white-controlled, Eurocentric education. Rather, the African American Studies movement was, and is, a kind of resurgence and extension of work by people like The Rev. Wilmot Blyden, Blyden's Ghanaian student Joseph E. Casely-Hayford, and Dr. Carter G. Woodson. Ultimately, Dozier argues, "Afrocentric Black Studies create a constant tension in the [West's educational] Academy due to inherent ideological differences."[24]

At its conclusion, it may be revealed that this work's analysis concurs in some way(s)—at least implicitly—with Dozier's position. Such possible or implicit concurrences, however, are not the foci of this study. Primarily, this work intersects with Dozier's in that it is concerned with determining philosophical and conceptual continuities-and-discontinuties between contemporary Afrocentric scholars' ideas and praxis, ideas and praxis of some of the scholars mentioned by Dozier, and ideas and praxis of other African people and scholars from the origins of humanity in Africa to the 1600s, and from the 1600s to the present.

NOTES

1. See articles by or that quote Afrocentricity's first framer, Molefi Kete Asante, such as Ellen K. Coughlin's "Scholars Work to Refine Africa-Centered View of the Life and History of Black Americans," *Chronicle of Higher Education*, 28 October 1987. Joseph A. Baldwin (professor and chairman of Psychology at Florida A & M University) and Dona Marimba Richards (professor of African Studies at Hunter College in New York City) are also quoted in the aforementioned article as supporters and developers of the Afrocentric perspective. Ronald Walters is also quoted in that same article; currently Walters is a professor of Political Science at the University of Maryland, and he utilizes an Afrocentric perspective in some of his work. Asante is also quoted in D. Rick Hancock's "African Studies Need to be Based on Afrocentric Viewpoints, Scholar Says to Black Studies Group," *Black Issues in Higher Education* (1 May 1988) and Stanley Bailey's "Afro-doctoral Program a Dream Come True," *Philadelphia Tribune*, 16 September 1988. Nilgun Okur, formally an assistant professor in the Department of African American Studies at Temple University is also quoted in the latter article as a supporter of the Afrocentric project. Barbara Sizemore, a University of Pittsburgh professor of Black Studies and former Superintendent of Washington, D.C. public schools, is sup-

portive implicitly, when she is quoted in Julie Johnson's "Curriculum Seeks to Lift Blacks' Self Image," *New York Times*, 8 March 1989. Maulana Karenga is also a staunch supporter and proponent of Afrocentric scholarship; such is articulated forthrightly in a 1 February 1990 letter from Dr. Karenga (Chairman, the Department of Black Studies, California State University, Long Beach) to Dr. Molefi Asante; the letter was prompted by a scholarly symposium celebrating the Twentieth Anniversary the *Journal of Black Studies* (of which Dr. Asante is editor). Franklyn G. Jenifer, former president of Howard University, is also supportive; see his "Afrocentricity Is No Cause For Alarm," *Washington Post*, 19 November 1990. Other supporters of the Afrocentric perspective include Cornell University's James Turner, Morehouse College's Charles Finch, M.D., Asa Hilliard III, Yosef ben-Jochannan, John Henrik Clarke, Jacob Carruthers, and others, all cited in Joye Mercer's "Nile Valley Scholars Bring New Light and Controversy to African Studies," *Black Issues in Higher Education* (28 February 1991): 1, 12-16. Julianne Malveaux is also implicitly supportive in her "Clash of Visions," *New Orleans Tribune*, June 1991. See also Molefi Asante's "Putting Africa at the Center," *Newsweek*, (23 September 1991), p. 46. Asante is also cited in other articles in the aforementioned issue of Newsweek—"African Dreams," "A Is for Ashanti, B Is for Black . . .," respectively. Jawanza Kunjufu a national African American educational consultant, is also supportive of the Afrocentric project; he is cited in the last noted *Newsweek* article. Also see the excellent rendering by Abu Shardow Abarry, ed., "Afrocentricity: Introduction," *Journal of Black Studies* (December 1990): 123-125.

2. See decided (and some relatively unwitting) opponents to Afrocentric thought and praxis. Consider comments by the late Nathan I. Huggins of Harvard University in *Chronicle of Higher Education*, an article cited at the beginning of the preceding "Note 1." In *New York Times* article cited in "Note 1," see subtly sophisticated oppositional statements by The University of Virginia's E. D. Hirsch, Jr. (author of best-selling books on [eurocentric] cultural literacy) and Yale University's James P. Comer (professor of Child Psychiatry). For indirect, implicit attacks on the Afrocentric perspective being utilized and taught in grade schools as well as graduate schools, see debilitating comments by The University of Virginia's Richard Rorty (professor of Humanities/Philosophy), Columbia University's Diane Ravitch (professor of Eduaction and History), and Elizabeth Coleman (president, Bennington College) in Joseph Berger's "Ibn Batuta and Sitar Challenging Columbus and Piano in Schools," *New York Times*, 12 April

1989. Also see a very telling, anti-Afrocentric curriculum and anti-authentic multicultural curriculum, full-page advertisement in *Chronicle of Higher Education*, 8 November 1989, p. A23; the ad's heading reads, "*IS THE CURRICULUM BIASED?* A Statement by the National Association of Scholars." Great misunderstanding and misinterpretation of the content and process of Afrocentric scholarship is evident in comments by Henry Louis Gates Jr. See the same in Adam Begley's "Henry Louis Gates Jr., Black Studies' New Star," *New York Times Magazine*, 1 April 1990; Gates' honest ignorance is perhaps most evident when he speaks of departments that embrace and utilize an Afrocentric perspective and method as "ghettoized programs where students and members of the faculty sit around and debate whether a white person can think a black thought." Diane Ravitch attacks and attempts to misrepresent, undercut, and deconstruct Afrocentric and multicultural education in her "Multiculturalism, E Pluribus Plures," *The American Scholar* (Summer 1990): 341-343, 337-354. Similarly, see John Leo's "A Fringe History of the World," *U.S. News & World Report*, 12 November 1990, pp. 25-26; also, Ravitch is cited in Leo's article. In the same vein, see Thomas Toch's "The Happening Department: Bush's Stellar Education Team," *U.S. News & World Report*, 22 April 1991, p. 22; Ravitch is also cited in Toch's article. Henry Louis Gates Jr. again indicates shallow understanding of—and therefore, essentially, that he does not understand—the content and intent of Afrocentric thought and praxis, in his "Beware of the New Pharaohs," *Newsweek*, 23 September 1991, p. 47.

3. Ibid.

4. See preceding Notes 1 and 2; also see Asante's response to Arthur Schlesinger in Asante's "The Painful Demise of Eurocentrism," *The World & I* (April 1992): 305-317.

5. Molefi Kete Asante, *Afrocentricity*, Revised ed. (Trenton, N.J.: Africa World Press, 1988), p. 6.

6. Molefi Kete Asante, *The Afrocentric Idea* (Philadelphia: Temple University Press, 1987), p. 6. Also, see page 125.

7. See *The Afrocentric Idea*. Give specific attention to the discussion on p. 125.

8. Ibid., p. 198.

9. The term "Africa centered" can be attributed to C. Tsehloane Keto, Deputy Vice-Chancellor and professor of History, Vista University, Pretoria, South Africa. Keto uses the term in his *The Africa Centered Perspective Of History* (Blackwood, N.J.: K. A. Publications, 1989): see p. 51. I first heard "Africa(n) centered" used at Temple University

in Philadelphia, between 1988 and 1989. The terms grow out of "Afrocentric." They vary slightly in meaning, however. In general, each is concerned with African people relating to all reality as self-aware, self-affirming, sane African people.

10. I first framed, defined, and began discussing "Afrocentric thought and praxis" and "incipient Afrocentric thought and praxis" in autumn 1988, in a paper entitled, "Afrocentric Thought and Praxis in the United States of America: A Brief Historical Survey of Major (Male) Contributions, A Projection of Future Directions and Promise," submitted for Department of African American Studies' course "Pro-Seminar in Graduate Studies in African American Studies," Temple University, 13 December 1988.

11. Ibid.

12. Ibid.

13. Asante authored the seminal *Afrocentricity: The Theory of Social Change* in 1980. Since then, he and a number of other scholars— Kariamu Welsh, Wade Nobles, Maulana Karenga, Dona Richards, Na'im Akbar, and others—have become identified as the primary proponents of Afrocentric scholarship.

14. See Holm Wolfram Neumann, "The American Negro—His Origins and His Present Status as a Hybrid or Secondary Race" (Ph.D. dissertation, Indiana University, 1962), *Dissertation Abstracts International* (23/06, p. 1871), *62*, 05066.

15. Bernard Magubane, "The American Negro's Conception of Africa: A Study in the Ideology of Pride and Prejudice" (Ph.D. dissertation, University of California, Los Angeles, 1967), *Dissertation Abstracts International* (28/02-A, p.818), *67*, 09655; Benson Ellsworth Penick, "Knowledge of Black Culture as a Factor in Attitudes and Behaviours of Whites and Blacks" (Ph.D. dissertation, Kansas State University, 1970), *Dissertation Abstracts International* (31/08-A, p. 4266), *71*, 04444; John Justo Murungi, "Two Views of History: A Study of the Relation of European and African Culture" (Ph.D. dissertation, The Pennsylvania State University, 1970), *Dissertation Abstracts International* (32/02-A, p. 1020), 71, 21780; Ione Dugger Vargus, "Revival of the Afro-American Society Movement" (Ph.D. dissertation, Brandeis University, Florence Heller Graduate School, 1971), *Dissertation Abstracts International* (32/03-A, p. 1664), 71, 22697; Nathaniel Sims, "Strategy For Teaching Afro-American Cultural Studies In The Humanities" (Ph.D. dissertation, University of Massachusetts, 1971), A.D.D., Publication No.: AAC023946.

16. Frederick William Preston, "Red, White, Black And Blue: The Concept of Race in American Sociology—An Exploration in the Sociol-

ogy of Knowledge" (Ph.D. dissertation, The Ohio State University, 1970), *Dissertation Abstracts International* (31/09-A, p. 4923), 71, 07541.

17. William Stanley Sutton, "The Evolution of the Black Studies Movement: With Specific Reference to the Establishment of the Black Studies Institute at The Ohio State University" (Ph.D. dissertation, Ohio University, 1972), *Dissertation Abstracts International* (33/04-A, p. 1451), 72, 26375; Lucius Turner Outlaw, "Language and the Transformation of Consciousness: Foundations for a Hermeneutics of Black Culture" (Ph.D. dissertation, Boston College, 1972), Dissertation Abstracts International (33/03-A, p.1199), 72, 24053. 20

18. Molefi Kete Asante, *Afrocentricity: The Theory of Social Change* (Washington, D.C. and Buffalo, NY: FAS Printing and Amulefi Publishing, 1980); Joseph Baldwin, *Afrikan (Black) Personality: From an Africentric Framework* (Tallahassee, Fla.: By the Author, Department of Psychology, Florida A & M University, 1980). See also Joseph A. Baldwin/Kobi K. K. Kambon, *African/Black Psychology in the American Context: An African-Centered Approach* (Tallahassee, Fla.: Nubian Nation Publications, 1998); this document is the book which resulted from the preceding historic manuscript.

19. Dorothy Kay Williamson, "Rhetorical Analysis of Selected Modern Black American Spokespersons on the Women's Liberation Movement" (Ph.D. dissertation, The Ohio State University, 1980), *Dissertation Abstracts International* (on compact disc) (41/07A, p. 3299), Publication No.: AAC8100283; Ethel Patricia Harris, "An Afrocentric View of the Rhetoric of Dick Gregory" (Ph.D. dissertation, The Ohio State University, 1982), *Dissertation Abstracts International* (on compact disc) (43/llA, p. 3455), Publication No.: AAC8305337; Mark Allen Fine, "The Effects Of Worldview On Adaptation To Single Parenthood" (Ph.D. dissertation, The Ohio State University, 1983), *Dissertation Abstracts International* (compact disc) (44/04B, p. 1235), Publication No.: AAC8318355; Garrett Laughton Turke, "Traditional African Psychological Styles in Middle Income African-Americans: An Africentric View of the Normal Black Personality as Measured by Rorschach Indices" (Ph.D. dissertation, University of Detroit, 1983), *Dissertation Abstracts International* (on compact disc) (44/09B, p. 2909), Publication No.: AAC8329119.

20. Ngwarsungu Chiwengo, "Peter Abrahams in Perspective (South Africa)" (Ph.D. dissertation, State University of New York at Buffalo, 1986), (0656); Pamela Joan Smith, "The Forest Of The Almighty: Being a Translation of D.O. Fagunwa's 'Igbo Olodumare' From Yoruba into

English" (Ph.D. dissertation, University of Washington, 1986), (0250).

21. Michael Van Cubie, "The Missing Link in the Afrocentric Model: Employment and the Role of the Black Father" (Ph.D. dissertation, The Wright Institute, 1988), *Dissertation Abstracts International* (on compact disc) (49/06B, p. 2373), Publication No.: AAC8807261.

22. Janice Denise Hamlet, "Religious Discourse as Cultural Narrative: A Critical Analysis of the Rhetoric of African-American Sermons" (Ph.D. dissertation, The Ohio State University, 1982), *Dissertation Abstracts International* (on compact disc) (51/OlA, p. 20), Publication No.: AAC9014431; Frenzella Elaine De Lancey, "Intertexuality and Willful Transformation as Narrative Strategies in African-American Women's Writing: From Whence the Imperative? (Jacobs, Hurston, Asante)" (Ph.D. dissertation, Temple University, 1989), *Dissertation Abstracts International* (on compact disc) (50/bA, p. 3226), Publication No.: AAC9007345; Ann Josephine Adams, "Sisters of the Light: The Importance of Spirituality in the Afra-American Novel" (Ph.D. dissertation, Indiana State University, 1989), *Dissertation Abstracts International* (on compact disc) (50/12A, p. 3948), Publication No.: AAC9012147.

23. In P. Oare Dozier, "The Politics of Knowledge: Selected Critiques of Western Education" (Ph.D. dissertation, University of Massachusetts, 1985), *Dissertation Abstracts International* (on compact disc) (46/03A, p. 633), Publication No.: AAC8509541.

24. Ibid.

Chapter 2

FOUNDATIONAL FRAMING

METHOD

This work utilizes Afrocentric method, one concerned with the cultivation of *harmony*.[1] As an orientation to data, this method is concerned with issues necessary to achieve human harmony.

According to Asante in *Kemet, Afrocentricity, and Knowledge*, Afrocentric method involves examination of phenomena utilizing one of "three knowledge areas": cultural/aesthetic, social/behavioral, or policy issues. As an intellectual history concerned with Afrocentric thought and praxis, this work deals with history, philosophy, and literature. It follows, then, that this text utilizes the cultural/aesthetic knowledge area.[2]

Afrocentric method involves determining which of the "seven general subject fields"—i.e., communication, history, culture, sociology, psychology, politics, or economics—holds one's chosen research concern. The research concern of this text, an intellectual history dealing with Afrocentric thought and praxis, is held within the fields of history, culture, communication, and politics.[3]

In assembling this text, there were seven goals:

1. to locate the idea of Afrocentricity historically;
2. to define Afrocentricity;
3. to determine Afrocentricity's major distinguishing principles;
4. to reflect on African history prior to the emergence of Afrocentricity and examine contributions antecedent to Afrocentricity;
5. to critique the said antecedent works, determining to what extent they are incipient Afrocentric offerings;
6. to demonstrate that Afrocentricity as well as its incipient ante-

cedents are equalizing, sane, legitimate contributions to the academy and the larger society;

7. to bring harmony to the relatively cacaphonous debate raging within the United States' higher and secondary educational systems.

The procedure utilized to gather data in an attempt to realize the seven preceding objectives is set forth below.

First—since the birth of Afrocentricity is precisely dated, citing the historic document by Molefi Asante—pertinent, contemporary documents by Molefi Asante and others, along with specific organizations central to the Afrocentric project are identified and discussed. Various definitions that the various sources set forth for Afrocentricity are noted. When excavating the said documents— context, audience, dominant themes, and styles of argumentation are also noted. When considering organizations—context, focus, and form of activity are noted as well.

In editing and refining the above, the principal characteristics of Afrocentric thought and praxis are drawn out. Once the major characteristics or principles are determined, they are used as a guiding analytical template or grid.

Then, using the established grid, three categories of antecedents to Afrocentric thought and praxis are excavated and discussed. Literary, political/activist, and academic/intellectual antecedents are considered; and explication is set forth as to how they might be understood as incipient Afrocentric offerings. In each category, there is analysis of one particular scholar's or one particular thinker-practitioner's thinking—or that scholar's or that thinker-practitioner's thinking *and* praxis. In some instances, analysis involves emphasizing a single work by one scholar or thinker-practitioner. In other instances, there is emphasis is on two or more works by the same scholar or the same thinker-practitioner.

The procedure for gathering data related to the antecedents involved: (1) identifying books, interviews, or speeches relevant to this study, (2) ascertaining the dates of those sources, and (3) examining the works within the parameters of the aforementioned grid. Speeches, novels, research writings, essays, and expository works by Aime Cesaire, Malcolm X, and Ayi Kwei Armah was utilized. The chosen works date from 1939-1979.

The works selected were limited because of time and space constraints; otherwise, works by Maria Stewart, Martin Delany, and Drusilla Dunjee Houston would have been included. Once the constraints were faced and adjustments made, works were chosen utilizing the following criteria and values: (1) it was imperative that the body of work to be examined include, at the very least, work by a continental African, work by an African from the Caribbean, and work by an African from the United States; (2) the body of work to be examined must span a reasonable length of time, i.e., no more that fifty years preceding Afrocentricity's appearance in 1980; and (3) the number of documents must be limited, so that this work is of reasonable, readable length. There was no hierarchical order to the four preceding criteria.

In addition to examining the antecedent documents via the aforementioned grid, the approach to each document encompassed two research questions: (1) What is the author's cosmological, axiological,[4] ontological, and telelogical orientation? (2) Does the document seek to establish authentic harmony among African people and others?

Along with the Afrocentric method, this study also employs historical-comparative analysis.[5] Tacitly, my method (and this entire project) is characterized and informed by introspection, retrospection, particular inquiry, and general inquiry.[6] All are integrated wholistically.

CHAPTER OUTLINES

A comprehensive outline of this work's chapters can be found in the "Preface." The outline of chapters in this section will commence with Chapter Three.

Chapter Three, "Afrocentricity: History, Definition, Scope," establishes most of this work's foundation. A history of Afrocentricity is set forth, beginning with Molefi Kete Asante and his seminal 1980 document *Afrocentricity: The Theory of Social Change.* His subsequent Afrocentric works are also examined. Important books by Kariamu Welsh-Asante and Maulana Karenga are also noted and examined. Afrocentricity is defined. Finally, the scope— the breadth, flexibility, and applicability—of Afrocentricity is discussed, particularly its influence within historical and important African organizations.

Chapter Four, "Major Principles," builds on Chapter Three, positing the primary pivotal principles of Afrocentric thought and praxis. Drawing meticulously from the documents examined in the preceding chapter, Chapter Four encircles or frames, names/identifies, and discusses in depth the major characteristics distinguishing Afrocentric thought and praxis.

Chapter Five, "Antecedents to Afrocentric Thought and Praxis," analyzes academic-intellectual, political-activist, and literary antecedents to Afrocentric thought and praxis by examining works of Cesaire, Malcolm X, and Armah, respectively.

Chapter Six, "Conclusion Summary and Commentary: In the Way," consists of a brief recapitulation of the five preceding chapters. It also contains commentary on the teachings and implications of this study and anticipatory commentary on the future of Afrocentric thought and praxis.

NOTES

1. See Molefi Kete Asante, *Kemet, Afrocentricity And Knowledge* (Trenton: Africa World Press, 1990), p. 26.
2. Ibid., pp. 18-23, 19-20.
3. Ibid., 12-14.
4. Ibid., pp. 8-10, 11, 8-12.
5. See Earl Babbie, *The Practice of Social Research*, 4th ed. (Belmont, Calif.: Wadsworth Publishing, 1986), pp. 290-295.
6. Asante, *Kemet*, pp. 27, 37-38.

Chapter 3

AFROCENTRICITY:
HISTORY, DEFINITION, SCOPE

The development of the *concept* of "Afrocentricity" must be attributed to Molefi Kete Asante. He introduces the concept in his 1980 text—*Afrocentricity: The Theory of Social Change*. In that concise but powerful work, Asante begins articulating, delineating, and defining a distinctive philosophy. That work, *Afrocentricity*, is the first document in modern history attempting intentional, explicit formulation of an African Centered approach to thinking, learning, living, and building. Indeed, twenty-one years after its initial publication, the document is still one of the most significant texts realizing systematic conceptualization of Afrocentric theory. Inarguably, the document serves as a historical marker in any discussion of Afrocentric theory and praxis.

In 1972, eight years prior to Asante's setting forth *Afrocentricity*, the beloved elder African American scholar John Henrik Clarke utilizes the term "Afro-centric." In an introduction to J. A. Rogers' *World's Great Men of Color, Volume II*, Clarke writes the following:

> There is now an international struggle on the part of people of African descent against racism and for a more honest look at their history. On university campuses and in international conferences they are demanding that their history be looked at from a [B]lack perspective or from an *Afro-centric* point of view. This has taken the struggle against racism to the world's intellectual centers, where the theoretical basis of racism started. This struggle has brought to us where we are now, standing on the "black and beautiful" plateau. From this position, [B]lack people will go into an-

other stage, much higher and more meaningful for [human]kind. After reclaiming their own humanity, I think [Black people] will make a contribution toward the reclamation of the history of [all humanity].[1] (emphasis mine)

Clarke's usage of "Afro-centric" has to do with historical perspective from an African vantage point, but it is not indicative of a total African-centered philosophy. It is also noteworthy that in the spring of 1995, at the African Heritage Studies Association's 27th Annual Conference, according to Asante, Clarke said, "There is no such thing as "Afro-centric."[2] That remark suggests there is only the slightest connection between Clarke's usage of the word "Afro-centric" in 1972 and Asante's work on the broad philosophy of "Afrocentricity" from 1980 to the present.

Five years prior to the publication of Asante's *Afrocentricity*, the term "Afrocentric" is used by the renowned Nigerian writer and social analyst Chinweizu. In 1975, in what was then the last chapter of his popular work, *The West and the Rest of Us: White Predators, Black Slaves, and the African Elite*, Chinweizu writes the following:

> One of the most devastating legacies of our satellization to the West is that our culture has become eccentric. Instead of being *Afrocentric* in our thoughts and actions, we [continental Africans] are Eurocentric.[3] (emphasis mine)

For four pages, Chinweizu continues to note how African people "have lost our ability to define ourselves,"[4] "[have] lost a clear and detailed sense of our identity [and have] lost our ability to create a point of view of the world strictly our own."[5] Finally, toward rectification of such debilitating realities, Chinweizu writes:

> That we must rapidly develop a strong *Afrocentric* view of the world and of ourselves should be obvious. We must approach all problems and issues from the viewpoint of our own interests. . . .[We] must work to liberate Africa, to create a liberated African culture, to foster a new global order within which we can stay liberated.[6] (emphasis mine)

All of the preceding is related to Asante's *Afrocentricity*. Similar to Clark's usage of "Afro-centric," however, Chinweizu's "Afrocentric" is a consciousness but not the substantive, meaningful philosophy of Asante's coherent rendering.

In 1978, two years prior to Asante's *Afrocentricity*, a brilliant African American philosopher writes an article outlining what is needed "for the deliberate development of a [B]lack cultural enlightenment." In the *Journal of the American Academy of Religion*, in an article entitled "Black Enlightenment: The Issues of Pluralism, Priorities and Empirical Correlation," Roy D. Morrison II, Ph.D. (University of Chicago, 1972), writes the following:

> [The] term [Black cultural enlightenment] is used to denote a state of psychological/intellectual freedom. The enlightened individual is free from internal guilt and emotional factors that restrain intellectual integrity. He or she is also free from external compulsion in the form of imported or donated categories and dishonest approaches to reality.
>
> If [B]lacks do not have their own indigenous instrumentalities for critical and constructive thought, they will remain victims of cultural and academic imperialisms inflicted by the majority culture.[7]

Morrison notes correctly, "authority and control lie with those who shape the categories by which men [and women] think." He also asserts astutely, "[B]lack enlightenment must not merely be against something; it must be for something. It must not exhaust itself in the battle with [white] racism; it must transcend that conflict and celebrate the fulfillment of [B]lack culture."[8]

Though Morrison does not utilize "Afro(-)centric," nor "Afrocentricity," nor any similar term etymologically, he seems to anticipate much of the infrastructure of Asante's seminal *Afrocentricity*.

In summary, the aforementioned works by Clarke, Chinweizu, and Morrison all relate to Asante's *Afrocentricity*. It is only Asante, however, who self-consciously sets forth a term, self-consciously defines the term, and self-consciously begins building a practical, far-reaching, functional, *usable theoretical, philosophical system*. It is also important to note that as early as 1969, while working as director of the Center for Afro-American Studies at UCLA, he was working at crystallizing Afrocentricity in an article titled, "Black Studies from a Black Perspective."[9]

Afrocentricity is published in 1980. The context of the times is that of portentous—if not ominous—transition. The African community in the United States of America is four years past the country's hypocritical, hypnotizing bicentennial. In 1980, African people in the United States are in the final year of some semblance of collective societal opportunity—as the measured liberal, Jimmy Carter, is to be replaced by the smiling ultraconservative, Ronald Reagan.

In 1980, in general, the African American intelligentsia seem to be in a rather befuddled lull. Understandably, many of the most courageous, risk-taking thinkers and scholars are necessarily pausing anxiously, to protect whatever physical and psychological health they still possess. Many other African American academicians and thinkers seem uncertain: Is the Black Power/Arts/Studies Movement really over? Are African people free enough—or at least as free as situationally possible? In the late 1960s through the early 1970s, was sufficient attention given to our being African people with many continuing connections to Africa—or is more attention and research called for?[10]

Into such a groping, somewhat nebulous, waiting period comes *Afrocentricity: The Theory of Social Change*. It is written to a waiting African community in the United States. In addition, the book is written for African people residing in all remaining quarters of the physical diaspora, for those residing on our home continent, and for all African people everywhere flailing in the psychological diaspora.

From commencement to conclusion, it is clear the book's primary audience is African people. Consider the following excerpts from various parts of the work:

> [Kariamu Welsh, writing the book's 'Foreword,' says,] The need for an Afrocentric philosophy is so great that it is impossible for me not to insist on every [B]lack person reading this book. [Molefi Asante explicates,] Afrocentricity... incorporate[s] . . . Pan-African examples. However, the book emerges from the experiences of African

> Americans and, therefore, finds most of its examples from
> that history. Our collective will secures the victory that we
> reach with our historical and cultural facts. . . . When you
> sit in classes and listen to lecturers speak of Keats, Yeats,
> Twain . . . you
> had better be able to call upon Baraka, Shange, Welsh . . .
> Ngugi. . . .
> Our anteriority is only significant because it re-affirms
> for us that if we once organized complex civilizations all
> over the continent of Africa, we can take those traditions
> and generate more advanced ideas.[11]

Clearly, the book is written for a Pan-African audience. Further, it is written especially for Africans seeking usable truth, that is, correct information that can be utilized in the work of transforming negative life situations into positive life realities. Finally, *Afrocentricity* speaks to every person, African as well as non-African, sincerely interested in encountering people-freeing, people-empowering, world-rectifying truth.

"The holding, reconstructing, and perpetual proficient development of African culture" can be understood as the core, omnipresent theme of *Afrocentricity*. Indeed, that theme so permeates the document, it cannot be isolated, extracted, and discussed with precision. It does appear, however, that there are at least four primary themes that can be distinguished and discussed. Arising out of and always tethered to the work's core omnipresent theme, the following particular-and-overlapping themes are posited:

•*Njia*
•*The Way of Heru*
•*Harmosis*
•*Manifesting Afrocentric Action Wholistically*

Njia is a theme that at once announces itself and begins being explicated right from the document's beginning. Indeed, the term is set forth in the first sentence of Chapter One. As philosophical concept and family/community practice, Njia is discussed near the conclusion of Chapter One; and it is referenced intermittently throughout the text. Finally, as a particular set of life-guiding, life-empowering affirmations and admonishments, Njia is set forth in ten different affirmational "Quarters," found on twelve of the document's eighteen closing pages.[12]

In discussing Njia, Asante writes:

> This book offers . . . a testament of Njia, the ideology of victorious thought. Njia [a Kiswhali word meaning "The Way"] is the collective expression of the Afrocentric worldview which is grounded in the historical experience of African people. . . Njia represents the inspired   Afrocentric spirit found in the traditions of African-Americans, and the spiritual survival of an African essence in America. . . . When we use Njia for our lives, we become essentially ruled by our own values and principles. Dispensing with alien views allows us to place Njia at our own center.
>
> . . . When Njia is accepted, all things seem new, old things no longer please or seem adequate. . . . A practice of Njia with the *Teachings of Njia* constitutes the beginning of reconstruction. ... It is necessary for the Afrocentric person to practice Njia for creative perfection. . . .[13] (emphasis his)

Njia is a sophisticated word symbol. It holds multiple meanings, and it can oscillate. Njia represents any one of, or various combinations of, the following: a word, a concept, a ritual, a document, a way of living as prescribed by a particular set of tenets. Regardless of what it means or represents at any moment, this is constant: Njia rests upon a commitment to *the primacy and victory of Afrocentric thought.* It is concerned with liberating and empowering the collective and personal consciousness of African people. *Njia* is a major and recurring theme throughout *Afrocentricity.*[14]

The Way of Heru is the creative, Afrocentric designation given to a second major theme in *Afrocentricity.* In the ancient, classical civilization of Kemet, Heru was a historical-mythical religio-spiritual person-power-principle. Heru subdued chaos, disharmony, and evil and re-established order, balance, and justice. In the spirit of Heru, Asante and *Afrocentricity* expect victory in the quest to reestablish order, balance, and justice within the lives and minds of African people.

With clear understanding of the challenge, Asante marshals

Heruean power proficient for the task: (1) *employing sophisticated,comprehensive critical cultural method*, (2) understanding that intrinsic in the work of African liberation is *the intentional wielding of conceptual power*. Consider Asante's clarity:

> Indeed culture is the most revolutionary stage of aware-
> ness . . . culture in the sense that Amilcar Cabral, Frantz
> Fanon, and Maulana Karenga have written about. This is
> at the macro-level of education and includes science, mu-
> sic, engineering, architecture, dance, art, philosophy, and
> economics. . . . We know that it is difficult to create freely
> when you use someone else's motifs, styles, images, and
> perspectives. Thus, Afrocentric awareness is total commit-
> ment to
> African liberation anywhere and everywhere by a consis-
> tent determined effort to repair any psychic, economic,
> physical, or cultural damage done to Africans. It is further
> a pro-active statement . . . .[15]

Further, Asante discusses the often unnoticed but immeasurably important matter of "Language Liberation." Consider too that Asante comments on, deconstructs, and reconstructs or reconceptualizes flawed or disempowering—usually Eurocentric—notions. For almost all of Chapter Three, deliberate attention is given to "Criticism and Science," "Consciousness," "Relationships," "Christian Church," "Race and Identity," "Marxism," "Science," and "Aesthetics."[16] Finally, when necessary, whatever is needed is simply created/conceptualized and set forth—new terms, new concepts, and so forth.[17]

Clearly, *Afrocentricity* is not naive, nor is it narrow or singular in its approach. It goes beyond examining "politics," or "econom-ics," or any other single and obvious arena. Asante understands that no one of those categories is the foundational cornerstone crush-ing African people; rather, all categories emerge from the metacategory—and reality—of culture. Consequently, Asante's method toward victory is thorough. His method rests upon sophis-ticated understanding, comprehensive critique, critical inquiry, and cultural clarity—*and*, the confidence to conceptualize and create.

document. Like Heru, Asante intends to resurrect and restore African people. *The Way of Heru* is a predominant theme in *Afrocentricity*.

Harmosis can be noted as a major theme in *Afrocentricity*. Harmosis, a term-concept this author first conceived and introduced in 1989, can be understood as "empowering, beneficial, harmonizing synthesis."[18] All synthesis is not necessarily empowering, constructive, beneficial. Whenever African people choose, appropriate, or are involved in synthesis, it must be synthesis that is strengthening and harmonizing for African people.[19] Clearly, then, African people need, must learn, and must enact Harmosis. This reality is indicated in much of *Afrocentricity*'s final chapter explicitly and in other parts of the book implicitly.

Consider the following positions articulated in *Afrocentricity*:

> A strategy is a long-term plan for achieving an objective while tactics are the science of arranging *and managing the details of human behavior*. Afrocentricity does not negate strategies or tactics; it recognizes their individual places in the overall thrust toward victory. The transcending action which takes us from the traditional to the revolutionary consciousness . . . [can] be called the eradication, blotting out, of the old and the opening up to the new. We *breakdown* in order to *breakthrough*. Neither action nor thought is good in and of itself, each must be accompanied by the other. [Harmosis is necessary.] The world has seen too much abuse . . . because of one element without the other. . . .[20] (emphasis his)

Asante continues explicating:

> The two fundamental aspects of the Afrocentric project are *innovation* and *tradition*. Both are essential to . . . humanizing the world. The generation of the new, the novel, is basic to the advancement of cultural ideas but [so] also is the maintenance of the traditional. Innovation permits us, indeed requires [of] us, the promotion of new themes and designs founded on the traditional motifs. Afrocentricity is the operative theory upon which we hang

our innovation and tradition.[21] (emphasis his)

Harmosis is a very recognizable theme in both of the preceding quotes. Consistently, there is recognition of and commitment to harmosizing dualities—dualities that many people often misunderstand as unrelated or antagonistic opposites, rather than as complementary pairs.

"Confraternity and Continuum" is a section of *Afrocentricity* that discusses the present and increasing harmosis—material, emotional, psychological, aesthetic, cultural, and other kinds of harmosis—between African Americans and continental Africans. Harmosis is also implied in other sections and passages of the book. Throughout *Afrocentricity, Harmosis* is a relatively subtle yet extremely present theme.[22]

Manifesting Afrocentric action wholistically is a predominant theme in Asante's work. It is perhaps most apparent in Afrocentricity's final chapter, "The Bases of Action." Asante is explicit and concise:

> There can be but one true objective for us in the contemporary era[:] to reconstruct our lives on an Afrocentric base. . . . *all* behaviour must be analyzed for their Afrocentric base. [emphasis mine] Each person [who becomes Afrocentric] chooses to become Afrocentric; this is the only way to accomplish it.[23] (emphasis his)

Asante continues, with boldness, conviction, and passion:

> . . . the Afrocentric cultural project is a wholistic plan to reconstruct and develop every dimension of the African world from the standpoint of Africa as subject rather than object. The task is for the lion-hearted. It requires discipline and devotion to the African cultural project . . . . We can achieve the humanizing mission of the earth by remembering that the idea for culture and civilization first went down the Nile from the interior of Africa. . . . Let the artist imagine, let the scientists expand, let the priests see visions, let the writers be free to create, and let an Afrocentric revolution be born![24]

The two preceding quotes make it clear that Afrocentric thought is to evidence itself, ultimately, in Afrocentric action. As individuals internalize Afrocentric thought, their actions and personal behavior become increasingly Afrocentric. As groups of people claim and give themselves to Afrocentric thought, collective Afrocentric actions result. In every sphere—unskilled and skilled, artistic and scientific, religio-spiritual and academic-scholastic—the permeative manifesting of Afrocentric action-behavior is desired.

In *Afrocentricity*'s "Preface," Asante states:

> [Afrocentricity is] a transforming agent in which all things
> that were old become new and a transformation of attitudes,
> beliefs, values, and behavior results.[25]

The above quotation suggests that the constant aim of Afrocentricity is to catalyze a wholistic metamorphosis within people. People's worldview—that is, the way they view and perceive life and the world, and their worldmovement—that is, the way they move throughout/navigate life and the world, are to be altered radically. People are to think, feel, and behave so that purposeful, humanizing actions and projects become habitual, expected, normal manifestations.

The comprehensive, wholistic manifesting of Afrocentric action is a prevalent theme in *Afrocentricity*.

Six styles of argumentation are employed predominantly within Afrocentric theory and praxis:
1. Sankofan argumentation
2. Nommoic argumentation
3. Maatic argumentation
4. Political-intellectual argumentation
5. African collective memory-perception argumentation
6. Explicit locational argumentation

These styles will be explained as the writings of Asante, Karenga, and Welsh-Asante are analyzed.

Sankofan argumentation and Nommoic argumentation are thepredominant styles employed within *Afrocentricity*.

"Sankofa" is an Akan term meaning "return to the source; go and get it and bring it here." Sankofan argumentation, then, is argumentation that is anchored in African history. Sankofan argumentation considers the African past, gleans its most instructive and constructive information, refines that information if necessary, then utilizes the information to achieve pro-African purposes in contemporary contexts.

Sankofan argumentation is employed at the outset of, and throughout, *Afrocentricitv*:

> We have within *our own history* the most sacred and holiest places on the earth. Afrocentricity directs us to visit them and meditate on the power of our ancestors. Afrocentricity is the belief in the centrality of Africans in post modern history. It is *our history*, our mythology . . . . During our reconstruction, we must not lose sight of our total Afrocentricity. It cannot develop further until we rid ourselves of all fantasies except those that grow out of *our own history*.[26] (emphasis mine)

For almost fourteen pages, Asante critiques great African leaders and their historic legacies. Booker T. Washington, Marcus Garvey, Martin Luther King, Jr., Elijah Muhammad, W. E. B. DuBois, Malcolm X, and Maulana Karenga are all discussed.[27]

Then, holding their contributions as a historical foundation, Asante posits the various historical and theoretical arguments and considerations that comprise *Afrocentricity*. Asante argues repeatedly it is imperative that African people reconstruct sanity in the present, by studying, recalling, and recounting the works of sanity produced by Africans of the past. The works of Aime Cesaire, Langston Hughes, Ngugi wa Thiongo, John Coltrane, Duke Ellington, David Walker, Amiri Baraka, and others are noted.[28] Sankofan argumentation is utilized throughout *Afrocentricity*.

Nommo is a word and a concept generating from the Dogon people.[29] It translates variously: "the word, word power, the power of the word, generative-productive word power, the magical power of the word, the magical force of the spoken word," and so forth. Nommoic argumentation can be understood as argumentation that employs definitional and semantic precision and sophistication. It introduces new words, new phrases, new concepts; and it re-introduces familiar concepts in fresh, creative-innovative ways. Nommoic argumentation invites and challenges African people—and ultimately all people—to think, perceive, conceive, create, speak, and finally to behave in new and more human ways.

Nommoic argumentation is employed throughout *Afrocentricity*. In the book's title, such argumentation is employed. " Afrocentricity" is a relatively new term for almost all English-utilizing people. Therefore, its fundamental definition is as creative and as potent as its introducer is able to make it. In positing "Afrocentricity"—and later, "Njia," "Afrology," and other concepts—Asante empowers himself and other Afrocentrists.[30] Immediately, he is free to define, create, and critique from an offensive position, from a position of strength. Asante's sophisticated use of language, the creation of new words and concepts, frees Asante of many constraints—especially the constraint of attempting to articulate a new humane reality utilizing old or familiar limited terms.

The employment of Nommoic arguments in *Afrocentricity* is quite conscious. Consider the following passage from the book's second chapter, "The Constituents of Power":

> Language is essentially the control of thought. It becomes impossible for us to direct our future until we control our language. . . . If language is not functional, then it should have no place in our vocabulary. In every revolution, the people have first seized the instruments of idea formation . What Nicholas Guillen did to Spanish, what . . .Pushkin did to Russian, what . . . Hughes did to English, and what Cesaire . . . did to French, suggest that it is in the soul of our people to seize and redirect language toward liberating ideas and thought.[31]

Nommoic arguments continue with clarity and intentionality:

> When the oppressor seeks to use language for the   manipulation of our reality; Nommo, for ourselves, and of ourselves must continue the   correct path to critical analysis. Our political doctrines must speak to [the] reality [of anti-African people warring upon us].
>
>   Since language is the instrument for conveying that truth, our language must be aggressive and innovative. The mas-

> siveness of [our task] can be met by skillful rhetoricians
> understanding the immensity of the problem. A mobilizing
> language would [overcome the divisions among African
> people and unite African people]. Afrocentric writers
> restructure the language to tell the truth.[32]

Asante's understanding of word power—or perhaps more precisely, his understanding of the communication of concepts—is broad and thorough. He argues that all channels of communication are to be utilized in overcoming racist repression. "[L]anguage, dedicated to such an end, regularly expanded with relevant ideas and symbols, is crucial to our liberation . . . ."[33] Nommoic argumentation is a predominant style of argumentation in *Afrocentricity.*

Molefi Asante's *The Afrocentric Idea* and his *Kemet, Afrocentricity and Knowledge* are African Centered books that must also be noted when discussing the Afrocentric project.

The Afrocentric Idea extends the work Asante initiated in *Afrocentricity.* Published in 1987, *The Idea* came forth in a context ripe and ready for its message. At least three major realities characterize the context:

1. African people in the United States were looking for more and more elucidating Afrocentric information (as Jesse Jackson's second American-centered run for the presidency was being tolerated-and-deconstructed for the second time),
2. European people in the United States were beginning to acknowledge the inevitability of this nation being populated extensively by people of many colors and cultures, and
3. The United States system of higher education was preparing to launch its relatively sophisticated campaign against (a) Afrocentricity, and (b) authentic multiculturalism.

Relative to audience, *The Afrocentric Idea* seems addressed primarily to professional academics, especially African and European academics. The book seems intended for local people secondarily. Relative to styles of argumentation, *The Afrocentric Idea* utilizes Nommoic arguments primarily, complemented by Sankofan arguments.

Locating his effort within, and stretching beyond, the tradition of the great Africans "David Walker, W.E.B. DuBois, Ida B. Wells, Cheikh Anta Diop, and George James," Asante continues working at constructing and framing a definite Afrocentric philosophy—a philosophy that serves to liberate African people and helps to humanize all people. *The Afrocentric Idea* centers on "orature," that is, "the total body of oral discourses, styles, and traditions of African people." The document notes that the orature of African Americans has been/is, most of all, a discourse "confront[ing] the human condition of oppression . . . ,"[34] discourse dealing with the reality that "[w]e are on a pilgrimage to regain freedom."[35] Arguing that orature must be examined as thoroughly as African literature, *The Afrocentric Idea* explicates, edifies, and extends African culture. Simultaneously, but secondarily, the document critiques some of the arrogance and contradictions that characterize Euro-Anglo culture and discourse.

The Afrocentric Idea culminates with the explication of the "quest for harmony [as] the predominant aspiration of African American orature and literature."[36] Indeed, the quest for harmony is the principal characteristic of African culture. Further, the core of the Afrocentric Idea—the core of Afrocentricity, Afrocentric philosophy—is a commitment to the quest for harmony.

Molefi Asante's *Kemet, Afrocentricity and Knowledge* was published in 1990. The volume was published in a context characterized by both affirmation and antagonism. Temple University's Department of African American Studies' doctoral program was two years old; and the efforts and work of Molefi Asante, the department's chairperson, were being lauded and affirmed nationally and internationally. Simultaneously, backwards-looking Eurocentric scholars and their hegemonic academic organizations were gathering and attacking authentic, academic-discourse-expanding efforts, such as *Kemet, Afrocentricity and Knowledge*.

The volume seems addressed primarily to an audience of African intellectuals or professional African academics, or professional academics-to-be, especially those interested in understanding or participating in the academic discipline-method called "Africalogy"/ ""Africology."[37] The predominant and constant theme of the book is the framing and explication of Africalogy—its methodological infrastructure ("interiors"), its historical foundation ("anteriors"), and its academic-and-social implications, ramifications, and intentions ("exteriors").[38] Relative to styles of argumentation, *Kemet, Afrocentricity and Knowledge* utilizes Nommoic arguments predominantly, complemented by Sankofan arguments.

At the very beginning of *Kemet, Afrocentricity and Knowledge,* Asante centers himself in African reality. He locates himself in the presence of the ancients—Amenomope, Ptahhotep, Thuthmosis III; in the aspirations of the incipient Afrocentrists—Garvey, DuBois, Blyden, Delany; in the vision of the supreme incipient Afrocentrist—Cheikh Anta Diop; in the company of the contemporary Afrocentric theorists Wade Nobles and Maulana Karenga; and at the feet of the immortal Person and Power Jehuty (Tehuti).[39] Further, Asante expresses his intent clearly, stating boldly and explicitly:

> The Afrocentric method seeks to transform human reality by ushering in a human openness to cultural pluralism which cannot exist without the unlocking of the minds for acceptance of an expansion of consciousness. I seek to overthrow parochialism, provincialism, and narrow Wotanic visions of the world by demonstrating the usefulness of an Afrocentric approach to questions of knowledge.[40]

In *Kemet, Afrocentricity and Knowledge*, Asante explicates that all over the planet "the exclusive Eurocentric view" is under the scrutiny of people who have achieved self-awareness. Increasing numbers of people are challenging Eurocentric arrogance and hegemony.[41] Unavoidably, the exclusivist Eurocentric perspective will be transformed and eclipsed; because a plurality of perspectives already exist, and they manifest themselves more distinctly and with greater sophistication every day.[42]

"Africalogy," *Kemet, Afrocentricity and Knowledge's* central concern, is defined as "the Afrocentric study of phenomena, events, ideas, and personalities related to Africa." As a discipline, Africalogy holds three interrelated foundational tenets:

1. Relative to centrism, Kemet is the primary "classical"—that is, anterior validating—referent.

2. Relative to inquiry, one must begin with the fact that African people are the parentpeople of humanity, and that African civilization is the parent civilization of world-global civilization.
3. Relative to centrism and inquiry, the particular cultural voice of the composite African people is utilized.[43]

Further, Asante states that Africalogy holds four principal issues as the arenas wherein inquiry ought to unfold: the cosmological, the epistemological, the axiological, and the aesthetic.[44]

In one of its clearest assertions, Asante explains in *Kemet, Afrocentricity and Knowledge* that Africalogy—African American Studies—is a "human science."[45]   It is a science—a discipline—with a heart. It does not wrap itself in pretentious claims of neutrality. Africalogy has integrity, is methodical, and is committed to a constructive agenda. Using history as the core "integrator"[46] of data, Africalogy "is committed to discovering in human experiences, historical and contemporary, all the ways African people have tried to make their physical, social, and cultural environments serve the end of harmony."[47] Africalogy is not dispassionate; it is intentional.

At the close of *Kemet, Afrocentricity and Knowledge*, Asante states the discipline's ultimate aims in succinct terms:

> Africalogy seeks to bring a new birth to the intellectual enterprise by encouraging scholarship to tear itself away from the imposition of a European domination, in fact, to place Europe in a normal context, separate from arrogance and within an arena of pluralism without hierarchy. . . .
>
> [Further,] Africalogy cannot achieve its purpose as a liberating discipline unless it is founded on assumptions that dignify humans rather than negate them. . . . Africalogists must critique but also in our research we must propose concrete actions that lead to the lessening of disharmony, suffering, misunderstanding, and dislocation.[47]

In *Kemet, Afrocentricity and Knowledge*, then, we see the greatest crystallization and systematic articulation of Afrocentric philosophical theory to date.

KARENGA

In 1982, Maulana Karenga published *Introduction to Black Stud-*

ies, a solid, systematic, well-constructed survey text.[49] This text is central to the Afrocentric project. James Turner noted, "Prof. Karenga has provided a comprehensive *Afro-centric* [emphasis mine] analysis of the seminal authors and the standard body of discipline-specific literature . . . of Black Studies." Turner lauded Karenga's effort further, saying of the document, "[It] was the most significant scholarly production in the field [of Black Studies] that year [1982]."[46] During the decade of the 1980s, the book may have been probably utilized in more African American Studies courses nationwide than any other document. As of April 1987, *Introduction to Black Studies* was in its fourth printing; and in 1993, a revised, enlarged, second edition was published.

In 1982, when the book was first published, the national context was that of increasing conservatism. The Reagan-Bush administration was two years into its initial term, unfolding its people-and-planet-reducing program. Homelessness was increasing; the construction of a sophisticated neo-feudalist society was in motion; and pricing and positioning of higher education just beyond the reach of millions of African and other local people was just about to begin. By setting forth a very straightforward and systematic discussion of Black Studies in the midst of such a context, Karenga's *Introduction to Black Studies* served to organize, protect, perpetuate, and even elevate African American Studies efforts during a slippery, insidious season.

The book seems addressed primarily to African students, professional African scholars, and others concerned predominantly with the historical and continuing reality of African people in the United States. Primarily, however, through *Introduction to Black Studies*, Karenga wishes to reach questing students. Such emphasis can be extracted from remarks in the text's "Preface":

> [This introductory text] seeks to provide the *student* with a concise but substantive intellectual base for a critical understanding and discussion of Black Studies. . . . stress is placed on inquiry and analysis as key to building the *student's* intellectual base in the discipline. . . . I have self-consciously used abundant references to introduce the *student* to the literature in the field and provide him/her with a bibliography which will facilitate research for term papers

bibliography which will facilitate research for term papers in Black Studies . . . .[51] (emphasis mine)

Additionally, implicitly, *Introduction to Black Studies* is addressed to a mature Afrocentric audience. Such is apparent when Karenga explicates the following:

This enterprise is self-consciously Afrocentric . . . . An Afro-centric approach is essentially intellectual inquiry and production centered on and in the image and interest of African peoples. [This enterprise also has a critical thrust and a corrective thrust.] The critical thrust is the advancing of . . . criticism of the established [Eurocentric] order of things . . . . And the corrective thrust is the correlative discovery and affirmation of the truth of the Black experience in its current and historical unfolding [and the] posing of correctives to problems internal to the discipline of Black Studies as well as to those which confront Black people, themselves.[52]

While *Introduction to Black Studies* is a "Kawaida" expression and can be understood as a tangible demonstration of it; Kawaida is not the theme of the document. Kawaida will be discussed later in this text.

One core theme galvanizes *Introduction to Black Studies*. The theme can be set forth as, "the citing, analyzing/ critiquing, and explicating of (a) African people's best efforts toward being fully, truly human on our own terms, *and* (b) our various victories/achievements in the course of such efforts." (It should be noted that Karenga's overwhelming focus is on African people in what is now called the United States of America; he gives some attention to continental Africans.)[53] The said theme takes particular form via three sub-themes: (1) the origins and place—that is, *location*—of the discipline of Black Studies; (2) the seven central subject areas of Black Studies—Black History, Black Religion, Black Social Organization, Black Politics, Black Economics, Black Creative Production, Black Psychology; and (3) Black Studies' current and coming challenges and opportunities.[54]

Three predominant styles of argumentation are prevalent in *In-*

tellectual."

Sankofan argumentation has been defined earlier in this paper. Karenga's employment of Sankofan argumentation style is prevalent throughout *Introduction to Black Studies*. He begins the document with a discussion of the *origins* of Black Studies.[55] Such discussion necessitates looking into history, gleaning appropriate information, and applying it to present concerns. Further, when Karenga begins discussing Black Studies' seven central subject areas, he begins with "Black History," noting:

> First, the core task of Black Studies . . . is the rescue and reconstruction of Black history and humanity. Secondly, Black Studies also begins with Black History because it is relevant, even indispensable to the introduction and development of all the other subject areas. Black History places them in perspective. . . . Moreover, each of the other   subject areas of Black Studies teaches its own particular history which in turn is a part of general Black History.   History reveals itself as the key social science, the social science on which all other social sciences depend.[56]

Consistently—whether considering Black History, Black Religion, Black Politics, Black Creative Production, or any of the other core subject areas—Karenga references African people's past historical and historic realities; he extracts information and insight therefrom; and he then connects the same with African people's present realities. Sankofan argumentation is employed repeatedly, intentionally.

Finally, in the book's conclusion, Karenga utilizes Sankofan argumentation, as he references the past to illuminate the present and beyond:

> . . . [W]hatever unsure steps or stumbling there was [within the Black Studies movement] in the past offers a wealth of lessons for the future which will aid a quicker-paced development. For as an African proverb says, "To stumble is not to fall but to go forward faster."[57]

Clearly, Sankofan argumentation is apparent throughout *Introduction to Black Studies*.

duction to Black Studies.

Maat is a Kemetic concept with multiple, yet related meanings, among them: "truth, justice, harmony, righteousness, balance."[58] At their core, all of these meanings hold that there is a divine design-invitation-and-imperative permeating all life: individuals and institutions, that is, all of society—even nature and the infinite cosmos—are to manifest justice, harmony.

Understanding Maat in the broadest sense, but focusing on one interpretation of the term while retaining the integrity of the term, one can that Maat is a divine and human expectation-requirement-"law" intrinsically incumbent upon all. In short, whether they answer or not, all persons and parts of society are "called by the Creator/the Neters-the Angels/the Orishas-Loas-Ancestors/the Universe" to function in an *exemplary, ethical, moral, just* manner at all times.

Maatic argumentation, then, is characterized by an explicit or implicit concern that harmony and justice ought to predominate throughout society. Maatic argumentation is prevalent in *Introduction to Black Studies.* In his consideration of each of Black Studies' seven subject areas—as well as in the book's first and final chapters—Karenga consistently explicates and argues African people's persistent focus upon matters of Maat.

In the book's "Black Religion" section, Karenga notes that African religion(s) emphasizes the harmonious integration of a person's personal responsibility and identity with her/his collective responsibility and identity as a member of the community and society. More specifically, as one of its highest ideals, African religion invites and encourages people to be just, to live in harmony, to realize one's highest potential by living in cooperation with the rest of the community. This ideal is apparent in the religio-spiritual teachings of (1) ancient and contemporary continental African people, such as the people of Kemet and the Dogon people, (2) Martin Luther King, Jr., (3) Black liberation theology, (4) Noble Drew Ali, (5) the Nation of Islam, and other African people and groups.[59] Karenga's explication of Black Religion is quite sensitive to African people's focus upon Maat.

Maatic argumentation is quite evident in the "Black Psychology" section of *Introduction to Black Studies.* Wasting no time, Karenga notes at the opening of the section's third paragraph:

The concerns of Black psychology revolve around the development of a discipline which not only studies the
behaviour of Black persons, but seeks to transform them
into self-conscious agents of their own mental and political liberation.[60]

Near the section's close, Karenga asserts and explains:

[Black people collectively must overcome a deficient self-
consciousness, i. e., a deficient consciousness/awareness
of ourselves relative to who we really are and what we are
really capable of doing/producing/building.] The demand
to end a deficient consciousness must be joined to a demand to eliminate the conditions which caused [and which
continue to try and cause] it. This is why Black [Afrocentric]
psychologists advocate the social intervention model of
psychology advanced by Fanon. . . who argued mental
health demanded a solution on both subjective (mental)
and objective (social) levels.[61]

In the two quotations noted above, and throughout the entirety of
the section, Karenga explicates and re-explicates that Black psychology, at its best, is concerned with Black people realizing mental and sociopolitical *liberation*.[62]

The realizing of liberation—of any sort—is the realizing of justice. So, as African people achieve mental and sociopolitical liberation, they achieve justice; they manifest Maat. And when people
are living and breathing liberation and justice, people are able to
manifest their best selves more consistently. Such people are able
to be, behave, build, and create in harmony; and Maat becomes an
immanent reality for them and not merely a transcendent vision.

Karenga utilizes Maatic argumentation throughout the Black
psychology section and in many other sections of *Introduction to
Black Studies*. Consistently, arguments rest and pivot upon hu-
mane-human, ethical-moral foundations. Maatic argumentation is
prevalent throughout the document.

Political-intellectual argumentation is also utilized in *Introduction to Black Studies*. "Political-intellectual" argumentation, as
defined by the author of the work in hand, (1) refers to argumenta-

AFROCENTRIC THOUGHT AND PRAXIS

tion addressing political economy-socioeconomic-sociopolitical *power* configurations, or (2) refers to argumentation speaking to matters of academic or scholarly honesty and integrity. Possibly, political argumentation and intellectual argumentation could be considered separately. In life, however, political realities and intellectual realities are often intertwined. Frequently, the work of academicians and scholars is used to undergird and/or guide the work of politicians—for better or for worse. Karenga is aware of this fact.

In the "Black Economics" section of *Introduction to Black Studies*, Karenga begins by noting that economics "penetrates every aspect of social life." He argues further that it is "relatively impossible and certainly unwise" for African people to make political decisions devoid of economic considerations. Karenga asserts that rather than merely studying economics; Africans must study *political economy*, that is, "the relationship between politics and economics and the power relations they express and produce." Political economy goes beyond considering economic process alone; rather, it also involves consideration of "economic policy and the race [*color*] and class [*financial and property*] interests this suggests." Such being clear, Karenga tells us, the study of Black economics necessitates studying "the politics which shape economics in both positive and negative ways."[63]

For the remainder of the section, Karenga (1)sets forth and dissects the systems-wide, intentional exploitation and oppression of the African American community by European Americans, and (2)critiques and proposes avenues of solution—especially Cooperative Economics (which DuBois proposed as early as 1940)—that African people can employ in order to attain positive rather than deficient political economy involvement. Throughout, Karenga is careful to critique various scholars' efforts relative to these matters. He is particularly critical of Thomas Sowell's and Julius Wilson's inaccurate—even dishonest—interpretations of African Americans' place in and experience of the political economy in the United States.[64]

Political-intellectual argumentation is present in the "Black Economics" section of *Introduction*; and it is also present in both the "Black Politics" and the "Black Social Organization" sections. Such argumentation is even present in the document's "Black Creative ties" section.

Throughout the "Black Creative Production" section, Karenga explicates and argues that Black art—particularly Black art, Black music, and Black literature—at its best, expresses African "peoples [collective] life-experiences and life-aspirations" in an empowering manner.[65] In Karenga's terms, this means that African artists have at least three obligations—whether or not they honor the obligations—when creating/performing:

1. to create/perform art that is centered in the best history and culture–"the [healthiest] image[s] and [the most human] interests"—of African people;
2. to create/perform art that speaks to African reality as it has been (the glorious and the inglorious), and as it is (the challenges), and as it ought be (full of alert, strong, sane, free African people and constructive African creations); and
3. to create/perform art that is functional rather than dysfunctional or neutral/abstract; that is, to create art which "demand[s] and urge[s] willing and conscious involvement" from African people in the struggle and work of building a new, better, more just world for African people (and ultimately, for all people).[66]

The preceding implies that while Black Art should entertain and inspire, it should necessarily and intentionally support the intellectual and political liberation of African people. Indeed, the above cuts away academically-intellectually dishonest notions of Black Art, or any art, as being apolitical, politically neutral "art for art's sake." Simple integrity demands we note there is no such thing as apolitical or politically neutral art.[67]

All art is political, because all art is conveying some message to people and evoking some response from people. Even so-called abstract art is political: it moves people toward liberation-balance, or oppression-imbalance, or nothing." If people are moved toward "nothing," that is, if the art or artist does not move-touch-reach people in the midst of a society which tends toward oppression and imbalance, then, in fact, the people are being moved toward oppression and imbalance. So, the real question is this: Is the artist's or art's message one of liberation for people who know oppression, and is the response an empowered response from people who know disempowerment, or, is the artist's or art's message and the audience's response antiliberation and antiempowerment? The preceding is both an intellectual and a political question; and Black art—at its best—confronts the question forthrightly.[68]

Considering African people's current historical situation, unavoidably and inextricably, Black art in particular and Black Studies in general find themselves in the midst of—and the vehicles of—intellectual and political and intellectual argumentation. Karenga demonstrates this, implicitly and explicitly, throughout the "Black Creative Production" and "Challenges and Possibilities" sections of *Introduction to Black Studies*. Consider his culminating words in the former section, "Black Creative Production":

> Thus, by teaching beauty in the midst of ugliness and strength and durability under stress and strain, [Sonia Sanchez, Mari Evans, and other Black artists and their art] inspire and teach [victorious, sane, human] possibilities[,] which . . . is the fundamental function of Black [Art].[69]

Consider Karenga's concluding words in the latter section, "Challenges and Possibilities" section:

> [Black intellectuals have] the vital task of intellectual production which leads to a critical explanation of the economic and institutional causes of Black oppression and the development of solutions. -/- [Black Studies places] hope and educational focus on the creation of a conscious, capable and committed body of Black intellectuals who will self-consciously intervene in social reality and history and shape them in the image and interest of Black people.[70]

As discussion of *Introduction to Black Studies* nears conclusion, it is imperative that Karenga's comments on Kawaida be noted and critiqued. It is equally imperative that his 1993 discussion of "The Concept of Afrocentricity" be noted and examined.

Karenga first articulated "Kawaida" in 1965. Toward a concise, fundamental definition, Karenga states:

> The ideology of Kawaida . . . is essentially a theory of cultural and social change . . . which seeks to draw from and synthesize the best in nationalist, Pan-Africanist and so-

cialist thought . . . ."[71]

Further, Kawaida is deemed both "ideology and practice." At its core, it contends and holds that the primary crisis in African life is "the cultural crisis, i.e., a crisis in views and, especially, values."[72] Additionally, Kawaida posits seven areas of thought and practice—culture—that African people must rebuild and recreate:

1. sacred and secular myth
2. history
3. social organization
4. economic organization
5. political organization
6. creative production (arts and sciences)
7. ethos (collective self-definition and conciousness)[73]

African people's current existential task, then, is to reconstruct and reconfigure the said areas "so that each area is in [African people's] *image* and *interests.*"[74]   By "image," we believe Karenga means "grounded in African people's historic movements and personalities."   And by "interests," we believe he means "in ways which help African people to live life sanely and victoriously." As the seven areas are so reconstructed and recreated, cultural revolution manifests.

A cultural revolution, Karenga explains, is 'the ideological and practical struggle to transform [a particular group of] people and to build structures to ensure, maintain and expand that transformation.' Further, as the cultural revolution unfolds satisfactorily, political revolution follows. Indeed, cultural revolution enables *and sustains* political revolution; as cultural revolution continually produces "transformed self-conscious participants," that is, people who can struggle and make real political change, people who are awake and functioning as "agents of their own liberation."[75]

All the preceding points of Kawaida being understood, here is perhaps the most pivotal, demanding, and catalytic point in Kawaida's framework: a "self-conscious vanguard" must lead the said cultural—and political—revolution. (A vanguard has also been called for by DuBois, E. Franklin Frazier, Harold Cruse, Chancellor Williams, and others, each scholar explicating the character and function of the vanguard in her/his own way.) Kawaida emphasizes that the vanguard must consist of African people who identify clearly and constantly with the realities and needs of grassroots African people. The vanguard must be disciplined and ever vigilant, so that it remains unmoved and uncompromised by the anti-human analysis and the seductive-money-materialism-self-numbing-comfort-values of those who hurt and dehumanize African people. As explicated by Kawaida, the vanguard has at least three major tasks:

1. the vanguard must "build on the strengths of Black culture . . .";

2. the people in the vanguard "must create an Afro-centric ideology which negates the ruling race/class ideology and provides the basis for a critical Afro-centric conception of reality and the possibilities and methods of changing it"; and

3. the vanguard must cultivate a national culture, which "distinguishes Blacks from their oppressors [and] aids them in" resurrecting the best of "their history and humanity and enables them to contribute to human history and achievement in their own unique way."[76]

All the preceding explication makes it clear that Kawaida, as ideology and practice, holds African culture as essential and pivotal in the wholistic liberation of African people. The preceding also demonstrates that Kawaida understands and explicates African culture—and its resurrection and re-creation—in a charged, challenging, *politicized* manner. Additionally, the vanguard that Kawaida calls for seems more mission-specific and more controversial than the more general "conscious, capable and committed Black intellectuals," noted earlier in *Introduction to Black Studies'* "Challenges and Possibilities" section.

Kawaida and Afrocentricity are similar. Like Kawaida, Afrocentricity holds African culture as essential and pivotal; however, Afrocentricity's handling of the matter is more theoretical and philosophical than political. Perhaps Kawaida might be thought of as a relatively specific, localizing land map; while Afrocentricity might be thought of as a broad, encompassing, view from the air.

It is noteworthy that while Kawaida precedes Afrocentricity in time, Afrocentricity precedes it—perhaps predictably—relative to broad appeal. What may be even more noteworthy, however, is that Afrocentriciy seems to fulfill one of Kawaida's pivotal proposals and recommendations. In Afrocentricity, Asante seems to be putting definite and firm foundations under Kawaida's faint or skeletal articulation. Afrocentricity seems to answer Kawaida's call for the "[creation] of an Afro-centric . . . social theory which . . . provides the basis for a *critical Afro-centric conception of reality* and the *possibilities and methods* [emphasis mine] of changing it."[77]

Clearly, Kawaida and Afrocentricity are similar but not the same. Kawaida is something of a precursor to Afrocentricity. It pre-dates but does not really anticipate Afrocentricity. Kawaida senses the need for something more, senses the need for "an Afro-centric social theory." Further, Kawaida's awareness of and simple articulation of the said need helps the emergence and unfolding of Afrocentricity. Consider now Karenga's explicit discussion of Afrocentricity.

Set forth in the second edition—it is not in the original edition—of *Introduction to Black Studies*, "The Concept of Afrocentricity" is found in the first chapter, under the heading, "Subsequent Developments."[78]

Karenga's discussion is informed, honest, and thoughtful. He notes that Asante posited in 1980 and has maintained since then that "Afrocentricity [is] the indispensable perspective of the Black Studies project . . . ." Further, citing James Stewart, Karenga asserts astutely that Afrocentricity should not be confused with "Afrocentrism." Citing James Stewart, Karenga explains that "Afrocentrism" is a term used most frequently in "ideological discourse between advocates and critics"—especially those engaged primarily in *popular* media or popular exchanges. Further, some people understand—or attempt to posit—Afrocentrism as being the African version or opposite of the oppressive, hegemonic European ideology known as "Eurocentrism." Whatever Afrocentrism is, it is not Afrocentricity, Afrocentricity is not Afrocentrism. Afrocentricity is an intellectual concept and category; it has "intellectual value"; and, as Stewart asserts, it adds to and contributes to "systematic intellectual approaches in the field" of Black Studies.[79]

Further into the section, Karenga sets forth his particular definition of Afrocentricity: "Afrocentricity can be defined as a quality of thought and practice rooted in the cultural image and human interests of African people." While Afrocentricity announces itself unapologetically, it does not arise from, rest on, or seek the obliteration, defamation, or false reduction of non-African people or reality. Rather, Afrocentricity strives to epitomize intellectual integrity. Karenga explicates:

> [As an intellectual concept,] Afrocentricity . . .contains both a *particular* and *universal* dimension. It self-consciously contributes a valuable particular [African] cultural insight and discourse to the multicultural project[,] and in the process. . . finds common [universal] ground with other cultures which can be cultivated and developed for [Africans' and all other humans'] mutual benefit.[80]

Finally, Karenga offers sensitive, sharp, useful critique. He points out that as Afrocentricity soars and blazes within the academic and intellectual community, there are at least five real temptations, tendencies, and challenges which must be navigated with integrity:

1. the temptation to posit Afrocentricity as "a dogma of authenticity" rather than [as] an orientation and methodology;
2. the tendency to exclude "the reality and value of the diversity of perspectives and approaches" extant within the discipline of Black Studies;
3. the temptation to promote one, unchanging, unvarying conception of African culture;
4. the tendency to emphasize African people's Continental African past, "at the expense of recognizing" African people's past and present   in the United States as central to and constitutive of African culture and the Afrocentric enterprise; and
5. the challenge of proving "its utility in intellectual production beyond declaration of its presence and aspirations."[81]

Karenga concludes his discussion noting that as Afrocentricity continues unfolding constructively, it will provide African people—and all people—a "more accurate and informative view of the African experience, [and it will] contribute to a more accurate and informative understanding of the human experience in all its rich and instructive diversity."[82]

Introduction to Black Studies should be considered a major Afrocentric work. In a few instances, the book's critical commentary does come within a wisp of sounding like apology; however, appreciating the author, such meticulous reasoning is more likely a conscious tempering of what might otherwise overwhelm.

That criticism noted, *Introduction to Black Studies* ought be understood as a most venerable, Afrocentric book. Far beyond competent, filled with insight and foresight, the volume's author is located firmly in the company of the African community's most forward-looking African anchored thinkers—Robert Benjamin Lewis, Hosea Easton, J.W.C. Pennington, Martin Delany, William Wells Brown, Edward Wilmot Blyden, Anna Julia Cooper, Nat Turner, George Wells Parker, Garvey, George G. M. James, Fanon, Diop, Madhubuti, Carruthers, Nobles, Hilliard, Linda James Myers, Obenga, and others. A conscious, confident, African based voice rings throughout *Introduction to Black Studies*. African people and African concerns are at its core. An African audience is primary. The arguments are clear. The critique is sure. The scope is comprehensive. *Introduction to Black Studies* is a sound, solid, academic-intellectual Afrocentric contribution.

KARIAMU WELSH-ASANTE

The work of Kariamu Welsh-Asante is central to the Afrocentric project. An essay in her 1985 document (with Molefi Asante), *African Culture: The Rhythms of Unity*, and an essay in her soon to be landmark document, *The African Aesthetic: Keeper of the Traditions*, are most pertinent for the purposes of this work.[83]

Welsh-Asante's 1985 essay, "Commonalities in African Dance: An Aesthetic Foundation," in *African Culture: The Rhythms of Unity* and her volume *The African Aesthetic: Keeper of the Traditions* and the essay, "The Aesthetic Conceptualization of *Nzuri*," are significant works in the Afrocentric school. Indeed, Welsh-Asante's 1985 work foreshadows her aforementioned 1993 work and points to numerous, additional, direction-setting contributions as the years unfold.[84]

Relative to context, in 1985, in the United States, the Reagan-Bush administration was into phase two—of three phases, three terms—of its unsophisticated-sophisticated deconstruction of African (and other) people's best efforts to humanize the United States.

Michael Jackson's mega hit album, *Thriller*, had soared—and continued soaring farther and farther—beyond the known universe of music sales (opening the door for large sales by Madonna, Bruce Springsteen, and others); and with Jackson having surgically altered (surgically de-Africanized) his physical appearance, the project of the intentional complexification-convolution and deification of popular culture was in effect.

Further, other forms of mass media were multiplying at an incredible pace. Twenty-four hour cable television was beginning to assert itself. National [conservative-liberal] Public [private-controlled?] Radio was growing steadily. Gannet's *USA Today* [uniperspective] national newspaper was in place and expanding. And a massive avalanche of rental videos was being injected into the country's consciousness.

As a result of the Eurostream/"mainstream" media's mushrooming, along with the essentially de-educating content of most of the media, European Americans were being brainwashed/braindirtied and seduced at an accelerated rate. They were being duped and seasoned into holding re-reified Eurocentric notions of "the American flag," "the American government," and "the American dream" as "realities" most worthy of their support and allegiance. Simultaneously and similarly, African people and other people of color in the United States were being seduced. All of the seductions had one common denominator, an implicit, unstated, consistently sent message: If you work hard, play hard, and refrain from reflective/deep/serious thoughts-words-and-actions, you will have attained the American dream—a smooth, fun-filled life.

Into such context, a context which might be considered "The Beginning of the Neo-Maafa," Welsh-Asante's bold, forward-looking "Commonalities in African Dance: An Aesthetic Foundation" emerged.

In 1993, the societal context was similar to that of 1985. There were some differences, however. By 1993, the citizenry of the United States was far more confused than in 1985—and understandably so. By 1993, multi-farious misinformation and disinformation campaigns were set before the people almost constantly. With society being almost totally computerized, even with good information being available, most people in the United States suffered from what this author calls *information saturation*. That is, they were inundated with all manner of useful-and-useless information *beyond their ability to consider and process the information*.

Further, by 1993—beginning around 1989—the Afrocentric Movement was the unabashed target of Eurocentric individuals and groups from every strata of United States society, i.e., from the academic Diane Ravitches, to the literary Arthur Schlesingers, to the clever-cloaked-conservative political Clintons, to the various anonymous locals who carry and work under the flag of Eurocentricity. From unadulterated Eurocentrism, to Eurocentrism masquerading as multiculturalism, to sincere-but-naive attempts at authentic multiculturalism—by 1993, the Afrocentric movement was a very present reality within United States society; but it was not necessarily a very desired reality. In the midst of such context, Welsh-Asante's optimistic essay, "The Aesthetic Conceptualization of *Nzuri,*" was published.

"Commonalities in African Dance: An Aesthetic Foundation" is addressed primarily to those who appreciate and who wish a more distinct, delineated, defensible, conscious understanding of African dance in particular and African aesthetics in general. "The Aesthetic Conceptualization of *Nzuri*" is addressed to those who wish a solid, broad, thoughtful theory and explication of a Pan African aesthetic—an Afrocentric aesthetic.

Primarily, Welsh-Asante's writings are intended for those who appreciate the importance *and* the power of defining African aesthetics from a centered African perspective. Her writings are not for those seeking hype and cheap excitement; her writings are intended for an inquisitive, thoughtful, Afrocentric audience.

One primary theme seems to reverberate throughout both "Commonalities in African Dance: An Aesthetic Foundation" and "The Aesthetic Conceptualization of *Nzuri*": the delineation and explication of centered African aesthetics. In the former essay, the theme unfolds in the assertion and explication of seven, foundational aesthetic "senses."[85]

In the latter essay, the theme is fulfilled by the positing, encircling, and explaining of three central aesthetic categories-realities set forth as "sources, aspects, and principles."[86]

The seven aesthetic senses, posited in "Commonalities in African Dance: An Aesthetic Foundation," apply primarily to African dance, but may be applicable to all African art forms. Before discussing the seven senses, however, it is necessary to discuss the oral principle. The seven senses are connected intimately to the catalytic oral principle, emerging as a result of it. The oral principle—or, oral tradition—ought to be understood (a) as "an art in and of itself," (b) as "a word of mouth phenomenon that preserves history and entertains in African culture," and (c) as appearing "in all disciplines of the arts as a subtle undercurrent." Welsh-Asante explains further:

> The oral tradition . . . is the organic, creative process, evident in all African artists. . . . The oral principle constitutes a fundamental principle in African aesthetics . . . [i]t concerns the process of creativity itself . . . . The derivatives of [the oral tradition] are seven aesthetic senses: polyrhythm, polycentrism, curvilinear, dimensional, epic memory, repetition, [and] holism.[87]

Polyrhythm is the first aesthetic sense that Welsh-Asante discusses. She states clearly and simply, "The rhythmic quality of the aesthetic is the most distinguishable of its qualities." Further, polyrhythm is a motion sense, holding that movement and rhythm cannot be separated. Particularly in African dance and music, Welsh-Asante explicates, "[in the] context of multiple rhythmics, people distinguish themselves from each other while they remain dynamically related." Additionally, the polyrhythmic sense holds that traditional African—and all centered African—artistic products manifest layers of rhythms, multiple and various complementary rhythms in the same space/time.[88]

Polycentrism is an aesthetic sense having to do with multiplication—of movement, and/or sound, and/or texture, and/or color—within the artistic product. Welsh-Asante explains that relative to traditional African dance—and all centered African dance—this sense holds that fast and slow can manifest together, with movement(s) coming from several directions simultaneously.[89]

The curvilinear sense, addresses shape, form, and structure. Citing the timeless African aphorisms, "Let the circle be unbro-

ken," and "[t]here is 'power' [metaphysical power] in the circle"—
Welsh-Asante notes that the "circular quality of the African artists'
world is ever apparent. The curvilinear sense, then, holds that traditional—and all centered—African artistic products possess a circular, curved, round quality. And all those curvilinear qualities are
similar [to] and resemble aspects of African society and mythology,
[and history]." African aesthetics is not devoid of utilization of
proportional, symmetrical, or profile-oriented form. Welsh-Asante
writes:

> There is calculation and methodology as well as precision,
> but neither masters the artist; rather, they serve the artist
> and the work of art in expediting the idea.[90]

Dimensionality is the fourth aesthetic sense posited by Welsh-
Asante. It concerns the graininess, coarseness, or fuzziness that a
participant feels, hears, or sees in an artistic product. The dimen-
sional sense concerns the metaphysical, with the presence beyond
the empirical presence of the artistic product; it is what is perceived rather than what can necessarily be proven. Welsh-Asante
explains:

> [The dimensional sense] is by definition extrasensory ....
> [It holds within it] a human quality, something extra that is
> present in harmony with the music, dance, or sculpture. It
> speaks in a physical, three-dimensional sense in Western
> terminology, but it is not measured dimension, but rather a
> perceived dimension.[91]

Epic memory is Welsh-Asante's fifth aesthetic sense. She asserts
that the epic memory sense *may* involve *some* historical re-enact-
ment of significant periods in the collective life-journey of African
people. This sense involves most of all, however, *retrieval of the
memory* that delivers African people's ethos, "pathos, feeling, and
experience, without telling the story literally." The epic memory
sense holds within it a metaphysical—a spiritual—dimension. Welsh-
Asante notes that it is not "religious," but it can involve ritual. The
epic memory sense involves the conscious and subconscious calling upon our *asili*—i.e., our ancestors, our gods, our collective Af-

rican mind, to allow energy—NTU—to flow so that the artist can create. Welsh-Asante explicates the matter:

> [The epic memory sense] is an innate recognition that the creative force is indeed a force and not the person performing the act of creation. The artist can reject it, kill it, or accept it, but the creative energies come from within in response to a spiritual initiator. The spiritual element is embodied in the epic memory sense.[92]

The holistic aesthetic sense, involves the fact that the *whole* of an artistic product—including the artist(s)—is of the utmost importance. According to Welsh-Asante, "Silence or stillness is as much a part of the music or dance as sound or movement." Compartmentalized segments of an artistic creation are not highlighted or accentuated over and above the whole artistic creation. The painter *and* the picture matter together; the *whole* artistic product is important. The singer *and* the song, *and* the pauses, dips, and peaks all matter *together*; the lead dancer(s), *and* the supporting dancer(s), *and* the dance, *and* the drumming, *and* the drummer all matter together—the *whole* artistic creation is important.[93] This point cannot be overemphasized.

The repetition sense, Welsh-Asante's seventh aesthetic sense, has to do with intensification. She explains that this sense "is not the refrain or chorus of a movement . . . ." Rather, this sense involves repeated reiteration of a note, a phrase, a sequence, a color, a shape, a movement, or even an entire dance or song.

Such repetition leads to saturation, or ecstacy-possession-euphoria, or satisfaction; and, let it be clear, African aesthetics certainly seek to satisfy. In fact, satisfaction is desired by and for the primary creative conduit(s)—the artist(s)—*and* the complementary, co-creative conduit, the audience.[94]

Near the close of "Commonalities in African Dance: An Aesthetic Foundation," Welsh-Asante states, "The oral principle and the seven senses combine to comprise an African aesthetic."[95] Welsh-Asante's statement can be taken as further support for this work's contention that the primary theme of the essay is "delineation and explication of centered African aesthetics."

In "The Aesthetic Conceptualization of *Nzuri*," the aforementioned theme is again primary and central. The term "Nzuri" holds that beauty and good are synonymous and interchangeable. In centered African culture, that which is considered good is considered beautiful. Goodness involves aesthetics; beauty involves ethics; they are bound inextricably. In powerful, clear, flowing prose, Welsh-Asante shares what she is doing in "The Aesthetic Conceptualization of *Nzuri*":

> Theories of African aesthetics are specific or general. The specific theories focus on ethnic group or nation. The general or Pan African aesthetic aims at individualizing the common characteristics that occur in the African aesthetic. It is not my goal to describe a fixed aesthetic that is Afrocentric but rather to determine what the issues and characteristic terms of an Afrocentric aesthetic might be.[96]

Welsh Asante continues on explaining that "literally thousands of African centered aesthetics" exist in the world. She points out further that "in the Diaspora there are aesthetics born out of deep structure shaped by surface structure that are decidedly African." Welsh-Asante then explains that she is intentionally using and mixing "Kiswahili, Shona and other African language terms," as they "demonstrate precisely" her "theory of an Afrocentric aesthetic that is Pan African in focus and perspective." Then, musing apparently in an intentional, didactic manner, Welsh-Asante posits, "Perhaps it is only the diasporan African who can conceptualize and contextualize different traditions under one rubric." Then, no longer musing, she asserts, "It is the diasporan African's privilege and position that allows her to see Africa as a [unified, cultural] concept as well as a diverse and multicultural continent."[97]

After setting forth the preparatory, core understandings noted in the two preceding paragraphs, Welsh-Asante places those understandings and positions on the following galvanizing explicatory foundation:

> This conscious vision and perspective of the African in America has guided, informed and inspired the African to reclaim Africa politically as well as historically and aesthetically. An understanding of the African aesthetic(s)   facili-

tates any paradigm or blueprint for artistic, literary and philosophical criticism and scholarship.[98]

In *Nzuri,* then, relative to the writing's primary theme, Welsh-Asante is concerned with centered African aesthetics generally. And she is concerned particularly with "delineation and explication of one, broad, centered African aesthetic: Nzuri."[99]

In explicating Nzuri, Welsh-Asante posits and explains three central aesthetic categories-realities: "sources, aspects, and principles." When diagrammed, the Nzuri model consists of four concentric circles, the three innermost circles being the holders of ontological *sources*, the outermost circle being the holder of seven determinative *aspects*. Beginning from the diagram's core, the innermost source circle holds *"spirit"*; the next source circle holds *"rhythm"*; and the third source circle holds *"creativity"*. The fourth, final, and outermost circle holds and consists of seven distinct-but-interrelated determinative-locational aspects: *form, method/technique, function, mode, motif, ethos,* and *meaning.* Additionally, the Oral, the *Ehe,* and the *Ashe* principles manifest and interact in various ways within the Nzuri model.[100]

Spirit, Rhythm, and Creativity are primary. Welsh-Asante states that those three ontological sources "are the key criteria in discussing any [centered] aesthetic for African people." She says they derive from her aforementioned *"epic memory"*—that relatively non-empirical reality that Larry Neal refers to as *"race memory,"* and which Robert Ferris Thompson refers to as *"ancestorism."*[101] Further, the three sources are *ntuonic.* They are infused with NTU–"the Life Force, the infinite cosmic energy" which permeates and flows through all beings and things, and which joins everything.[102]

It seems that spirit is pristine. Then, rhythm manifests and ascends from within spirit; then, creativity ripples forth from within rhythm. As the first manifestation of NTU, *spirit* transcends neat empirical discussion. It is within *and* beyond empirical understanding. Spirit is connected intimately to—what the ancient Kemetic people designated as—the K(R)A, that is, the soul. Spirit does not "die" or cease to exist; indeed, it cannot die. Further, spirit cannot be seen, quantified, or measured within empirical epistemology and frames of knowing.

Though unseen, it joins things and holds things together, gives things order—and it is a prerequisite on the way to creativity. Welsh-Asante states, "[S]pirit is the metaphysical experience of humans, and as such, it provides an ethereal extension to both the super world of deities and the inner world of [humans and our] ideas, thoughts and emotions."[103] Spirit permeates all. Clearly, it is difficult to explicate spirit fully. Sometimes, spirit can be sensed or felt more easily than it can be discussed or explicated.

Rhythm is similar to spirit. In its similarity to spirit, rhythm—or, a satisfactory "sense of rhythm"—"gels human reality," explicates Welsh-Asante. [Spirit births rhythm; rhythm is harmonious movement; spirit includes harmonious movement as well as harmonious and profound stillness.] Welsh-Asante asserts and explicates with confidence and clarity:

> Rhythm is integral to the life force of every African. . . . The relationship between Africans and rhythm is not only constant but it is essential. It is not a question of having rhythm or not having rhythm but how well does one negotiate rhythm in life and in the artistic expressions of life. On time or off time is a . . . result of a . . . basic relationship with rhythm.[104]

As visible or subtle harmonious movement, then, rhythm is ntuonic life force or energy that guides and permeates "acts of creation and the material results of artistic thought." Indeed, according to Welsh-Asante, the "relationship to rhythm is key not only in dance and music but in visual arts, architecture, theater, literature and film."[105]

In Welsh-Asante's Nzuri model, *creativity* is the third ontological source. Creativity is similar to spirit and rhythm, in that it is invisible. Yet, creativity gives rise to that which is visible. We cannot see "creativity," but we can see the creations that creativity produces and enables. Welsh-Asante says, "[creativity] is one of the material manifestations of spirit and rhythm, the two . . . sources [which precede it]."[106]

African artists are great carriers of creativity, so they create much. Equal to creativity, however, is "what has been created and who evaluates what has been created."[107] As African artists create,   (a) at their best, their creations reflect authentic African culture predominantly; and   (b) their creations are best evaluated by the African community, that is, by Africans competent relative to knowing—those able to see, hear, and determine authentic African culture. Within African aesthetics, Welsh-Asante says, "creativity is both communal and individual"; creations affirm and serve both the community and the individual creator(s).[108]

Further, Welsh-Asante notes, creativity is "an expansive concept"; as it stretches the artist and her/his vision of the world. Creativity enables the artist to produce creations that are rooted in the artist's particular, predominant ancestral culture, and which can be accessed and appreciated simultaneously by people from all the world's cultures. Welsh-Asante makes the matter clear when she asserts:

> Finally, creativity is the metatext for creation itself[;] and through man's and society's creative expressions, clarity is shed on the Supreme Being's master plan.[109]

Nzuri, as mentioned above, posits seven aspects: form, method/ technique, function, mode, motif, ethos, and meaning. The seven aspects, in addition to guiding the creation of art, allow classificatory determinations to be made. Once an artistic product manifests, the seven aspects enable evaluators to locate—or designate— the art product.

Welsh-Asante's *form* aspect is concerned with the artistic product's structure, and/or shape, and/or composition. The *method/ technique* aspect specifies the "practical, physical, and material means" employed to realize the artistic product, e.g., the writing and rehearsal of lyrics and music; the utilization and rehearsal of human voices, live instruments, and computer programmed instruments; the conceptualization and actual rehearsing of dance or choreography, poetry, prose, and so forth. *Function* is concerned with how the artistic product operates in relation to individuals and the community: Does it educate, entertain, "edutain," inspire, affirm, empower, encourage, and so forth?   *Mode* is concerned with the manner in which the artistic product is expressed, e.g., through music, words, dance, painting, and so forth. The *motif* aspect is concerned with the incorporation and utilization of symbols—in the artistic product—"which reflect a specific culture and heritage." Welsh-Asante's *ethos* aspect is concerned with the quality—intensity, type, clarity—of NTU ("spirt, emotion, energy") that the artistic product emanates or exudes. Her *meaning* aspect is concerned with the significance of the artistic product "in relationship to individual[s] and [the] community."[110]

As we finish noting the seven *aspects* of Welsh-Asante's Nzuri model, it is important that we note her, *Umfundalai* ("the essential"), an Afrocentric "artistic school of thought" that, says Welsh-Asante, is relevant "in all of the art forms." It is an African centered "technique used to devise or create a specific character or persona in an artistic product." *Umfundalai*, when utilized, helps ensure that the seven aspects are centered. Welsh-Asante began developing Umfundalai over twenty years ago.[111]

Relative to the *principles* within the Nzuri model, the *Oral* principle denotes the *transmission*-maintenance-and-continuity of traditional African art forms, "including storytelling, music, dance and literature." The *Ashe* principle denotes *affirmation* of African traditions "through reinforcement" of African artistic products. The *Ehe* principle denotes "discovery and renewal." It is a critical—and positive—Afrocentric response to an artist and her/his artistic product; it indicates that an artistic expression is new or creative, even as it is "contained and continued within the value parameters of [authentic-traditional African] society." "The *Ashe*, *Ehe*, and Oral principles," Welsh-Asante explains, "are concepts that interact within the *Nzuri* model." According to Welsh-Asante, they "emanate out of the [model's] sources and generate a support system for the *Nzuri* model['s] aspects." Finally, permeating the principles of the Nzuri model is the *Nommo Spiritual mode*—"the manifestaion of energy in all of its varied forms . . . spoken and unspoken, movement and gesticulation."[112]

Welsh-Asante's "The Aesthetic Conceptualization of Nzuri"has a single, overarching theme. The thirteen preceding paragraphs demonstrate that theme: delineation and explication of one, broad, centered African aesthetic theory: Nzuri.

Two styles of argumentation are predominant in Welsh-Asante's writings:

•African collective memory-perception argumentation
•Explicit locational—*umojan*—argumentation

"African Collective Memory-Perception," as I am positing the term, holds that African people share memory-perception. This term is akin to, but is not nearly as intricate as, Wade Nobles' "deep structure" designation.[113] As African people are linked externally, relative to our shared historical-experiential journey (journeying from societies, where peace, harmony, and progress predominated, to actual living configurations wherein pain, imbalance, and "survival" are too prevalent), so are we are linked internally, relative to a shared memory-perceptual base. Our common memory base consists of shared or common feelings, attitudes, and proclivities. Our common perceptual base consists of shared or common responses to tangible—and intangible—stimuli.

We are not talking necessarily about memory and perception relative to specific facts, specific events, specific people. Rather, we are noting that there is an incredible internal-interior memory-perception link—African collective memory-perception—that seems to exist among African persons generally. One manifestation of this link is revealed in the common-shared way(s) that African people perceive and respond to African artistic expressions. [Consider the popular African variety show, "Showtime at the Apollo." If an artist interfaces harmoniously or disharmoniously with the African-collective-memory and the African-collective-perception of the African audience, then she or he receives a response from the African collective (audience), that being approval or disapproval, accordingly.]

African collective memory-perception argumentation, then—perhaps predictably—is argumentation that depends upon and presupposes Welsh-Asante's epic memory sense. Close reading of "An Aesthetic Foundation" yields that almost all explication in the essay is linked to epic memory. Epic memory is pivotal; it is essential for the entire discussion. Consider the following, telling excerpts:

> . . . *epic memory* . . . contributes to the ideal in the African
> artistic expression. Perfection cannot be achieved unless
> the experience or *memory* sense is drawn upon. It is the

"body" of the work itself. . . . [*epic memory* retrieves and] delivers to the [audience] . . . pathos, feeling, and experience without telling the literal story. . . .[*Epic memory*] unearths the emotional feeling realm without limiting the artists or the audience. . . .[*Epic memory*] in the arts is the reconciliation of the metaphysical with the physical . . . . [*Epic memory*] flows into and overlaps with experience, preceding, feeding, and imprinting the African aesthetic qualities.[114] (emphasis mine)

[Centered African dances of all types, from all over the globe have] a commonality [that] can be established. Intrinsic in this commonality is the *ancestral connection* through *epic memory* and oral tradition, even though these dances represent different languages, people, geographies, and cultures.[115](Emphasis mine.)

Welsh-Asante continues:

[There are non-empirical parts in African aesthetics that] provide the African aesthetic with its complexity and the reasons for its nondocumentability in strictly Western terms. There is great difficulty in documenting . . . the extrasensory dimensions of an art form which is creative by definition . . . . The nonmeasured, but ultraperceivable senses are difficult to define . . . .

[I]t is not merely the skill that makes the [artist] . . . [it is] the history, *the memory*. The ontological aspect of African aesthetics is *memory*. The blues, the presence of *memory* recreated in the southern United States environment of Africans, and the samba, a 6/8 rhythm in dance, is continued and expanded from *memory*.[116] (Emphasis mine)

Explication and understanding of the seven aesthetic senses—and more—to varying degrees, depend upon the epic memory sense. Further, epic memory prevails in and through Welsh-Asante herself, enabling her (a) to encircle, to "name"—to *remember*, to *perceive*, to sense-identify-and-delineate—the African aesthetic senses, and (b) to communicate the same—and more—so that we can distinguish and grasp similarly. And epic memory functions in the African audience enabling African people to receive clearly what Welsh-Asante is communicating. Effective communication of empirical *and* nonempirical aesthetic information and understanding by way of the empirical page, is a form of African collective memory-perception argumentation. And this form of argumentation is prevalent in "An Aesthetic Foundation."

Location has to do with place—place relative to ideas, ideals, myth, history, symbols, icons, and more. Molefi Asante asserts, "All knowledge results from an occasion of encounter in place. . . . [and] place [is] a rightly shaped perspective that allows the Afrocentrist to put African ideals and values at the center of inquiry [and explication]."[117] In his *Malcolm X as Cultural Hero and Other Afrocentric Essays*, Asante states further, "Location tells you where someone is, that is, where they are standing. [Location gives] certain markers of identity."[118]

Explicit locational argumentation, then, at its best, is argumentation utilizing explicit African-centered language, names, terms, and philosophical assumptions or stances. Explicit locational argumentation is apparent, systematic, and nearly constant in its self-reinforcement and self-announcement, as it invites the reader or audience to come and see and consider—and even understand—from a centered African place, from a place planted on and supported by African ideals and positive African values. Explicit locational argumentation is argumentation with integrity. Minimally, explicit locational—Umojan—argumentation reinforces consistency and unity—Umoja—within the writer. Maximally, it reinforces unity—Umoja—within the writer *and* between the writer and her or his audience.

In explicit locational argumentation, the African speaker or writer makes her/his case utilizing African language terms frequently and centrally—rather than utilizing French, or German, or other non-African terms most frequently or centrally in the discussion. Welsh-Asante is explicit and "deliberate [in her] use and mix of Kiswahili, Shona, and other African language terms" in making and explicating her argument in "Nzuri."[119] Further, consider the appellation of her aesthetic model—"Nzuri," and the names of parts of the model—the "Ashe" principle, the "Ehe" principle. Consider too her various examples/references, when making various points, throughout the text: the *Sabaar* dance of the Wolof; the *Gure* dance of the Chopi; the Kikuyu women; the Mende girls; *Kente/Adinkra/Adire* designs;

the *Umfundalai*, the *Ntu*, the *Gelede* of Nigeria, the *Lindjen* dance of the Wolof, the *Mbakumba* dance of the Karanga of Zimbabwe, *Shango, Obatala*, the *Mbira* dance of the Shona.[120](emphasis hers)

In "Nzuri," centered African concepts and conceptions of reality are primary and predominant—rather than secondary, sporadic, peripheral. Indeed, African ontological understanding—that is, ancient and traditional African assumptions about the nature of Being and being—permeates the document. Consider that fundamental and foundational to "any aesthetic for African people" is the indivisible synthesis of "Spirit, rhythm, and creativity"[121]—such position is rooted firmly in the most ancient African (Twaic, Kemetic, and other) cosmological-philosophical understandings. Consider also the explicit location evident as Welsh-Asante cites and calls on great, positive, late and present, anchored/ing artistic African personages: Gwendolyn Brooks, Katherine Dunham, Coltrane, Wole Soyinka, DuBois, and Tubman.[122] Her location is explicit, clear, definite; she is Africa(n) centered. Welsh-Asante does not call on/ reach for Adrienne Rich, Barishnikov, Benny Goodman, Keats, William James, and Ulysses Grant, as such appellations would locate her away from herself. And when one is located away from one's self, away from one's cultural-historical center, then one is dislocated, mislocated, even misoriented.

Consider the following, disciplined stance, a stance based on and located in the heart of Africans' ancient and continuing commitment to *Ubora* ("excellence"). Welsh-Asante asserts that "critical . . . analytical skills from an Afrocentric perspective" are required to truly understand, fully appreciate, and properly perpetuate African art and aesthetics. Unreflective personal opinion, or spontaneous or elementary emotion, or simple positive or negative feelings, are not enough. If one wishes to have an authentic grasp of centered African aesthetics, it is imperative that one have "a knowledge of symbols, history, geography, language and conceptual actions such as time, space and elements."[123]

Another example of explicit location is Welsh-Asante's notation that the supreme affirmation in "traditional and contemporary African societies" is the *"Reward of Recognition"* [emphasis hers]. The Reward of Recognition occurs when the community, the art, and the artist are affirmed; and all are affirmed when their intersection produces creativity anchored firmly to knowing, remembrance, resemblance, and empathy. The *Reward of Recognition* includes criticism of the creation; and again, it is essential that the creation reflect and resemble the community—that is, the ancestors, those present, and those to be born.[124] Such conception is African centered; its positing such is explicit location. Our assertion that explicit locational argumentation redominates within "Nzuri" may be supported most explicitly when Welsh-Asante states:

> The need to define an Afrocentric aesthetic is in direct response to the continuous *dislocation* [emphasis hers] of Africans from their own particular and collective centers. . . . The essays in this volume[—and this essay in particular—] speak to the need for Africa to look within to create *express symbols and images* that allow Africans *an immediate route* to properly communicate to future generations.[125] (Emphasis mine)

Ultimately, collective memory/perception-based arguments can be understood as contained within locational arguments. Nonetheless, collective memory/perception-based arguments are sufficiently distinct to warrant independent consideration. Both types of argumentation are utilized in both Welsh-Asante documents. In "Commonalities in African Dance: An Aesthetic Foundation," however, collective memory/perception-based arguments predominate; while in "The Aesthetic Conceptualization of *Nzuri*" explicit locational arguments predominate.

Welsh-Asante's "Commonalities in African Dance: An Aesthetic Foundation" and her "The Aesthetic Conceptualization of *Nzuri*" are complementary writings, as they support and enhance each other. More importantly, they are Afrocentric writings. They deal with African centered aesthetics; and the philosophical, conceptual, and consequential reality of African centered aesthetics is that such *awakens*—and will continue to awaken—Black people; and when African people awaken to the truth of themselves, there is Afrocentric theory birthing Afrocentric consciousness and praxis! Further, as centered aesthetics are asserted, the march of European aesthetics will be confined essentially to the European community. The reality of hierarchical aesthetics will be transformed.

A number of different aesthetics will exist simultaneously, horizontally, dynamically, harmoniously.

Welsh-Asante's writings are manifestations of Afrocentricity. They are clear and bold, as they claim, hold, and ascend from an African centered perspective. As the documents are set forth, Welsh-Asante draws generally from the history, language, mythology, values, creative motif, ethos, deep and surface structure, and galvanizing traditions of African people. She also draws upon relevant non-African sources resonant with the most constructive traditional African values. Further, she does not merely parrot or replicate ancient African perspectives and set them forth, irrelevantly and ineffectively, in the contemporary context. Instead, Welsh-Asante demonstrates necessary contextual sophistication; as she draws from ancient and contemporary traditions, synthesizes the most constructive of the same with contemporary needs *while being careful to retain the integrity of the traditions*; then, finally she and shares the product, creation, or re-creation with the African and world community.

Additionally, Welsh-Asante expends a minimum of energy confronting the contradictions arising out of the white-racist/colorist-anti-African West. Most of her energy is given instead to asserting the African truth and allowing it to generate the beautiful, the good, the harmonious. Of course, as such an offensive rather than defensive process unfolds, worldviews collide periodically; and various Eurocentric contradictions are exposed and revealed automatically.

Welsh-Asante is fully self-conscious as she delineates, orders, and offers her aesthetic. It seems that Welsh-Asante is entering the town that Zora Neale Hurston longed for, the one that Larry Neal envisioned. It can be said, then, because of their work, Welsh-Asante is doing her work.

In "An Aesthetic Foundation," Welsh-Asante shares, "Pride and self-satisfaction come from the harmony [one achieves via one's art/work] with the ancestors, nature, family and village."[126] Such being true, Welsh-Asante can be proud and satisfied within herself, because she has indeed achieved and facilitated great harmony via *both* of her writings. Welsh-Asante's "Commonalities in African Dance: An Aesthetic Foundation," and her "The Aesthetic Conceptualization of *Nzuri*," are major contributions to Afrocentric metatheory in general and gigantic contributions to Afrocentric Aesthetic theory in particular. The works' significance to the Afrocentric project will only increase as time unfolds.

Before concluding this chapter, the major 1994 work of Marimba Ani (Dona Richards)—*Yurugu: An African-centered Critique of European Cultural Thought and Behavior*—will be commented upon briefly. It is, and its reputation will increase as, a very important Afrocentric document. A number of her earlier writings, such as *Let the Circle Be Unbroken:The Implications of African Spirituality in the Diaspora*, also contribute much to the Afrocentric project as well.[127]

Yurugu is an important book for the Afrocentric project. In the mythology of the Dogon people, Yurugu—also known as "Ogo"—is a restless, impatient, anxious entity. He/It is responsible for disharmony and disorder in the universe and cosmos. *Yurugu* is important for at least two major reasons: (1) Like much of Ani's work, it utilizes indigenous African words and terms as it introduces useful African centered concepts and terms; and (2) it is probably the most creative, *forthright*, comprehensive, meticulous, mature, systematic, Afrocentric analysis and critique of Europeans to date. For over 600 pages, Ani x-rays and examines the foundational and core ontological and epistemological assumptions of Europeans and their reality.

Ani questions and answers *why* and *how* Europeans manifest and create the violational, impositional, unfulfilling experience known as "Eurocentric reality."   With great boldness, she adresses and answers why Europeans are as they are, and how have they violated and imposed themselves on majority peoples so successfully and continually. She invites us to join her in considering the peculiar-yet-constant content and the oscillating contours of the collective European psyche—and the predictable behavior that manifests as a result. In her own words, Ani says of her effort:

> [It is] a critical study of the totality that is European culture; [my intention is] to lay bare its ideological underpinnings, its inner workings, the mechanisms that facilitate its functioning. . . .The objective of this study is to place the European experience under scrutiny in order to reveal its nature. We turn the tables by transforming "subject" into

"object," and in the process we are ourselves transformed into victors rather than victims. We emerge from the yoke of European conceptual modalities that have prevented us from the realization of [that which Molefi Asante refers to as] the "collective conscious will" of our people.[128]

Once African and other majority people understand *clearly* how and what makes Europeans "tick," then, the European way is exposed utterly. Its mystery is removed. Its massiveness is reduced. European control and hegemony are dismantled, deconstructed, and discarded more readily; and there is an acceleration of the manifestation of a world where harmony and sanity prevail.

Yurugu is a work that advances the Afrocentric project in general and Afrocentric thought in particular. It is a forward moving, offensive work. It is not a reactionary effort. The document is not a simple lament; it is not a romantic sorrow song. The book does not catalogue the hideous, horrendous, wicked effects of Eurocentrism upon African people and other people of color. Rather, it focuses proactively upon dissection and delineation of the wicked, unhealthy phenomenon of Eurocentrism itself. *Yurugu* excavates and explicates the interior workings—the subterranean caverns, *dungeons!*—of the thought that creates-sustains-perpetuates-and-propagates European culture. Ani walks and strides deliberately, disrespectfully, slowly, sacrilegiously, incisively, and professionally upon European (un)holy ground. Ani explicates her effort further:

> This study of Europe is an intentionally aggressive polemic. It is an assault upon the European paradigm; a repudiation of its essence. It is initiated with the intention of contributing to the demystification necessary for those of us who would liberate ourselves [and our people] from European intellectual imperialism.[129]

Ani notes that Europe's political confusion of Africa—and much of the rest of the planet which is not Europe—"has been accompanied by a relentless cultural and psychological rape and by devastating economic exploitation." Ani continues, pointing out that beneath the just noted "deadly onslaught lies *a stultifying intellectual mystification*" [emphasis mine] that paralyzes the thinking of the political victims of Europe. Indeed, this evasive mystification prevents the victims of Europe "from thinking in a manner that would lead to authentic self-determination."[129a] With piercing insight, Ani explicates a simple, immeasurably critical truth:

> The secret Europeans discovered early in their history is that *culture carries rules for thinking*, and that if you could impose your culture on your victims you could limit the creativity of their [thinking and] vision, destroying their ability to act with will and intent and in their own interest. The truth is that we are all "intellectuals," all potential visionaries.[130] (emphasis mine)

After asserting her thesis and intentions, Ani makes clear some of her essential ideological, and philosophical commitments:

> This study was not approached objectively. It is not possible to be objective towards Europe. Certainly the victims of its cultural, political, and economic imperialism are not objective, if they are sane. . . .
> The claim that [is made here] is not to a spurious "objectivity," but to honesty. I, therefore, have made no attempt to camouflage either my relationship to Europe or my goal in undertaking this study.[131]
> . . . [This study is grounded] in African-centeredness. "Afrocentricity" is a way of viewing reality that analyzes phenomena using the interest of African people as a reference point, as stated by Asante. African-centeredness provides the theoretical framework within which the dominant modes of European expression have been set for analysis [in this work]. This process establishes a system for critical evaluation. Its standards are severe. Its questions uncompromising.[132]

Three major, interrelated concepts galvanize and guide Ani's work: *asili, utamawazo*, and *utamaroho*.[133] *Asili,* is a Kiswahili word with a number of related meanings—"beginning," "seed," "source," "germ," "origin," "essence," "nature." Taking the term and utilizing it as a conceptual tool for cultural analysis, Ani explicates that Asili can be held as referring to "the explanatory principle in a culture." It is important to note that Ani's discussion of the Asili does *not* include notions on the genesis of the Asili itself: how it came into existence. Her discussion encompasses (a) existence of the Asili, (b) delineation of the Asili and how it functions. Asili is "like a template that carries within it the pattern or archetypical model" for a culture's development. It can be understood as "the DNA of [a] culture." Ani says the asili "acts as a screen, incorporating or rejecting innovations, depending on their compatibility with [the asili's] own essential nature."[133a] Ani explicates further:

> *Asili* is a synthesizing concept in that it allows us to explain and to see the way in which various aspects of a culture relate and how they cohere. *Asili* allows us to distinguish the peripheral, the anomalous, the idiosyncratic, and at the same time *asili* allows us to interpret patterns of collective thought and behavior. *Asili* is both a concept and a cultural reality.
> . . .*asili* is not [merely] an idea . . . . It is a force, an energy [which can be perceived and experienced]. *Asili* is the primary factor of cultural development and an essential explanatory principle in cultural theory.[134] (emphasis hers)

Utamawazo and *utamaroho*, terms which Professor Ibrahim Sherif and Professor Jaffer Kassimali helped Ani create the *asili* concept. Utamawazo is a word Ani created by borrowing from the Kiswahili words *utamundi* ("culture," "civilization") and "wazo" ("thought"). She says *utamawazo* is a word designed to hold and posit the concept "thought as determined by culture." Ani created *utamaroho* by synthesizing the aforementioned *utamundi* and another Kiswahili word, *roho* ("spirit-life"). *Utamaroho,* as posited by Ani, means "the spirit-life of a culture," "the collective personality" of a culture's members.[135]

Going deeper, utamawazo can be understood as being *similar* to "worldview;" because it does involve emphasis on (1) particular nonempirical—ontological—presuppositions, and (2) "the way in which [a] culture presents its members with definitions and conceptions with which to order experience." Ani says utamawazo goes farther than worldview, however, because utamawazo "places more emphasis on *conscious mental operations* [emphasis mine] and refers to the way in which both speculative and nonspeculative thought is structured by ideology and bio-cultural experience."[135a] Ani explicates further:

> *Utamawazo* allows us to demonstrate the ideological consistency of the premises of [a] culture and to identify those premises as they tend to be standardized expressions of a single cultural entity. . . . [Utamawazo] focuses on epistemological definitions in the belief that as culture acts to fix definitions of truth and truth-process, the culture constructs a universe of   authorization that rejects and incorporates ideas with reference to a cultural predisposition in intent and style. . . . *Utamawazo*, then, cannot be understood unless it is placed in the context of *asili*.[136] (emphasis hers)

In short, utamawazo "accounts for perspective."[137] It is the way that members of a culture—must—see and perceive collectively. It is the imperative—almost unavoidable—pattern of the thought, and ultimately the behavior, of the members of a culture.

Ani argues that while *utamawazo* is cognitive in expression, "*utamaroho* is affective." Further, it is a collective reality. Utamaroho can be understood, then, as the unconscious, subconscious, instinctive, collective response—and sometimes reaction— by the members of a culture as they meet life, as they are met and confronted by life and life circumstances. Ani makes the matter clearer by explaining, "[Utamaroho can be understood as] the idea that a . . . culture, or group of people possess an immaterial (nonphysical) substance that determines their unique character or 'nature.' But the physical and nonphysical essence[s] [are] here linked as . . . in the concept of a 'gene' which carries 'memory.' "[137a] Perhaps Ani is clearest when she explicates the matter this way:

> [*Utamaroho* is the] vital force of a culture, set in motion by the *Asili*. It is the thrust or energy source of a culture[,] giv[ing] it its emotional tone and motivat[ing] the collective behavior of its members. Both the *Utamawazo* and *Utamaroho* are born out of the *Asili* and, in turn, affirm it. They should not be thought of as distinct from the *Asili* but as manifestations of it.[138] (emphasis hers)

The three aforementioned powerful conceptual tools, plus her unapologetic and intentional reliance upon the work of other Afrocentric thinkers, her blatant subjective trust in her own life experience, and the ability to write clearly, are all more than Ani needs to accomplish her task.

In the course of her book, she names, deconstructs, demystifies, and thereby disempowers the major ideological pillars—the keys, the core, the decisive deep structure aspects—undergirding and unifying European cultural thought and behavior. Ani sets forth, defines, and dissects a number of terms and concepts that are pivotal for anyone wishing to understand the workings of Eurocentric reality. Those terms and concepts include "the Cultural Other," "Dichotomization," "Lineality," "Objectification," "Reductionism," and "Yurugu."[139] The following chapter titles and sub-titles within chapters give indication of Ani's "scalpel and laser" approach, evincing her seriousness in confronting, decloaking, and dehooding the workings of Eurocentric reality. Consider the following partial list of titles: "Desacralization of Nature: Despiritualization of the Human," "Religion and Ideology" (probably the most important chapter), "Christianity, Colonialism, and Cultural Imperialism: 'Heathen,' 'Native,' and 'Primitive,' " "Aesthetic: The Power of Symbols," "An Aesthetic of Control," " 'White,' 'Good,' and 'Beautiful,' " "The Myth of a Universal Aesthetic," "Hypocrisy as a Way of Life."

In summary, Ani's Afrocentric critique meets Eurocentric cultural thought and behavior head on. She exposes Oz's facade; she identifies and removes the curtains from the control booth. She cuts away illusory intellectual barbed wire. With solid, searing analysis, she melts away what many thought was immovable iron, impenetrable steel. She encircles and illuminates the contradictions, carves a sophisticated path through the oscillating yet tamable European intellectual jungle, cracks codes and hacks into the European intellectual-cultural mainframe; and the evidence is clear: the structure of European cultural thought is quite vulnerable.

The decision rests with the people and intellectual-cultural custodians of Europe. They can continue on the fruitless and ridiculous path of Eurocentric reification, or they can work consciously at the intentional transmutation of their Asili. Eurocentric reification no longer works.

Afrocentricity enables Afrocentric scholars to understand such reification now. Equipped with the tool of Afrocentricity, increasing numbers of African scholars are enervating all destructive, imprisoning reified European terms, concepts, and forms. European people will either transform or alter European cultural thought and behavior so that harmonious co-existence with African people and the other majority peoples of the Earth occurs; or, an immeasurably difficult future awaits all the people on the Earth.

In *Yurugu: An African-centered Critique of European Cultural Thought and Behavior*, Marimba Ani has given us a proficient, intellectual Afrocentric document.

NATIONAL AND INTERNATIONAL ORGANIZATIONS

Currently, there are three national organizations—and myriad local organizations—that affirm and assist the Afrocentric project. The African Heritage Studies Association (AHSA), The National Council for Black Studies (NCBS), and the Association for the Study of Classical African Civilizations (ASCAC) are the major organizations that have substantive understanding of the propagation of Afrocentricity. The aforementioned organizations are guided by African scholars. It is appropriate, therefore, to examine each of the three, noting each organization's originating context, each organization's constituency focus, and each organization's primary-distinguishing-defining activities.

The African Heritage Studies Association (AHSA) came into being in 1969. It was founded by Dr. John Henrik Clarke and other African scholars committed to the authentic liberation of African people. Once Dr. Clarke and others realized that the African Studies Association (ASA)—an organization founded in 1957 by European American scholars for the Eurocentric study of Africa—had made itself "the validating agency in the United States for all matters African, political and academic," AHSA's birth and formation was imperative. It is noteworthy that ASA came into being just as a number of African countries were achieving independence. Indeed, some scholars hold that ASA was and is a white, CIA/government-controlled organization.[140]

The context of AHSA's birth and subsequent early formation can be understood as a context of crisis, change, and challenge. It was a context of crisis because African people in the United States were still reeling from and dealing with the assassinations of El Hajj Malik El Shabazz (Minister Malcolm X) and The Rev. Dr. Martin Luther King, Jr. As musician-poet Gil Scott-Heron says of the late 1960s-early 1970s, ". . . all Black leaders who dared stand up wuz in jail, in the courtroom, or gone."[141]

It was a context of change; because the young students of the Civil Rights and Black Power-Black Arts Movements were continuing to work for, push for, and speak for change—change from a dehumanizing, oppressing, hierarchical, white people-focused society and world to a humanizing, freeing, horizontal, Black-and-all-people-focused society and world. Consequently, African scholars were being pushed indirectly and directly to be identifiably relevant relative to the academic, social, and political needs of African people.

Finally, AHSA's birth and foundational formation occurred within a context of challenge; because, fundamentally, ASA dared and challenged AHSA to be.[142] AHSA's second annual conference was a critical gathering but also a very successful one. On May 1-3, 1970, at Howard University, attendance was high, and "the programming was excellent." Ties with the ASA had been severed consciously and necessarily, and the people gave every indication that they were ready to continue moving forward independently. According to Cyprian Lamar Rowe, a participant in the pivotal May 1970 conference (and by 1978 an assistant professor in the—then—Department of Pan-African Studies at Temple University):

> The formation of the African Heritage Studies Association constitutes the reclaiming of [B]lack lives and the AHSA has made the statement that [Black] people must ultimately be in charge of their own destiny.[143]

AHSA's focus—its central constituency, the people involved in the organization and the people served by the organization—has remained consistent from the organization's inception to the present. AHSA's focus consists of African scholars, students, and community transformers—community activists. The organization understands the necessity of African scholars and African community transformers working together, reinforcing and complementing each other's work, to better and advance the lives of African people.

A number of activities distinguish and define the AHSA. The organization holds an annual conference wherein established scholars, undergraduate and graduate students, and community transformers are invited to present papers, organize panels, or conduct workshops. Periodically, conference papers are gathered, bound, and published. Additionally, AHSA affirms and encourages those African scholars, grade school teachers, and grade school administrators who work at creating Afrocentric programs, as well as those who write, research, and teach information relevant and empowering for African people. The multifarious constructive, creative local efforts of community transformers to make life just and human for African people are also affirmed, encouraged, and supported by AHSA.[144]

Years ago, AHSA "was seeking *new theories and approaches to the study of Africa*" [emphasis mine]. Today, Afrocentric theory and Afrocentric approaches to the study of Africa have been found—and they continue to expand and grow stronger. Years ago, AHSA held that "[We who are African people] must begin to make our assumptions about life, the world, et cetera, the basic assumptions . . . everything [that we do relative to Black education] must grow radically out of our [African people's] experience." Today, Afrocentricity rests on the assertion that for African people, viewing all of life through African eyes is the height of sanity, an utter necessity, and the key to personal and group liberation. According to Cyprian Rowe, in 1970 at the second AHSA conference, Chike Onwuachi proclaimed, "We must bring about a centralization of our ethnic effort. We must sustain the spiritual resources of our past."[145] Today, an ever-increasing "centralization of our ethnic effort" is a reality: continental Africans and diasporan Africans all over the globe embrace and utilize the ancestor-honoring, pan-African theory of Afrocentricity.

Almost twenty-five years ago, African scholars, students, and local community workers were nurtured and cultivated by AHSA. Today, many of those same people are avid supporters and participants in the Afrocentric project. It is no wonder, then, that AHSA embraces and espouses Afrocentricity; for while AHSA may not be a monolithic, homogeneous seed bed that leads directly into the

Afrocentric project, it is undeniable that the organization assists and contributes greatly to the spread of Afrocentricity and the unfolding of the Afrocentric project.

The first conference of the National Council for Black Studies (NCBS) was held in 1976. The context of the organization's birth can be understood as a context of construction in the midst of deconstruction.

In 1976, the United States celebrated its bicentennial, In that same year, Eurocentric rulers and custodians of the United States began—or continued—a serious, relatively insidious, intentional assault upon the various gains made by African people from the 1950s, the beginning of the modern Civil Rights Movement, through about 1975 or 1976, the waning days of the Civil Rights-Black Power-and-Black Arts Movements. Almost simultaneously—and actually earlier, the Chairperson of the Department of Afro-American Studies at the University of North Carolina at Charlotte, Dr. Bertha Maxwell, and other African scholars, saw or foresaw how the said assault would result in reduction and deconstruction of many of the gains African people made in higher education—*unless* African scholars made creation and construction of a national professional organization an immediate priority.[146]

With great foresight, from 1975-1976, Dr. Maxwell and other astute and self-determined African scholars—some of whom were already members of AHSA—worked at constructing, and did in fact construct, the National Council for Black Studies, (NCBS) was/is a much-needed "national professional organization" for pro-African higher education. While Eurocentric persons worked at deconstruction of pro-African higher education, and in the midst of numerous African business ventures, publications, people, and movements being attacked and deconstructed, NCBS was conceived and constructed.[147]

The NCBS' focus consists of African scholars from all fields and disciplines, scholar-activists, and African American Studies (Black Studies) administrative units. NCBS is committed to assisting and enabling the strengthening of existing—and the creation of new—African centered Black Studies units within the academic community, as well as Afrocentric academic programs based within local communities. Further, NCBS' leadership understands that the contributions of scholars, scholar-activists, and administrators are *all* needed to help and ensure that the NCBS discharges its work as thoroughly and as effectively as possible.[148]

A number of activities distinguish the NCBS. Similar to the AHSA, it holds an annual conference for African scholars, scholar-activists, students, and administrators. Additionally, NCBS publishes (a) a newsletter, "The Voice of Black Studies," (b) a scholarly journal, *The Afrocentric Scholar: The Journal of the National Council for Black Studies*, and (c) special documents and surveys noting the state of Black Studies. The NCBS also has a number of foundation—such as Ford Foundation—sponsored programs, including the Summer Faculty Institute, a program wherein new African American Studies faculty are introduced to Afrocentric approaches to thinking, writing, teaching, and researching. Further, the organization affirms efforts by local African people and groups, and works with other national African organizations committed to the uplifting and centering of African people. Finally, it is important to note that NCBS has established evaluation and accreditation standards for African American Studies programs and departments; this may be the organization's most controversial and most progressive activity.[149]

The NCBS has always worked to rectify and enhance the study of African people. More specifically, the organization has always worked "to promote and strengthen academic and community programs in the area of Black Studies."[150] Around 1988, however, the organization sharpened its focus. NCBS began making it clear to its members and others that the organization was holding and utilizing an Afrocentric perspective and approach in its efforts. The *National Council for Black Studies Constitution and Bylaws* states explicitly:

> The National Council for Black Studies is a professional organization that defines, promotes and enriches Black Studies as a vehicle to further the development of people of African descent. As such, it attempts to integrate scholarship and political advocacy from an [*A*]*frocentric* perspective to affect public policy and contribute to the liberation of African people in Africa and throughout the diaspora.[151] (emphasis mine)

As a tangible indication of its Afrocentric self-understanding, the NCBS held its First International—its 17th Annual—Conference in Accra, Ghana, West Africa, in 1993. In 1994, the organization held a Second International—its 18th Annual—Conference at Georgetown, Guyana, in South America. The organization's Afrocentric self-understanding helps African scholars, and the African community as a whole, attain and maintain an independent posture. It frees Africans from being at the costly mercy of Eurocentric organizations, publications, conferences, and so forth.

Considering the preceding, and considering that the organization has established a national office—replete with full-time staff persons—it is clear that the NCBS has great organizational commitment, clarity, stability, and visibility. Further, and finally, when it is considered that the organization clarified and specified its core philosophical commitments more than a decade ago, then it becomes clear that NCBS—with its motto, "Promoting Academic Excellence and Social Responsibility"—is a serious participant in the national and global Afrocentric project.

The Association for the Study of Classical African Civilizations (ASCAC) was established February 1984, in Los Angeles, California, at a gathering designated, "The First Annual Ancient Egyptian Studies Conference." The gathering was co-chaired by Maulana Karenga and Jacob Carruthers. Yosef ben-Jochannan, John Henrik Clarke, and other leading African scholars. ASCAC 1995 literature states, "[ASCAC] was inspired by Dr. Yosef ben-Jochannan, called forth by Dr. Maulana Karenga, operationalized by Dr. Jacob Carruthers, given an economic imperative by [ASCAC'S] Eastern Region, named with historical accuracy by Dr. John Henrik Clarke, and institutionalized by Nzingha Ratibisha Heru."[152]

The context of the organization's birth can be understood as extreme socio-political regression and horrendous socio-economic oppression infiltrated by profound hope, indomitable determination, informational insurrection, and psychological resurrection.

In 1984, Ronald Reagan's unabashedly Eurocentric administration was concluding its first term and beginning a second. For most African people, that reality bespoke dire times. Specifically, that reality portended the maintenance and furtherance of extreme sociopolitical regression and horrendous socio-economic oppression.

Simultaneously, however, for some Africans, that monstrous reality meant that it was absolutely imperative that the African community collect itself and overcome great odds and gigantic obstacles—again. For some Africans, dire times are not to be accepted or bowed to; rather, such difficult seasons are to be challenged—and infiltrated with profound hope and indomitable determination. Looking back, explaining some of the energy and impetus behind the aforementioned 1984 gathering, Jacob Carruthers—director of the Kemetic Institute in Chicago, and ASCAC's first president—tells us:

> Only the determined intellectual resistance waged by the 19th century Black Nationalists in the western hemisphere prevented the complete take over of the Nile Valley culture by [white] intellectual emirates who accompanied the Napoleonic invasion of Kemet (Egypt) in 1798. Those old African scrappers never left the high ground of the Nile Valley heritage[;] and now their spirit . . . beckons us to come back to the Black Land [and reestablish our birthright of collective sanity, collective dignity, and collective prominence—in the United States and around the world].[153]

In 1984, then, Carruthers, Karenga, and others began heeding the beckoning of our nineteenth century Black Nationalist ancestors—people like Robert Benjamin Lewis (1834, 1844), Hosea Easton (1837), J. W. C. Pennington (1841), William Wells Brown (1874), and Edward Wilmot Blyden (1884). Karenga, Carruthers and others determined to puncture the looming and expanding white-anti-African-nightmare, determined to mount a most serious informational insurrection, determined to catalyze the psychological resurrection of millions of African people in and beyond the United States.

ASCAC was born in 1984, in a context of regression and oppression—*infiltrated by intentional informational correction and insurrection, coupled with the beginning of the mass resurrection of millions of Africans' African mind.* And at its inception, ASCAC determined that it would encourage, support, and contribute continually to "the organization of African people throughout the world toward the rescue of the African heritage and the restoration of African civilization."[154]

ASCAC's focus consists of local people, college and university students, and local-national-and-international African scholars interested in serious, systematic study of classical African civilizations. ("Classical," in this instance, means "noteworthy and influential during and beyond a society's most prominent time.") Calling itself an "African centered organization," ASCAC states in its literature:

> The aim and thrust of *ASCAC* is to bring together scholars, thinkers, planners, artists, students, scientists, technicians and most significantly, dedicated workers to promote and preserve our ancient African heritage [by studying] African civilization and [by developing and promoting an African worldview.[155]

It is especially noteworthy and quite impressive that ASCAC invites and encourages the membership and active participation of nonscholars. When committed local people, energetic students, and generous learned scholars work together—a powerful and productive synergy is released. Indeed, when those three communities work in concert, incredible and beautiful things can happen. Much of the work and many of the accomplishments of the Africans of the 1960s and early 1970s make the matter clear. So, not only is ASCAC's multifaceted, intergenerational focus a demonstration of Afrocentricity applied—it also bodes well for the organization's and African people's collective future.

ASCAC is distinguished and defined by a number of activities. Like AHSA and NCBS, ASCAC offers annual conferences for its members and potential members. The organization's First International (its Fourth Annual) Conference took place in Kemet, Egypt, July 1987. The location of the First International Conference is noteworthy for at least two reasons. First, it indicates a tangible heeding of Diop's admonition that African people must begin by claiming and coming to understand Kemet—as such will enable us to (a)understand all of Africa, (b)place Africa and ourselves properly in world history, (c)renew African culture, and (d)build a healthy future for Africa and African people everywhere. Second, from ASCAC's inception through the present time, while there has been and will be research on various classical African civilizations, most of the organization's classical African civilizations research has centered on Kemet.

In addition to offering regional, national, and international conferences, ASCAC is distinguished by its position endorsing and promoting African-centered (Afrocentric) curriculum in public, private, and independent schools. Further, complementing its publication—in book form—of selected papers from select national conferences, the organization publishes occasional papers in *Critical Commentaries: A Series of Shared Insights on the Important, Pivotal and Controversial Issues of Our Time.* ASCAC also publishes *Serekh: Promoting An African Worldview,* a quarterly newsletter. Four major, ongoing, project research and application areas are part of the organization's structure and function: the Research Commission, the Education Commission, the Creative Production Commission, and the Spiritual Development Commission.[156] Finally, within designated regions, ongoing local African centered Study Groups exist—and they may be the most outstanding activity of ASCAC. In ASCAC's Mid-Atlantic region, in Philadelphia, Pennsylvania there is a diligent group of local people who are dedicated relative to reading-studying-critiquing-and-applying major African centered documents. Indeed, that same Study Group also sponsors an ongoing lecture series, "Nile Valley Contributions to World Civilizations."[157]

It is in and through all of the aforementioned activities that ASCAC contributes to the work of recentering African history-culture-and-people on the world stage. ASCAC is an Afrocentric organization committed to a bold vision, a vision that will be realized by many months and years of intergenerational and transgenerational work. It is clear that ASCAC supports the Afrocentric project—hear Jacob Carruthers:

> . . . through ASCAC . . . we will reestablish our spirit and cultural foundations. Such a restoration will in turn give African people the intellectual and theoretical framework for the development of institutions and movements that will   enable us to "retake our fame [in the tradition of our greatest, most constructive, most human African ancestors]."[158]

There are other scholars—such as Abu Abarry, Kobi K.K. Kambon (Joseph A. Baldwin), Wade Nobles, Linda James Myers, Na'im Akbar, Asa Hilliard, and C.T. Keto—who are proponents and practicioners of Afrocentric thought and Afrocentric praxis. There are other, smaller, more localized organizations that support the Afrocentric project. Consider "PACE"—the Pan African Cultural and Educational Institute, Inc.—located in Hamilton, New York, catalyzed by African scholars and students at Colgate University. PACE and organizations like it help further the intellectual growth and popular expansion of the Afrocentric project.[159]   While all the people and organizations involved in Afrocentric thought and praxis have not been and cannot be cited and noted, this chapter nonetheless has attempted to examine the most fundamental.

In the next chapter, all of the preceding elements will be considered and the principal principles or characteristics distinguishing Afrocentric thought and praxis will be extracted and set forth as a guiding analytical grid.

NOTES

1.   J. A. Rogers, *World's Great Men of Color, Volume II* (New York: Macmillan, 1972), pp. xxiii-xxiv. It is also important to note here Daudi Ajani ya Azibo, "Articulating the Distinction between Black Studies and the Study of Blacks," *The Afrocentric Scholar: The Journal for the National Council for Black Studies* Volume 1/ Number 2 (May 1992): 64-97. In Azibo's very important and meticulous essay, on page 88, Azibo cites Lorenzo Martin's research which notes, " '[A]s early as 1971 Dr. Chancellor Williams had 'written [history] from an Afrocentric [perspective].' "   See Lorenzo Martin, "Arab Imperialism," *The Afrocentric World Review*, 1 (1) (1973): 43-46. Additionally, in Azibo's aforementioned essay, on pages 87-88, Azibo notes that in 1973 Dr. Jacob Carruthers and the Association of African Historians (AAH) published a journal entitled *The Afrocentric Word Review*. Azibo notes, "[The AAH was concerned with Africentricity or Afrocentricity; and the AAH defined its position this way]: 'Putting Black interests first, [is] the view of Afrocentrality . . . Afrocentrism strives for . . . a collective identity [and is] founded on Black ideas, rather the the ideas of non-Blacks

... [and] the best place to begin this endeavor is with our collective experience, rather than the preconceived theories of aliens.' " See Association of African Historians, "Prefatory Remarks to our Readers," *The Afrocentric World Review,* 1 (1) (1973): 1-2. Finally, in Azibo's essay, on page 88, Azibo notes Dr. Wade Nobles' creation of "An Afro-Centric Analysis of the Black Family" an African Centered theory and practical application of that conceptual creation as early as 1978. See Wade Nobles, "Toward an Empirical and Theoretical Framework for Defining Black Families," *Journal of Marriage and the Family* (November 1978): 686, 679-688. In all of the above, Azibo is concerned with attempting to establish that the term and concept "Afrocentric" or "Afrocentricity" existed in some form prior to Asante's extensive articulation and development of Afrocentricity in 1980.

2. This important remark by Dr. Clarke was shared with this writer by Dr. Molefi Kete Asante. The writer of this paper was present for two days of the 1995 AHSA Conference but was not present the day that Clarke made the noted remark.

3. Chinweizu, *The West and the Rest of Us: White Predators, Black Slaves, and the African Elite* (Lagos, Nigeria: Pero Press, 1975, 1987), p. 492.

4. Ibid., p. 493.

5. Ibid., p. 495.

6. Ibid., pp. 496-497, 505.

7. Roy D. Morrison II, "Black Enlightenment: The Issues of Pluralism, Priorities and Empirical Correlation," *Journal of the American Academy of Religion* XLV/2 Supplement (June 1978): 219-220.

8. Ibid., pp. 221, 223.

9. Molefi Asante shared this information with me during a formal meeting, at Temple University, Thursday, June 23, 1994. A number of Asante's other articles show his working on crystallization of the concept of "Afrocentricity" prior to 1980; see Molefi K. Asante, "Socio-Historical Perspectives of Black Rhetoric," *Quarterly Journal of Speech* (October 1970); see M.K. Asante, "Markings of an African Concept of Rhetoric," *Today's Speech* (March 1971); see M.K. Asante, "Toward a Revolutionary   Rhetoric," in *Return to Vision,* ed. Richard L. Cherry (New York: Houghton Mifflin, 1971); and see M.K. Asante, "Systematic Nationalism: A Legitimate Strategy for National Selfhood," *Journal of Black Studies* (September 1978).

10. See Vincent Harding, *There Is a River* (New York: Vintage Books, 1982), pp. xxv-xxvi; Manning Marable, *How Capitalism Underde-*

veloped Black America *(Problems in Race, Political; Economy and Society* (Boston: South End Press), pp. 215-228; Manning Marable, *Race, Reform and Rebellion: The Second Reconstruction in Black America, 1945-1982* (Jackson: University Press of Mississippi, 1984, 1989), pp. 168-199, 200-212; Haki R. Madhubuti, *Earthquakes and Sunrise Missions: Poetry and Essays of Black Renewal, 1973-1983* (Chicago: Third World Press, 1984), pp. 17-33, 133-135, 145-154, 171-175; Alphonso Pinkney, *The Myth of Black Progress* (New York: Cambridge University Press, 1986); Claudia Tate, *Black Women Writers at Work* (New York: Continuum Publishing Corporation, 1985), 133, 135-137; Joanne M. Braxton and Andree Nicole McLaughlin, *Wild Women in the Whirlwind: Afra-American Culture and the Contemporary Literary Renaissance* (New Brunswick, N.J.: Rutgers University Press, 1990), pp. 361, 357-362.

11.   See Asante, *Afrocentricity* (New Revised Edition 1988), pp. vii, ix, 42, 106-107, respectively. Further, throughout the book, Asante speaks of "us," "we," "our."

12.   Ibid., pp. 1, 21-24, 52, 109-120.

13.   Ibid., pp. ix, 21-22, 25.

14.   Ibid. Also, pay close attention to pp. 24-30, "Toward Collective Consciousness."

15.   Ibid., p. 50.

16.   Ibid., pp. 31-34, 45-47, 50-58, 71-84.

17.   Ibid. Consider especially the discussion of "Afrology"—the term that preceded "Africalogy"—on pp. 58-65. Indeed, this entire document involves the intentional wielding of conceptual power, the making of symbols and meaning.

18.   I created the term and concept "harmosis" early in 1989. "Harmosis" was introduced formally in March 1990, in a paper entitled, *The Afrocentric African American Male: Messenger and Manifestation of MA'AT*; the paper was presented at the Twentieth Year Symposium of The University of Virginia's Black Student Alliance. It is now published—with some revisions—in *Testimony: Young African-Americans on Self-Discovery and Black Identity*, ed. Natasha Tarpley (Boston: Beacon Press, 1995), pp. 248-258.

19.   Ibid.

20.   Asante, *Afrocentricity*, pp. 85, 100-101, 103.

21.   Ibid., p. 104.

22.   Ibid., pp. 65-69. Also, see Harmosis implied in the discussion of "Negritude," pp. 69-71, and in "Relationships," pp. 52-58. Also see notation of the necessity of Harmosis between "logic and emotion" (p. 43), and "mind and matter, spirit and fact, truth and opinion" (p.

38).
23. Ibid., pp. 85, 86, 101.
24. Ibid., pp. 105, 106-107.
25. Ibid., p. 2.
26. Ibid., pp. 4, 6, 7, respectively.
27. Ibid., pp. 7-21.
28. Ibid., pp. 40-42.
29. See Marcel Griaule, *Conversations with Ogotemmeli: An Introduction to Dogon Religious Ideas* (London: Oxford University Press, 1980).
30. Asante, *Afrocentricity*, pp. 1-2, 21-30, 58-69.
31. Ibid., pp. 31, 32, respectively.
32. Ibid., pp. 32, 33, 35, 36, respectively.
33. Ibid., p. 37.
34. Asante, *The Afrocentric Idea*, pp. vii, 19, 81, 157.
35. Ibid., p. 159.
36. Ibid., p. 157.
37. Asante, *Kemet, Afrocentricity and Knowledge*, p. ix.
38. Ibid., pp. 3-40, 43-158, 161-193.
39. Ibid., pp. v, vii.
40. Ibid., pp. v, vi.
41. Ibid., p. vi.
42. See self-aware, self-conscious Native American centered and Latino-centered perspectives set forth in Vine Deloria, Jr., *God Is Red* (New York: Dell Publishing, 1983), and in Gustavo Gutierrez, *We Drink from Our Own Wells (The Spiritual Journey of a People)* (Maryknoll, N.Y.: Orbis Books, 1985), respectively.
43. Ibid., pp. 14, 12.
44. Ibid., pp. 8-12.
45. Ibid., p. 7.
46. Ibid., p. 30.
47. Ibid., p. 7.
48. Ibid., pp. 192, 193.
49. Maulana Karenga, *Introduction to Black Studies* (Los Angeles: Kawaida Publications, Fourth Printing, April 1987).
50. Ibid., see liner notes on book's back flap.
51. Ibid., pp. xii, xiii.
52. Ibid., p. xiii.
53. Ibid., pp. 353-354, 361-368.
54. Ibid., pp. 17-41, 42-349, 358-376.
55. Ibid., pp. 17-24.
56. Ibid., pp. 42, 43, 47.

57. Ibid., p. 373.
58. Maulana Karenga and Jacob Carruthers, eds., *Kemet and the African Worldview: Research, Rescue and Restoration [Selected Papers of the First and Second Conferences of the Association for the Study of Classical African Civilizations, 24-26 February 1984 (6224 AFE), Los Angeles, and 1-3 March 1985 (6225 AFE), Chicago]* (Los Angeles: University of Sankore Press, 1986), pp. 89, 90-92, 94.
59. Karenga, *Introduction*, pp. 162-163, 164-197.
60. Ibid., pp. 322-323.
61. Ibid., p. 345.
62. Ibid., pp. 322-349.
63. Ibid., pp. 264-265.
64. Ibid., pp. 265-277, 277-290, 284-286, 268-271.
65. Ibid., p. 291.
66. Ibid., pp. 293, 295, 291-295.
67. Ibid.
68. See Larry Neal, *Visions of a Liberated Future: Black Arts Movement Writings* (New York: Thunder's Mouth Press, 1989), pp. 62-66, 67-78.
69. Ibid., p. 316.
70. Ibid., pp. 372, 373.
71. Ibid., p. 133.
72. Ibid.
73. Ibid., p. 207.
74. Ibid.
75. Ibid.
76. Ibid., pp. 207-208.
77. Ibid.
78. Maulana Karenga, *Introduction to Black Studies*, 2nd ed. (Los Angeles: University of Sankore Press, 1990), pp. 34-38.
79. Ibid., pp. 35, 36. Also see James B. Stewart, "Reaching for Higher Ground: Toward an Understanding of Black/African Studies," *The Afrocentric Scholar*, 1 (1) (1992): 1-63.
80. Ibid., p. 36.
81. Ibid., pp. 37-38.

82. Ibid., p. 38. For additional examples of Karenga's contribution to the Afrocentric project see Maulana Karenga, *The African American Holiday of Kwanzaa: A Celebration of Family, Community, and Culture* (Los Angeles: University of Sankore Press, 1988); *The Book of Coming Forth by Day: The Ethics of the Declarations of*

Innocence, trans. and commentary by M. Karenga (Los Angeles: University of Sankore Press, 1990); also see document cited earlier—M. Karenga and J. Carruthers, eds., *Kemet and the African Worldview;* Maulana Karenga, ed., *Reconstructing Kemetic Culture: Papers, Perspectives, Projects [Selected Papers of the Proceedings of the Conferences of the Association for the Study of Classical African Civilizations, Including the Fourth Conference, Aswan, Egypt, 1987 (6227 A.F.E.)]* (Los Angeles: University of Sankore Press, 1990); and *Selections from the Husia: Sacred Wisdom of Ancient Egypt*, selected and retrans. by M. Karenga (Los Angeles: University of Sankore Press, 1984,1989).

83. Kariamu Welsh-Asante, "Commonalities in African Dance: An Aesthetic Foundation," in *African Culture: The Rhythms of Unity*, eds. Molefi Kete Asante and Kariamu Welsh-Asante (Westport, Conn.: Greenwood Press, 1985), pp.71-82; Kariamu Welsh-Asante, "The Aesthetic Conceptualization of *Nzuri*," *The African Aesthetic: Keeper of the Traditions*, ed. Kariamu Welsh-Asante (Westport, Conn.: Greenwood Press, 1993), pp. 1-20.

84. Welsh-Asante, "Dance Aesthetic Foundation," *African Culture*, p. x.

85. Ibid., pp. 72, 74, 74-81.

86. Welsh-Asante, "Aesthetic of *Nzuri*," *African Keeper Traditions*, pp. 10-13.

87. Welsh-Asante, "Dance Foundation," pp. 73-74.

88. Ibid., p. 74.

89. Ibid., pp. 74-75.

90. Ibid., pp.75, 76, 75-77.

91. Ibid., pp. 77-78, 77-79.

92. Ibid., pp. 79-80.

93. Ibid., pp.80-81.

94. Ibid., p. 81.

95. Ibid.

96. Welsh-Asante, "Aesthetic of *Nzuri*," p. 1.

97. Ibid.

98. Ibid.

99. Ibid., pp. 17, 9-18.

100. Ibid., p. 10.

101. Ibid., p. 4.

102. Ibid., p. 11.

103. Ibid.

104. Ibid., p. 12.

105. Ibid.

106. Ibid., p. 13,
107. Ibid., p. 12.
108. Ibid., p. 13,
109. Ibid.
110. Ibid., p. 11.
111. Ibid., pp. 9, 11, 9.
112. Ibid., p. 13, 10.
113. See Wade Nobles, Lawford L. Goddard, and William E. Cavill, III, *The KM Ebit Husia: Authoritative Utterances for the Black Family* (Oakland: The Institute for the Advanced Study of Black Family Life and Culture, Inc., 1985); note, especially, pp. 6-8.
114. Welsh-Asante, "Dance Foundation," pp. 79-80.
115. Ibid., p. 71.
116. Ibid., pp. 78, 79.
117. *Kemet, Afrocentricity*, p. 5.
118. Molefi Kete Asante, "On Afrocentric Metatheory," in Molefi Kete Asante, *Malcolm X as Cultural Hero and Other Afrocentric Essays* (Trenton: Africa World Press, 1993), p. 100.
119. Welsh-Asante, "*Nzuri*," p. 1.
120. Ibid., pp. 3, 6, 8, 9, 11, 13, 16, 17.
121. Ibid., p. 4.
122. Ibid., p. 8.
123. Ibid., p. 9.
124. Ibid., pp. 16-17.
125. Ibid., p. 6.
126. Welsh-Asante, "Dance Foundation," p. 79.
127. Marimba Ani (Dona Richards), *Yurugu: An African-Centered Critique of European Cultural Thought and Political Behavior* (Trenton: Africa World Press, 1994); Dona Marimba Richards, *Let the Circle be Unbroken: The Implications of African Spirituality in the Diaspora* (Trenton: Red Sea Press, 1989).
128. Ani (Richards), *Yurugu*, pp. 3, 24.
129. Ibid., p. 1.
129a. *Yurugu*, p. 1.
130. Ibid.
131. Ibid., p. 23.
132. Ibid., p. 24.
133. Ibid., pp. 11-21. Also, Dr. Dona Marimba Richards—Marimba Ani— shared and explicated these three pivotal terms while lecturing at Temple University, Sunday, October 18, 1989, five years prior to publication of *Yurugu*.
133a. *Yurugu*, pp. 11-12, xxv.

134. *Yurugu*, pp. 12, 13.
135. Ibid., pp. 13, 14, 15.
135a. *Yurugu*, pp. 14-15.
136. Ibid., pp. 15.
137. Ibid.
137a. *Yurugu*, pp. 15-16.
138. *Yurugu*, p. xxv.
139. *Yurugu*, pp. xxv, xxvii-xxviii, 230, 293, 301, 339, 402-416, 478, 32-36, 105, 56-69, 524-528, 556-560.
140. Cyprian Lamar Rowe, *Crisis in African Studies: The Birth of the African Heritage Studies Association* (Buffalo: Black Academy Press, 1970), p. 3. Also, for a thorough explication of AHSA's beginnings, see John Henrik Clarke, "The African Heritage Studies Association (AHSA): Some Notes on the Conflict with the African Studies Association (ASA) and the Fight to Reclaim African History," *Issue: A Quarterly Journal of Africanist Opinion*, vol. vi, number 2/3 (Summer/Fall 1976): 5-11. Cyprian Rowe's explanation is in harmony with Clarke's; and, essentially, it conveys the same information. John Henrik Clarke's sharing, however, is far more meticulous and comprehensive, giving information on the years preceding the AHSA's birth and on the years following its birth. The writer of this paper discovered the aforementioned essay by Dr. Clarke late; consequently, it is not quoted directly in the body of this text. Since Dr. Clarke was a, if not *the*, catalytic force in AHSA's inception, his essay is most authoritative. As an example of his comments, consider some of his concluding words on pp. 10-11 of his essay: "History, properly understood and utilized, is power—a force for liberation or slavery, depending on how it is used or misused. . . . The intent of the [AHSA] is to use African history to effect a world union of African people. . . . We know there is no way to move a people from slavery to self-awareness without engaging in political expedience and revolutionary coali-tions. . . . It is not enough to be united unless that unity has some meaning and goal. We had a common heritage before and after [Europeans captured us and traded us about]. We will have to make creative uses of this heritage. . . . It will be our function as scholar-activists to put the components of our heritage together to wield an instrument of liberation."
141. Gil Scott-Heron, *So Far, So Good* (Chicago: Third World Press, 1990), p. 68.
142. See John Henrik Clarke, "The African Heritage Studies Association (AHSA): Some Notes on the Conflict with the African Studies Association (ASA) and the Fight to Reclaim African History."

143. Rowe, *Birth of African Heritage*, p. 3. Also seee John Henrik Clarke's, "The (AHSA): Some Notes."
144. From 1989-1997, I had a number of conversations with the late Dr. Charshee McIntyre, professor at SUNY Old Westbury and a past president of AHSA. In those conversations, she shared and underscored the forms, the depth, and the breadth of AHSA's activities. Also, for a brief listing of the variety of AHSA attendees, see AHSA conference advertisement in The National Council of Black Studies, Inc.'s "The Voice of Black Studies Newsletter," vol. 18, number 3 (Winter 1993): 11.
145. Rowe, pp. 7, 8, 9.
146. Karenga, *Introduction Black Studies*, 2nd ed., p. 31. Also see Carolyn M. Leonard and William A. Little, eds., *National Council for Black Studies, Inc. Constitution and Bylaws* (Bloomington: National Council for Black Studies, Inc., Memorial Hall East 129, Indiana University, 1988), p. 1.
147. Karenga, *Introduction*, 2nd ed., pp. 31-32; *NCBS Bylaws*, p. 1. Also see Pennsylvania State University professor James B. Stewart, "The Field and Function of Black Studies," paper prepared for the William Trotter Institute for the Study of Black Culture at the University of Massachusetts, July 1987, p. 3. (typewritten)
148. See *NCBS Bylaws*; also see Carolyn M. Leonard and William A. Little, eds., *National Council for Black Studies, Inc. Organizational Handbook* (Bloomington: National Council of Black Studies, Inc., Memorial Hall East 129, Indiana University, 1988); also see James Stewart, "Field and Function," p. 3.; also see Karenga, *Introduction*, 2nd ed., p. 32.
149. James Stewart, pp. 3-9; *NCBS Organizational Handbook*, p. 79; Karenga, *Introduction*, 2nd ed., pp. 33-34.
150. *NCBS Bylaws*, p. 5.
151. Ibid., p. 3.
152. See "... building for eternity ASCAC Association for the Study of Classical African Civilizations," official organizational tri-fold brochure (Philadelphia: ASCAC, P.O. Box 130 42511, 19101, 1995); it introduces ASCAC, giving a brief overview of its history, purpose, objectives, significance, and mission. See Karenga and Carruthers, eds. *Kemet Worldview*, p. xi; Karenga, *Reconstructing Kemetic*, p. ix; also see the Association for the Study of Classical African Civilizations' conference packet, "Fourth Annual ASCAC Conference, July 8-10, 1987 (6227 A.F.K.-After the Founding of KEMET), Aswan, Egypt; also, this is handled excellently—and concisely—by a professor holding a Ph.D. at Alabama A & M, James Wesley Johnson,

"Kawaida and Kuminalism: Basis for a New Ecumenism" (Department of History and Political Science, Alabama A & M University, 1990), pp. 15-16.

153. *Kemet Worldview*, p. xi.

154. Ibid.

155. See ASCAC Spring 1994 promotional mailing to ASCAC members and potential members; also see Jacob Carruthers, ed., "Constitution of The Association for the Study of Classical African Civilizations, Article II (Purpose)" April 1985—a copy can be obtained from "ASCAC Foundation, 3624 Country Club Drive, Los Angeles, CA 90019," or from the writer of this work. Also see Nzingha Ratibisha Heru, "From the President's Office," *Serekh: Promoting an African Worldview* vol. 5, no. 1 (1994):1; and see "ASCAC Mission Statement"—it can be obtained from the address listed earlier in this paragraph.

156. For example, see Jacob Carruthers, "Carruthers on Schlesinger," *Critical Commentaries* (Los Angeles: ASCAC Foundation, 1991, 1992); also see Karenga, *Reconstructing*, pp. 179-222.

157. This information is readily available to me, as I am a member (and was a regional officer—past vice president and former interim president of the Mid-Atlantic region; and former National Executive Board Member—1987-1992) of ASCAC.

158. *Kemet Worldview*, p. xii.

159. See brochure, *Pan African Cultural Educational Institute.* The *PACE* brochure lists as its Founders: "Eulas Boyd, MS and Dr. Elleni Telda, President"; it lists as its Council of Elders: "Dr. John Henrik Clarke and Emama Mignon L. I. Ford"; and it lists as its contact address: "RD. 1 Box 155A. Hamilton, New York." I received this brochure from Dr. Elleni Telda—then of Colgate University—after she spoke at a Cheikh Anta Diop Conference in Philadelphia, Pa., Spring 1990.

Chapter 4

MAJOR PRINCIPLES

This chapter discusses the major principles that embody Afrocentric thought and praxis. From the major points, themes, and styles of argumentation identified in the preceding chapter, that is, from critical analysis of texts and thematic analysis of writings of Asante, Karenga, Welsh-Asante, and Ani, thirteen principles emerge as most salient:
1. The Meta-Constants: Humanizing and Harmonizing
2. The Primacy of African People and African Civilization
3. An African Audience as the Priority Audience
4. Njia as Theme
5. The Way of Heru as Theme
6. Harmosis as Mode
7. Wholistic Afrocentric Action as Goal
8. Sankofan Approach
9. Nommoic Creativity
10. Maatic Argumentation
11. Explicit Locational Indicators Intentionality
12. African Collective Memory-Perception Competence
13. Nzuri as Invitation and Standard

These thirteen principles comprise *the Gray Template*; and they relate to the intellectual history of Afrocentric thought and praxis as they identify the essential infrastructure of Afrocentric thought and praxis. Also, with the principles identified systematically, non-Afrocentrists may gain a clearer understanding of the Afrocentric project; and new or additional discussion may be sparked among Afrocentric scholars.

Moreover, *the Gray Template* forms the framework of the thirteen principles, containing within it unambiguous intellectual responses to so-called intellectual arguments against Afrocentric thought and praxis. The major assumptions and arguments against the Afrocentric movement are held in the following representative sample, from academics and writers of national stature, i.e., from Henry Louis Gates, Diane Ravitch, and John Leo, respectively:

1. [the assumption that Afrocentric thought and praxis consists of scholars wearing] Kente cloth
and celebrating Kwanzaa instead of Christmas;
2. [the argument that the goal of the Afrocentric movement is to create] race/color-based curricula;
3. [the assumption and argument that Afrocentric thought and praxis consist of] the systematic propagation of fantasy [false] history and bizarre [non-intellectual] theories . . . .[1]

Those arguments are generally mis-informed or ill-informed. Offering ready, effective clarification, the Template's thirteen principles answer and deconstruct those and other fallacious arguments against Afrocentric thought and praxis.

Finally, the Template's principles illustrate and delineate how Afro-centric thinkers, writers, and practitioners are allowed maximum intellectual space, creative freedom, and functional liberty; while simultaneously, the principles help them remain accountable to and connected intentionally and unapologetically to the collective composite African cultural base.

For the remainder of this chapter, the thirteen principles of *the Gray Template* are explicated meticulously and expounded upon in depth. The priority principle that distinguishes Afrocentric thought and praxis is *the Meta-Constants: Humanizing and Harmonizing*. This principle is the priority principle, because Afrocentric thought and praxis strive constantly to humanize and harmonize. Humanizing and harmonizing are the overarching omnipresent constants of Afrocentric thought and praxis.

The quintessential intent of Afrocentric thought and praxis is to humanize and to harmonize. This particular principle is non-negotiable. Any effort or product qualifying as Afrocentric demonstrates the intent to humanize African people. Any such effort also demonstrates a commitment to restoring and maintaining harmony within African persons and the African community, and thereafter, between the African community, the ecosphere, and all communities.[2]

Does that particular theory invite African people to stand tall and realize their full potential? Does that poem or that book of poems, ultimately, help restore harmony within African persons and the African community? Does that particular organization, activity, or practice encourage or equip African people to be fully human and to cultivate or create true harmony? Does the effort or product, implicitly, invite, encourage, or challenge African people to align themselves with the ancient but ever relevant teachings of the Per Em Hru's [The Book of Coming Forth by Day's] "Declarations of Virtues,"[3]—teachings, which, when honored and embodied, produce exemplary, harmonious and human people, as well as an exemplary, harmonious, and human society? The answer to each of those questions is an unambiguous affirmative, if the effort or product is to be classified as Afrocentric.

Further, it is important to note that while being fully human and achieving authentic harmony may involve some figurative and some literal sacrifice, the focus is upon living. There is no implicit commitment to foolish, "Afropean Christian," and various other romantic notions of sacrifice and/or martyrdom. African people's being fully human may include being rewarded with profound humanness in another dimension, in a another life in a hereafter; simultaneously, being fully human is certainly about African people living life on human, humane terms now. Experiencing harmony and living harmoniously are not realities only to be pined for and postponed until the next life; they are realities intended for African people in this life as well.

To be considered Afrocentric, a written or literary rendering of whatever sort, or orature, an organization, or an activity must hold and reflect *The Meta-Constants: Humanizing and Harmonizing.* At its core, any effort must point to, emphasize, encourage, and build upon the humanizing and harmonizing character, function, role, and destiny of African people.[4]

The Primacy of African People and African Civilization is another major principle. Afrocentric thinkers, writers, and practitioners are clear about the fact that African people are the parentpeople of humanity; and African civilization is the parentcivilization of world civilization. Specifically, this reality is indicated clearly in Afrocentric work, whenever the work implies or references the origins of people or civilization.

Clarity is requisite relative to this matter. There is no reason for uncertainty or fuzziness of perspective. There is no need to lean toward Tibet, or China, or Indonesia, or Western Asia (often called "the Middle East"), or any place other than Africa as the birthplace of human beings and civilization. The paleontological, anthropological, archeological, and historical evidence is clear: true human beings, homo sapien sapiens, appear in Africa prior to appearing elsewhere on the Earth. Indeed, an African *monogenesis*—one common point of origin—for all the people now on the Earth was suggested many centuries ago in ancient African sacred texts, and in more recent times by African people such as Drusilla Dunjee Houston (1920s), John G. Jackson (1930s, 1970s), and Cheikh Anta Diop (1950s-1980s), and by Europeans such as Richard Leakey and Bruce Williams. Even popular, European American magazines like *Newsweek*, with an article by John Tierney, Linda Wright, and others, (January 11, 1988), and *U.S. News and World Report*, with an article by William Allman, (February 27, 1989), have printed articles in recent years admitting the African—female—origin of humanity as we know it.[5]

We can cite the Australopithecus Afarensis find, known popularly as "Lucy," but more appropriately by the Afrocentric Ethiopian name(s), Dinqnesh or Birkinesh ("You are the most wonderful"). Or, we can cite the more recent Australopithecus Ramidus find. The fact remains the same: All human beings now on the Earth have as their primordial-original-first parent an African person(s) indigenous to and living in central and eastern Africa. These are the most current empirical facts, and with the exception of an approximate 200 year, general "white out" from the 1700s into the 1900s, similar facts have been authoritative from the most ancient times.[6]

Archeological and historical evidence is equally clear about Africa being the birthplace of civilization. When consideration is given to the central-and-eastern African Twa people—the parentpeople of all humanity, a people short of stature, a people characterized as peaceful, harmonious, and most "God-like" by the ancient people of KMT [Kemet] (Egypt) as well as by some modern people, then it becomes easy to understand that civilization was imparted to the

Earth through them. Indeed, it is through the Twa that the world received the first ingredient necessary for the building of human relationships and empirical institutions: human harmony. Even today, as in ancient times, when the Twa are unperturbed and undisturbed, they are people who exemplify a peaceful and civil approach to interpersonal and group relationships.[7]

Eventually, the empirical data tells us, from the Twa come the people who raised the magnificent civilization of ancient Ethiopia—which birthed Ta Seti in Nubia and later KMT, at least as early as 4241 B.C.E. Further, we know that it is Ethiopia's prodigious daughter and the Twa's granddaughter, KMT, which gifted the world with highly refined implements for living: writing, mathematics, farming, personology (psychology), medicinal arts and medical science, astronomy, art, zoology, engineering, poetry, architecture, and more.[8] We know, too, that when these implements for living are applied rightly, the result is "civilization."

"Civilization" develops (a)when people live together harmoniously and evolve to ever higher levels of constructive consciousness and behavior, and (b)when people establish institutions that assist the community in maintaining and spreading harmony in the multifarious spheres in which life unfolds. Civilization is an ordering of relationships that leads to ever-increasing expressions of justice, harmony, and sanity.

Chaosization, in contrast to civilization, is an ordering of relationships between people and between people and the environment that—on the surface–resembles civilization. Upon closer examination, however, chaosization proves a disordered or misordered ordering of relationships that leads to truncated expressions of justice, false expressions of harmony, distorted-insane expressions of sanity. In short, chaosization is people living together in an almost surreal state of managed chaos, in a state of relatively stable confusion, in a state of sophisticated-buffered barbarism.[9]

Africa did not give the world chaosization. Africa birthed and gave the Earth civilization. All Afrocentric thinkers, writers, and practitioners must know, bear witness to, and beam forth these truths.

Another major principle in Afrocentric thought and praxis is *An African Audience as the Priority Audience.* This principle is simple yet very important. Of course, Afrocentric efforts can reach or address any audience; or Afrocentric efforts can touch multifarious audiences simultaneously. It is critical, however, that Afrocentric thinkers, writers, and practitioners are intentional about holding African people as the priority audience for their efforts.[10]

This principle is pragmatic. It is not narrow. This principle reminds and ensures that Afrocentric efforts and enterprises serve to elevate African people. There are too many instances in recent—and not so recent—African history when persons and movements concerned centrally with African people's welfare went through phases or culminated with African people as a peripheral concern, with non-African people as the central concern.

As an example, consider what happened with some of the contemporary voices of Black Theology. During the 1970s, some of the most prominent Black theologians burst onto the national and international scene, addressing themselves unapologetically to African people and the concerns of African people. Generally, they were relevant and received and appreciated by African people; and they were noticed by non-African people. After a few years, however, some of these African scholars were writing books that continued to deal with Black Theology, supposedly; but the books were not speaking to African people. Some of the scholars had begun—perhaps unintentionally or subconsciously—to seek the approval or response of European scholars. That is, apparently, they felt it important to demonstrate to themselves and/or to European scholars that they could discuss and explicate European theologians and European theology intelligibly.[11]

Undeniably, African theologians must be and are so conversant. In fact, at this point in history, Africans who hold the Ph.D. in the area of theology have to prove competence in European theology on the way to specializing in African or Black theology. The point, however, is this: while it is fine that European and other non-African persons or groups access African scholars' efforts, *African people ought always be an African scholars' priority audience.* African people do not benefit optimally when they are less than the priority audience of African scholars' efforts.

Afrocentric practitioners, writers, and thinkers should be intentional and forever vigilant relative to addressing themselves to and writing/working on behalf of African people primarily. *A non-African audience or a global audience is secondary; a Pan-Afri-*

can audience or a particular African audience is primary. Jacob Carruthers, the Afrocentric scholar at the Kemetic Institute in Chicago and at Northeastern Illinois University, citing the courageous and uncompromising David Walker, speaks to the matter in this way: "let us follow the example of Walker and . . . extend our message to '[all African] men, women and children, of every nation, language and tongue under the sun.' "[12] With African people as the priority audience, the African community is assured of being the priority beneficiary of the Afrocentric ones' best efforts, gifts, talents, skills, contributions.

Njia as Theme is a principle distinguishing Afrocentric thought and praxis. Afrocentric thinking, writing, and practice give evidence of Njia—"The Way" that rests upon the primacy of victorious thought. Put another way, Afrocentric thought and praxis are characterized by a *profound optimism.* That optimism results from Njia. Whether Njia is explicit or implicit, Afrocentric thought and praxis are committed to and emanate the idea of the attainability of victory.[13]

Njia as Theme means that at a time when life conditions are incredibly dire for most African people, Afrocentric writers, practitioners, and thinkers begin by determining victory can be had. They begin by committing themselves and their efforts to victory; they then travel the journey to victory. For example, an Afrocentric writer might write a collection of multidimensional stories or poems dealing with joy, pain, love, war, victory, defeat, suspense, adventure. The culmination of the collection, however—the essence of the collection—the predominant and defining voice of the collection is victorious. The final word is a victorious word. Afrocentric writers do not follow the tradition of the Greek tragedies.

Afrocentric thinkers are not proponents of dread or pessimistic existentialism. Afrocentric practitioners do not practice nor teach accomodationism, the chosen way of those who are cowardly, those who fear or who cannot envision wholistic freedom and authentic independence.

Consider ancient Ethiopia, Zimbabwe (Monomotapa), KMT, Songhai, Mali, and the Mossi States. They thrived because they held Njia as their theme. Consider African people in South America, Central America, and North America in the late 1800s and early

1900s. They emerged from the Maafa,[14] because they held and lived Njia as their theme. Marcus Garvey's Universal Negro Improvement Association, Septima Clarke and grassroots African people of South Carolina, the Student Nonviolent Coordinating Committee, the Black Panther Party for Self-Defense, Muhammad Ali, Sonia Sanchez and Haki Madhubuti and other tenacious members of the Black Arts Movement, and many other known and anonymous African people gifted the African community with, and continue gifting the African community with, important contributions—because they held, and continue holding, Njia as their theme!

Clearly, Njia as Theme does not mean that Afrocentric thought and praxis are naive or unidimensional. Further, it does not mean that Afrocentric efforts view the world through African violet-colored glasses, ignoring the massive, mountainous challenges facing African people. It means that the idea of failure or failing is never set forth as the central, crowning, culminating idea. It means that pessimism has no esteemed or honored place in Afrocentric thought and praxis.

Njia as Theme is a principle that may be explicit or implied. In either instance, the central, lasting thought is a thought which elevates African people. The essential, reverberating word is a victorious word for African people. The signature message demonstrated by the practitioner is: Stay strong, African people. We are overcoming. We come from a great people. We carry greatness within us. We will be great again. We can do this. Yebo! [Yebo is a Zulu word meaning, "Yes"].[15]

Finally, then, *Njia as Theme* is a principle which ensures that Afrocentric thought and praxis go beyond simple, *myopic notions of mere survival*. More specifically, it is a principle which *ensures that Afrocentric thought and praxis* consist of efforts, words, a vision, and consistent practice centered on forward, relentless, optimistic thriving unto *victory*.

Another major principle that distinguishes Afrocentric thought and praxis is *The Way of Heru as Theme.* As explicated earlier in this work, The Way of Heru involves doing the work of resurrecting and restoring African people with confidence. Further, it consists of (a)the employment of sophisticated comprehensive critical cultural method, and (b)the intentional wielding of conceptual power.[16]

The Way of Heru as Theme is present in a work when the work is confident, rather than doubtful, engaged in re-establishing order, balance, and strength within the minds and lives of African people. An Afrocentric thinker does not wonder whether African people will ever know again the sanity and stability which characterized their journey on the Earth for thousands of years. Rather, an Afrocentric thinker asserts: African people will realize again—and are even now in the complicated multifaceted process of realizing again—their traditional sanity, stability, and excellence as a people.

Further, an Afrocentric thinker undergirds her or his preceding assertion with an insightful view of what must occur, and what is occurring, for the re-establishment of consistent greatness among African people. And while the Afrocentric thinker's insightful view may emphasize one or more matters; it is certain to emphasize that culture is the core, foundational matter that must be understood. An insightful Afrocentric thinker might posit that African people's traditional greatness will be actualized in contemporary times when they unify and utilize their collective economic power. To unify authentically and then to utilize their collective economic power wisely and effectively African people must disengage from European culture.

African people must disengage and discard European notions of "African unity," "what unity ought to consist of," "how collective economic power ought to be utilized," and so forth. Simultaneously, an insightful Afrocentric thinker might explicate that African people must learn, trust, apply, and embody the most empowering aspects of African culture.[17]

Additionally, an Afrocentric thinker might explicate that African people must again be strong people who live constructive empirical and transcendent African cultural values: for example, saving money; purchasing existential necessities first and a few luxuries sometime in the future; being people who love and are proud of ourselves, people who possess integrity, reliability, trustworthiness; people who understand that African parents must be and represent today what they expect African children to be tomorrow; utilizing collective ecconomic power to buy land and to build Afrocentric educational institutions and non-exploitive businesses and industries.[18]

Finally, an Afrocentric thinker might assert that when and where

African people know and live the best and most human aspects of African culture, African people will again realize—and are already realizing—their historical legacy as a great, sane, and excellent people.[19]

Further, The Way of Heru as Theme is present when an Afrocentric thinker wields conceptual power intentionally and boldly. In the work of raising and restoring African people to their traditional state of greatness, an Afrocentric thinker where possible redefines and recreates concepts and words. An Afrocentric thinker, such as Marimba Ani, might explain, "From the African point of view, a people are not considered a great people because they produce a few wealthy individuals; rather, a people are considered a great people because they do not allow large numbers of their people to know destitution." This conceptualization of "collective greatness" is almost diametrically opposite the understanding of collective greatness which Europeans and European informational machinery offer African people daily.[20]

Thinking, writing, and practice qualifying as Afrocentric give evidence of the Way of Heru as Theme. It is important to note, however, that the Way of Heru as Theme is a very demanding principl. Therefore, it is more or less evident in an Afrocentric thinkers', writers', or practitioners' work, depending on her or his skill at critical cultural analysis, and depending on her or his ability to wield conceptual power with boldness and precision.

Harmosis as Mode is a principle which distinguishes Afrocentric thought and praxis. *Harmosis, as defined earlier in this text, is the harmonious synthesis of ancient and traditional African cultural ideals and approaches to life with constructive contemporary cultural possibilities and approaches to life. It is synthesis that benefits and empowers African people, and that does not compromise or injure the integrity of African culture.*[21]

Synthesis is not necessarily or automatically beneficial to African people. Some synthesis does not empower African people. Indeed, some synthesis injures, weakens, or disrupts African people and African culture. Rather than moving African people and culture to higher more functional places, some synthesis moves African people and culture to low, dysfunctional places.

Consider the synthesis of contemporary technology and traditional technology in the making of music. Consider the utilization of electronic computer-generated drumbeats in some of the contemporary music being made by African musicians. Synthesizing electronic drumbeats with live human vocal music allows for music to be made more efficiently, as fewer human beings are needed; fewer musicians' contracts are drawn up; and the challenges of human error and/or musicians' mood swings are reduced. Simultaneously, the particular feeling and possibility of improvisation that a live human drummer brings to a musical effort is lost. Admittedly, in some instances, computer generated drumbeats do not seem to weaken a piece of music. In other instances, the absence of live, human-generated drumbeats is an obvious artistic liability.

In all instances, however, human musicians are injured; because they are not called to work. Further, if electronic drumbeats become standard, African people and African culture risk losing the proper technical skill; and where there is no proper drumming—or no drumming at all—there is a great loss of spirit, and power, and other tangible and transcendant gifts that our Ancestors send through the drum.[22]   Mere synthesis, then, is not necessarily beneficial. Harmosis is required; because Harmosis is empowering, functional,beneficial, harmonizing synthesis.

Though he discusses the matter more extensively and utilizes different language, James T. ("Jimmy") Stewart understands Harmosis, positing in 1968 that the most effective African music—jazz, specifically—epitomizes some of the most effective or revolutionary African people. It can be inferred, then, that much of the music made by Africans living in the United States—especially jazz—is the epitome of Harmosis. Indeed, because the best African music functions empirically, inspiring and catalyzing us to constructive action, and because it functions non-empirically, evoking feelings and sentiments that link us to people, times, places, and activities which we do not "know" experientially, and because it is created by collectives of musicians and is enjoyed most profoundly by collectives of listeners—for these reasons, African music may demonstrate Harmosis more effectively than any other form of expression or activity. Asserting that the cost of not achieving Harmosis may be "early graves . . . dissipation and dissolution [and even] willful self-destruction," Stewart notes that in the case of Charlie Parker, "there was a dichotomy between his genius and

[Eurocentric] society. . . . [and tragedy resulted because] he couldn't find the adequate model of being [he couldn't find Harmosis as mode]."[23]

Harmosis is evident in the work of Afrocentric practitioners, writers, and thinkers. They appropriate the most constructive and sane aspects of ancient and traditional African civilization and culture. Then, where appropriate—that is, where Harmosis will result—they synthesize the ancient and traditional with the contemporary and new. The new Afrocentric product is then utilized and applied (1) to navigate and solve current and coming challenges, and (2) in the creation of beauty in the midst of the various challenges. That is how Afrocentric thinkers, practitioners, and writers work and create. They are vigilant in maintaining Harmosis as Mode. Another principle in Afrocentric thought and praxis is *Wholistic Afrocentric Action as Goal.* This is a simple principle; yet, it is an essential and pivotal principle, because the goal of all Afrocentric endeavors is to produce persons and a people who move, behave, *act* in an Afrocentric manner in *every sphere of life.*[24]

The late, incipient Afrocentric scholar Carter G. Woodson is very clear about the pivotal nature of action or acting, when he asserts, "When you control a man's thinking you do not have to worry about his actions. You do not have to tell him not to stand here or go yonder. He will find his 'proper place' and stay in it. You do not need to send him to the back door. He will go without being told. In fact, if there is no back door, he will cut one for his special benefit."[25] Woodson's lucid words, echoing across the decades, make it clear that the message that predominates in the mind determines and directs the actions of the body. The reason for controlling a person's thinking is to reach the ultimate goal of controlling that person's actions. The goal is not merely to have a person think she or he is a slave; the goal is to have that person act and behave as a slave.[26]

Since the actions of a person or a group are the final determinants of that person's or that group's empirical experience of life, Afrocentric writers, thinkers and practitioners work to influence action. They work to have women and men think they can go in a front door. More than that, they work to have women and men think about building their own doors, and businesses, and whatever else they desire, coming and going as they choose. As the pivotal goal of having people think such liberating Afrocentric thoughts, Afrocentric practitioners, writers, and thinkers work to have the people *act* in every viable Afrocentric way so that the people's empirical experience of reality is positive.[27]

Additionally, they work to influence behavior and action wholistically. Afrocentric thinkers, writers, and practitioners do not work for a compartmentalized, or segmented, or partial goal. They work for an organic and wholistic goal. Specifically, the theorist wants ultimately to see her or his theory result in individuals and communities structuring their lives and their living—their actions—so that they are Afrocentric in every dimension. The writer wants ultimately to help people and communities live their lives in healthy Afrocentric ways. The Afrocentric practitioner wants ultimately to cultivate and grow Afrocentric practice within people and communities to the point that every action is a constructive Afrocentric action.[28]

Understanding that people and persons can be taught and invited to think, write, and act in Afrocentric ways, in some situations, some of the time—Afrocentric thinkers, writers, and practitioners believe the people can be taught and encouraged to act and behave in Afrocentric ways in all situations, all of the time. *Wholistic Afrocentric Action as Goal* is a principle distinguishing Afrocentric thought and praxis.

Afrocentric thought and praxis also hold *Sankofan Approach* as a major principle. This principle ensures that Afrocentric thought and praxis begin with African history. Specifically, it helps Afrocentric practitioners, thinkers, and writers undergird their work with and anchor their work in the best of the African past. Further, the Sankofan Approach principle ensures that Afrocentric thought and praxis have and maintain integrity, as it protects Afrocentric thought and praxis from external encroachment or invasion.[29]

All praxis—that is, all thoughtful, constructive practice, behavior, and activity, as well as all thought—that is, all intellectual and literary endeavors, begin with and derive from and are attached to some historical context, some historical base. Though some people posit the contrary, thought and praxis are not "contextless" or ahistorical.[30] They emerge from some location. Explicitly and/or implicitly, all efforts emerge from a particular or a predominant historical place. Efforts come forth from some history, from some guiding "story." Afrocentric practitioners, thinkers, and writers are profoundly aware of and sensitive to this simple, powerful fact.

Utilizing the Sankofan Approach, Afrocentric practitioners approach their work consciously and intentionally. They approach their work with all of African history from which to draw. Afrocentric practitioners should begin by studying the practical models of the Twa, Imhotep, Queen Tiye, Nzingha and her supporters, Bishop Richard Allen and his supporters, General Toussaint L'Ouverture and his supporters, Denmark Vesey, Nat Turner and his supporters, Gabriel Prosser, Zimbabwe's Nehunda and her supporters, Laurence C. Jones and the Piney Woods School, Marcus Garvey and supporters, the Mau Mau, Patrice Lumumba, Malcolm and his supporters, King and his supporters, Amilcar Cabral and his supporters, and others. They develop genuine familiarity with ancient and recent, continental and diasporan, African history. Then, drawing first and most from that history—rather than from some other history—Afrocentric practitioners build, enact, and continually refine effective, practical models.[31]

Similarly, Afrocentric philosophers and theorists should begin by considering the historical and historic wisdom of Amen-o-mope, Du Bois, McLeod Bethune, Diop, Karenga, Welsing, Asante, and others. Likewise, Afrocentric writers—whether they are writing poetry, short stories, novels, plays, or whatever—should begin by considering the historical and historic work of past and recent African writers.

So, the *Sankofan Approach begins with African history. It does not consist, however, of simply having a surface or conversational familiarity with the African past. It includes drawing on that past functionally, anchoring efforts in that past—gleaning the most instructive and constructive information from the African past, refining that information as necessary, and then utilizing the information along with one's particular personal desires to achieve pro-African purposes in the present and future.*

By beginning with African history, Afrocentric thought and praxis build upon themselves. The foundation, and the core, and the product are all African. Though incredibly basic, such an approach is also rigorously self-reinforcing. Consequently, it involves very little reliance upon exterior sources. Being so self-generating and so self-contained, the Sankofan Approach assures Afrocentric thought and praxis of retaining and maintaining their integrity—that is, their proper "shape," strength, and function—perhaps perpetually. Non-African or anti-African sources cannot encroach or invade, because they are forever visible as non-African. *The Sankofan Approach is neither whimsical nor random. The Sankofan Approach is deliberate and conscious.*

Nommoic Creativity is a distinguishing principle of Afrocentric thought and praxis, concerned with the creative-empowered-and-empowering use of words and the *strategic creation of concepts.*[32] It contains within it the understanding that words contain power; and, used rightly, words can be more formidable than physical force. Used rightly, words can achieve and accomplish what many strong hands, arms, legs, and backs cannot.

Nommoic Creativity introduces new words, new phrases, and new concepts into the realms of thought and praxis; and it re-introduces familiar concepts in fresh, creative and innovative ways. Moreover, because it stretches and moves so boldly beyond the established bounds of—especially English and occidental—language, it involves definitional and semantic precision and sophistication. Additionally, this principle ensures that Afrocentric thought and praxis remain vibrant and forward moving. Finally, along with creativity and power, Nommoic Creativity opens the way to freedom and life. While it inspires and excites, it also invites and challenges African people, and ultimately all people, to think, speak, perceive, conceive, create, and live in freer, more life-oriented ways. This is a profound principle.

Nommoic Creativity is an essential element in the work kits of African-centered writers. Among African writers, Nommoic Creativity may be personified in the work—the writing and the oratory—of Sonia Sanchez, poet and scholar.[33] One of the leaders in setting language free, Sanchez began demystifying English language and literature in the middle 1960s. She determined that words were not sacred just because they resided on a page, or existed in a book, or just because white people wrote them and recited them as sonnets or whatever else. Sanchez determined and demonstrated for us that words and language are sacred when they are used in a sacred manner. That is, words are sacred when they are used in such a fashion that they free, liberate, *help, and heal* African people—and thereafter, others who are sincere in their quest for personal and global sanity and justice. She was one of the first to burst the bonds and sever the chains that Europeans wrapped around the English language.

Sanchez and a wave of brave, visionary sisters and brothers freed words, freed the language. They mastered and used old European forms whenever they wished; and they discarded and strode over them whenever they chose, as they penned and pioneered new forms, new tones, new images, new voices—new, bold, "blackly Black" voices. They did as they pleased. They were free.

Consider, for example, excerpts from Sanchez's 1987 "elegy (for MOVE and Philadelphia)":

> philadelphia
>   a disguised southern city
> . . . c'mon girl hurry on down to osage st
> they're roasting in the fire
> smell the dreadlocks and blk/skins
> roasting in the fire.
> . . . how does one scream in thunder?
> . . . look. over there. one eye
> . . . hide us O Lord
> deliver us from our nakedness.
> exile us from our laughter
> give us this day our rest from seduction
> peeling us down to our veins.
> . . . who anointeth this city with napalm?
> who giveth this city in holy infanticide?
> . . . there are people
> . . . collecting skeletons from waiting rooms
> lying in wait. for honor and peace.
> one day.[34]

In the preceding selection, and in numerous others, Sanchez does what she must to communicate with us really, to touch us deeply.

Sanchez *newspells*[35] words—spells familiar words in a new way—clipping them in some places, elongating them in others. She skates-stomps-dances-and-cartwheels on the page, turns corners at full speed in full control, accelerates and makes u-turns simultaneously, then comes to a soft smooth slow close—or a piercing-jarring hushed halt. Look closely at excerpts from her "Indianapolis/Summer/1969/Poem":

> don't it all come down
> to e/co/no/mics.
>   like. it is fo
> money that those young brothas on
> illinois &
>   ohio sts
>   allow they selves to
>   be picked up
>   cruised around
>   till they
>   asses open in tune
>   to holy rec/tum/
>   dom.
>   . . .   u dig?
>   . . .   if brothas
> programmed sistuhs fo love
> instead of fucken/hood
> . . . if we programmed/
>   loved/each
>   other in com/mun/al ways
>   so that no
>   blk/person starved
>   or killed
>   each other . . .
>   then may
>   be   it wud all
> come down to some
>   thing else
> like RE VO LU TION.
>   i mean if.
>   like. yeh.[36]

Her words and word pictures hammer us with hard, simple, honesty. They transport and transfix us with optimum optimism. All the while, in all instances, Sanchez is working words on us, opening our heads, widening our hearts, preparing us and enabling us to receive and ingest larger and greater doses and portions of life and freedom. Sanchez's writing—and her oratory—demonstrates extraordinary empathy, polyrythmic and polycentric creativity, regular repitition, relentless boldness, authentic freshness, and a profound ability to communicate and evoke liberated responses to life circumstances. Her writing personifies Nommoic Creativity.

Among African centered thinkers, some of the best examples of Nommoic Creativity are found in the work of Molefi Asante and Marimba Ani.[37] Asante and Ani evidence advanced awareness of the power and the vast utility that this principle affords. Consider Asante's creation and popularization of the term and concept "Afrocentricity." It has altered the intellectual and educational landscape of the United States of America, and it is moving toward impacting many more nations on the planet.[38]

Consistently, Asante utilizes words innovatively and invents words creatively. Similarly, Ani presents us with new concepts, strategically and fastidiously constructed. Consider Ani's conceptualization of "asili," "utamaroho," and "utamawazo." In her book, *Yurugu*, those concepts enable a most creative critique of Europeans *from beyond* the bounds of *their language and conceptual possibilities!*[39] Ani and Asante realize that *when well-worn words are used in novel ways, and when new words are cast, and when conceptualization proceeds from an innovative conceptual base and through a new conceptual screen, then energized images and more liberated thoughts begin to manifest in people's minds.*

As long as fresh, energized activity is occurring in people's minds, the people's future is open, vibrant, and every good *possibility is achievable*. African-centered thinkers understand that Nommoic Creativity is not about clever inconsequential rhetoric, cheap cerebral titillation, nor cute semantic manipulation. It is about a profound understanding of the incredibly positive effect which words and concepts, set forth meticulously, can have on people and the empirical world. Works by Ani and Asante demonstrate a thorough grasp—and unreserved utilization—of the Nommoic Creativity principle.

African centered practitioners utilize the Nommoic Creativity principle constantly. Whether facilitating a naming ceremony, a Kwanzaa celebration, a wedding, a rites-of-passage class, or participating in various other Afrocentric activities, African centered practitioners know that performance and behaviour become stronger and are maintained longer when people have new words and vitalized concepts imprinted in their psyche.

Consider, for example, an African centered practitioner who works with young people and who is committed to equipping young people with a mindset which will help them navigate through the insanity of drugs, to a life of sanity and service to the African community. Such a practitioner, understanding and utilizing the Nommoic Creativity principle, refrains from offering words like the following to young people, "Just say 'no' to drugs. That way, you will have a good life." Such words lack vitality. They are too familiar, shallow, and without substance.

Instead, an African-centered practitioner might offer words similar to the following to young people:

> Young sisters and brothers, here is a truth: Each of you is a manifestation of MAAT. Each of you actually contains in your physical body and in your mind truth, wisdom, justice, and balance. The Amen and the Neters created you that way. That means all the power, strength, and courage you need is already within you. It is not in the sky, or in outer space, or in any book; it is within you. What you need is within you. Repeat this truth to yourself over and over everyday. Keep an Ankh with you, and look at it every day, as a reminder of this truth. As each of you requires of yourself—and helps the others of of you—to remember and trust these truths and enact these instructions, you will be equipped to handle the debilitating seductions of drug use and drug dealing.[40]

Words like the preceding are relatively familiar, yet fresh. Without committing the major error of inaccessibilty, they are creative enough and innovative enough as to pique the curiosity and solicit questions from young people; for once they are genuinely engaged, the aforementioned practitioner knows the probability is high that she or he can equip, guide, and assist them safely through the danger zone of drugs.

In 1980, Molefi Asante posited the following: "[L]anguage, dedicated to [overcoming racist repression and realizing wholistic African freedom], regularly expanded with relevant ideas and symbols, is crucial to our liberation . . . ."[41] His position was—and is—correct; and it underscores the position that Nommoic Creativity is a central element in Afrocentric thought and praxis.

Maatic Argumentation is another principle distinguishing Afrocentric thought and praxis. As a major principle, it is is concerned specifically with *Maat*, in this instance, *justice* prevailing throughout society. It is not unconcerned with peace, or ecological conservation, or the possible extinction of the whales, or other important matters. Its priority concern, *however, is justice for and between human beings.*[42]

Afrocentric thinkers are concerned about African people experiencing Maat throughout the life journey. Afrocentric theorists are not building and setting forth models and constructs that equip African people to secure piece-meal-momentary-episodic-encounters-with-the-fragrance-of-justice-but-not-the-substance-of-justice. Further, they are not working to enable African people to perpetrate injustice upon non-African people. Afrocentric theorists are building and positing constructs and models that enable African people to achieve wholistic liberation and justice for African people, and which enable African people to extend justice to others.[43]

Afrocentric writers are concerned similarly. They do not write merely about flowers, fields of clover, sunsets, streams, lakes, and mountains. They write about the necessity that Maat (justice) be achieved and maintained in its various forms: justice between African couples, justice between African leaders and African communities, justice for African people everywhere.

Further, Afrocentric writers are not determined by what is. They do not write merely of the pervasive absence of justice in most African people's lives and in the collective life of the African community—and then say, we are just writing about life. *Beyond what is, Afrocentric writers write also of what* can be, what should be, what will be. They announce, "We are writing about life as it is; and more than that, we are writing *about life as it must become and as it is becoming."* Afrocentric writers understand that justice does not simply "appear" like the sun or morning dew; and then, once it has appeared, it is their charge to write about it. Rather, *Afrocentric writers understand* that their charge is to write continually about justice. They *understand that by writing about justice, they hasten its coming.* Afrocentric writers do not simply reflect life in their essays, stories, and poetry; they impact, influence, and shape life—and Maatic Argumentation is one of the tools that they wield.

Maat is a constant goal of Afrocentric practitioners. Afrocentric practitioners expend their effort so that African persons and the African community know how to secure, and do in fact secure, justice. Afrocentric practitioners *apply* the Afrocentric perspective, so that Maat—justice—is more than a word. Afrocentric practitioners work so that African people experience and can continually secure justice. They *practice* and train others in the practice of the Afrocentric perspective, so that justice becomes an experiential norm, a regular reality.

Indeed, a central point of praxis is that praxis leads to justice! *Praxis*—that is, *thoughtful reflection combined with constructive practice, behaviour, and action*—results in Maat/justice. For Afrocentric practitioners, then, *Maatic* Argumentation consists of the articulation of justice, the demonstration of justice, the securing of justice, and the training of others in the articulation-demonstration-and-*securing of justice.*

The *Explicit Locational Indicators Intentionality* principle distinguishes Afrocentric theory and praxis. This principle holds that Afrocentric writers, thinkers, and practitioners are intentional about locating their efforts in an explicit Afrocentric place.[44] That is, as often as efforts allow—without losing, diminishing, or artificializing the integrity and sincerity of the efforts—those committed to the Afrocentric project systematically employ African centered terms, metaphors, names, symbols, ontological and epistemological assumptions, and teleological stances.

By locating their efforts explicitly and intentionally, writers, thinkers, and practitioners reinforce consistency and unity within themselves, invite others to come-see-and-consider on African terms, and demonstrate locational integrity to any who are observing and evaluating.

Consider an Afrocentric writer creating a novel. That writer's novel will have female characters with names such as "Zakiya," "Aziza," "Folayan," "Ezinma," "Nyokabi," "Ife," and "Tuwalole," and male characters with names such as "Ehioze," "Adigun," "Ajagbe," "Okonkwo," "Mwamba," "Njoroge," and "Olu." The activity of the novel might be set in Cameroon, Senegal, Rwanda,

Burundi, Somalia, Brazil, Haiti; in Egypt, in Alabama, in Ohio, in Mississippi, in the Southeastern neighborhoods of Washington, D.C., or in the Northern or Western neighborhoods of Philadelphia. Consider the work of Buchi Emecheta, Toni Cade Bambara, Chinua Achebe, and Ngugi wa Thiongo. By giving characters such names, by setting action in such countries and cities, and by employing similar approaches to metaphors and other aspects of the novel, the Afrocentric writer indicates that the novel is being located in an African place explicitly and intentionally.[45]

An Afrocentric thinker sensitive to the Explicit Locational Indicators Intentionality principle offers her/his theory replete with her/his African centered ontological and epistemological assumptions stated explicitly. *Ontological assumptions* are premises about being, premises about the essential substance and nature of life and reality. *Epistemological assumptions* are positions relative to what qualifies as knowledge and how knowledge is obtained.

Consider an Afrocentric thinker building a theory. She/He begins with ontology—because the pattern-setting African ancients began with ontology. Consider the primary ontological injunction over the entry portals of many ancient African temple-schools: "Man/Woman, Know Yourself [Your Being]."[46] In their wisdom, the ancients discovered and determined that consequential thinking, being, and behavior—in contrast to mental wandering, inert being, or meaningless behavior—begin with ontology. They knew that a person's or a people's ontological assumptions serve as the primary rudder guiding—or misguiding—that person's or that group's life.

Afrocentric thinkers—while offering theory that varies depending upon their unique personalities and particular areas of concern, and while setting the matter forth in their own words—share a common ontological core, the core around which all Afrocentric theory adheres. That common African centered ontological core holds, essentially, the following:

> Being/being/life/reality begins with an infinite, invisible, intelligent, unfathomable-yet-beneficent Source. Further, while that Source is non-empirical and invisible, It produce empirical, material reality and allows empirical, material reality to exist. Additionally, the non-empirical, invisible Source—known by a variety of ap-

pellations, such as Spirit, Amon, Amun, Amen, Kheper, Khepri, Olodumare, Allah, Tunkashila, God, Creator, Neters, Orisas, Loas, angels, spiritual forces-laws-powers-principles, ancestors, spirits, and so on—permeates empirical, visible reality. That is, the unseen, invisible Source precedes, produces, and sustains visible, material reality. Human beings are part of the Source, have intrinsic worth, and may be in flow with the Source or out of alignment with the Source. Being in flow with the Source is preferable. The Source is, predominantly, good.[47]

Following ontology, an Afrocentric thinker sets forth her epistemology. After sharing explicitly and necessarily the perspective that informs her work relative to the essential substance and nature of being, and life, and reality itself, she shares the perspective informing her work relative to what knowledge is and how it is obtained. Just as her ontology resonates with the ancients', so does her African-centered epistemology. In her own words, the thinker (a)asserts that knowledge is information which helps people order and navigate the life journey effectively and with integrity, and (b)asserts that knowledge is arrived at and obtained via controlled empirical methods, via collective subjective life experiences, and via collective and/or individual subjective non-empirical sources— such as dreams, intuition, "vibes," and so forth—sources proven valid among African people for millennia.[48]

After intentional and explicit location of the ontological and epistemological assumptions and premises informing the core of her theory, the Afrocentric thinker continues on and builds and offers her particular, unique theory or theoretical model.[49] As noted previously, the said location reinforces consistency and unity within the thinker and her effort. It also announces the effort to others and invites them to come and see and consider on African terms; and it demonstrates profound locational integrity—rather than incomplete location, locational deceit, locational ambivalence, locational oscillation, or simple locational confusion.

Finally, consider Afrocentric practitioners. They demonstrate utilization of the Explicit Locational Indicators Intentionality principle by anchoring—and by announcing the anchoring of—their efforts to an African centered teleology. *Teleology has to do with the ultimate purpose of human life.* The guiding teleology of some non-African people might be to be the world's best conquerors and subjugate and absorb all other cultures on the Earth; or to be prolific consumers, consuming the Earth's natural resources and people-made products as fast as possible in quantities as conspicuous as possible. The teleology of African people is exceedingly different from that. The essential teleology of African people—as set forth and practiced by ancient Africans and as articulated more or less imperfectly by contemporary African people—is for humans to become and be like "God." African-centered teleology posits that simultaneous with the major focus of people's lives—such as marriage, parenting, career, being a student, or whatever—people are to grow, unfold, and evolve into higher beings. That is, people are to grow and become beings who embody and who are able to demonstrate the mundane and the transcendent attributes and ideals of (a constructive, good) "God."[50]

An *African-centered teleological stance distinguishes* Afrocentric practitioners from other practitioners. Other practitioners work to fulfill and to train others to fulfill ultimate purposes noticeably different from the ultimate purposes of African people; but an African centered teleological stance is the only stance which makes sense for African people. Indeed, as we are learning rather slowly and quite painfully, it is the only teleological stance that *functions optimally for African people.* When African people practice and work to fulfill non-African teleologies, we discover that we are not happy as time passes. We lose our joy; we hurt; and our lives evince painful disarray.

In addition to locating themselves and their efforts intentionally and explicitly by articulating and living an African centered teleology, Afrocentric practitioners locate themselves intentionally by honoring and utilizing explicit African symbols. Consider, for example, ignoring the ancestors, wearing European clothing, the posting of a red-white-and-blue flag, and bringing closure to a gathering with the words, "See you next time."[51] Such gestures and symbols are explicit intentional locational indicators of a non-African sort. In contrast, consider the intentional veneration of ancestors by pouring libation, wearing of African clothing, posting a red-black-and-green flag, and bringing a praxis gathering to culmination and closure by having the participants hold hands in a circle and declare,

"Tumalize Duara!" (a Kiswahili term meaning "Let the Circle Be Unbroken," or "Keep Our Circle United").[52] All of those visible and audible symbols are explicit African centered locational indicators. They announce clearly where the practitioners are, and they reinforce the practitioners in their location.

The *Explicit Locational Indicators Intentionality* principle contains within it the understanding that African centered efforts ought to rely minimally upon non-African ways and means of communication. This is necessary; because the greater the reliance upon non-African ways and means of communication, the greater the limitations as to how far, how *fast, and how well a liberated African reality can be built.* Additionally, because it is possible for an effort to be Afrocentric yet scant relative to explicit Afrocentric locational indicators,[53] *this principle pushes all involved in* Afrocentric thought and praxis to be intentional in maximizing the explicit Afrocentric content of their efforts. Thereby, there is maximization of the impact and effectiveness of their efforts. Finally then, as Afrocentric thought and praxis depend increasingly upon African ways and means of communicating, African humanity will be able to realize even higher, uncharted, constructive levels of humanness.

For Afrocentric writers, thinkers, and practitioners, the Explicit Locational Indicators Intentionality principle is a demanding and enhancing principle. *African Collective Memory-Perception Competence* is another distinguishing principle of Afrocentric theory and praxis. This principle holds that as *African people are linked* externally relative to our shared historical-experiential journey, so are we linked internally relative to a shared memory-and-perceptual base. African people share a common memory base consisting of shared, common feelings, attitudes, and proclivities or propensities; and we share a common perceptual base consisting of shared and common responses to *tangible and intangible stimuli.* This principle depends upon and presupposes Kariamu Welsh-Asante's Epic Memory Sense.[54]

The African Collective Memory-Perception Competence principle, then, *requires that the work of Afrocentric* thinkers, writers, and practitioners demonstrate awareness of the reality that African pen people share memory and perception. Further, it requires that their work (a)demonstrate competence relative to touching and activating the collective memory of African people, and (b) demonstrate competence relative to attracting a knowing and affirmative collective *perceptual response from African people.*

Afrocentric thinkers construct theories that can accommodate and that are broad enough to contain the principle. They posit theories that resonate with African people's collective memory. The theories, therefore, are logical and make good sense to African people; they do not find the theories unintelligible or irrelevant. Additionally, Afrocentric thinkers posit theories that evoke a positive, empowered response from African people. Specifically, the theories draw forth a response from African people wherein (1)the people perceive that they can re-achieve their former greatness as a people; and (2)the people are stirred and catalyzed to daily, incremental behavior and action, whereby they ultimately actualize their total possibility and glorious destiny as a people.

As an example, consider Asante's theoretical work,[55] which makes sense to numerous African people—males and females, of varying educational backgrounds, of all economic strata, all over the United States and in other parts of the world. For another example of how the African Collective Memory-Perception Competence operates principle in Afrocentric writing, consider Maya Angelou's poem, "And Still I Rise."[56]

Admittedly, the author has never declared herself an Afrocentric writer. Nonetheless, the poem, though not a total Afrocentric effort technically—nor was it necessarily written to be–still demonstrates the African Collective Memory-Perception Competence principle beautifully and powerfully.

African people's collective memory—epic memory—is given voice throughout the poem. It is perhaps at its start and at its close, however, that the poem activates and engages African people's collective memory most explicitly:

> You may write me down in history
> With your bitter, twisted lies,
> You may trod me in the very dirt
> But still, like dust, I'll rise.

> . . . Out of the huts of history's shame

I rise
Up from a past that's rooted in pain
I rise . . .

Bringing the gifts that my ancestors gave,
I am the dream and the hope of the slave.
I rise.
I rise.
I rise.[57]

This writer knows of no adult African person who has read or heard those words and has not resonated with those words. It seems that almost every adult African person encountering "And Still I Rise" holds in memory the struggle, pain, promise, and the indomitable surge toward victory that the poem contains and engenders.

There is also a common, collective perceptual response to "And Still I Rise." The collective perception of the poem is that it reflects African people's collective journey—and the essence of our multifarious personal journeys—correctly. The collective response to the poem is that its predominant theme—that African people possess infinite strength reserves and an eternal indomitable actional optimism—is also correct. When African people read or hear this piece of writing—those with formal education as well as those with little or no formal education, those living in the United States as well as those living in other parts of the world—*consistently*, African people respond with knowing nods of the head and/or vehement verbal approval and affirmation.

"And Still I Rise" demonstrates awareness of the reality that African people share memory and perception. It touches and activates the collective epic memory of African people, and African people perceive and respond to it knowingly. It effectively communicates empirical and non-empirical understanding and information via the tangible empirical page. "And Still I Rise," then, is an excellent example of a piece of writing wherein the African Collective Memory-Perception Competence principle is satisfied.

Afrocentric practitioners satisfy this principle when they suggest and demonstrate exemplary behavior which African people's collective memory recognizes and finds identifiable.

Consider a practitioner suggesting and demonstrating for people positive liberating self-talk. Consider an Afrocentric practitioner repeating and rehearsing to herself or himself daily:

> I am black and beautiful and African and incredible. I can do all things well, because *Ubora* (a Kiswahili term meaning "excellence") is the legacy left me by our Ancestors. And since Ubora is what our Ancestors demonstrated for me and us, I am walking and working so that Ubora in all things is the predominate reality of our present. Thereby, I can ensure that our future is a future wherein Ubora in all things, rather than mediocrity in all things, is our normal way. Thereby, I can ensure that our future is one wherein we give each other Ubora consistently, and wherein we expect Ubora from each other consistently.

As a practitioner demonstrates such practice, and as she or he invites others to try the practice of positive self-talk, the practitioner indicates awareness of the fact that African people share memory and perception. More specifically, the practitioner indicates understanding of the fact that African people's collective memory resonates to the proper and powerful utilization of speech. Further, *if the* practitioners's positive self-talk produces consistent positive behavior in the practitioner, a common affirming and positive perception, reception, and response to the *practitioner's practice will be forthcoming from African people.*

Consider Malcolm X. He exemplified the practice of positive, constructive self-talk and strong, consistent constructive behavior. His practice touched and activated the collective memory of African people. His practice was perceived, received, and responded to positively by numerous African people—many of whom expressed themselves publicly, and many more who expressed their approval covertly. While he might be best classified as an incipient Afrocentric practitioner, Malcolm X's satisfaction of the African Collective Memory-Perception Competence principle was not incipient. It was fully developed. Indeed, it was so highly developed, that it impacted the lives of millions of African people in his generation, as well as additional millions of African people many years after his assassination.

When an Afrocentric practitioner satisfies the African Collective Memory-Perception Competence principle, much good results. Her or his practice encourages and teaches others to practice similarly. It produces sanity and joy among African people in the present and speeds up the wholistic liberation of African people in the very near future. The African Collective Memory-Perception Competence principle is critical to Afrocentric theory and praxis.

Another principle that distinguishes Afrocentric theory and praxis is *Nzuri as Invitation and Standard.* As noted earlier in this text, "Nzuri" is a term holding that beauty and good are synonymous; most specifically, that which is considered good is also considered beautiful. In centered African culture, goodness involves aesthetics, and beauty involves ethics. They are bound inextricably.[58] As a principle, then, *Nzuri as Invitation and Standard* encourages Afrocentric practitioners, thinkers, and writers (a)to sprinkle their work with—and to weave into the fabric of their work—invitations to a true understanding of Nzuri; and (b)to have their work reflect, affirm, and/or demonstrate Nzuri *as an attainable standard worth holding and practicing.* Afrocentric practitioners know the truth of Nzuri. They know that beauty is as beauty does. Consequently, they strive to practice that truth consistently. As they achieve consistency, they train others in the practice.

Consider a female practitioner—a dance teacher—teaching a class of adolescent girls traditional African dances. The practitioner treats all the girls well and affirms all the girls, as they pour themselves into the work, aspiring to master the dances. Simultaneously, the dance expert is careful not to affirm the girls relative to their physical or facial attractiveness. Rather, the Afrocentric practitioner affirms the girls as "beautiful" as they treat each other and others with respect and consideration consistently. As a consequence, the dance group develops an internal peace and harmony—rather than a tense hierarchy—at which other dance groups and other people marvel. The Afrocentric practitioner understands Nzuri.[59]

She understands that a person may or may not be physically and/or facially attractive—the designation "attractive" being relative. Further, she understands that the designation that matters, and that is not necessarily relative is "beautiful"; a person is affirmed as "beautiful" when that person manifests constructive behavior and good actions consistently. In addition, the practitioner understands that as time passes, with the young girls remaining under her tutelage, they can absorb her dance technique and her living technique. As time passes, the young girls understand and live Nzuri as their teacher—an Afrocentric practitioner—does; and as more time passes, the young girls can pass it on to younger girls following them. Thereby, beauty and sanity grow and increase in the dance classes; and then beauty and sanity evolve, seeping out beyond the dance classes, into the community.

Without force or coercion, then, the Afrocentric practitioner— in this example, a dance teacher—invites others to Nzuri, by weaving almost invisible invitations into the fabric of her work, her dance class. Simultaneously, with great love and seamless skill, she demonstrates that Nzuri is an attainable standard worth holding and practicing.

Afrocentric thinkers include the Nzuri as Invitation and Standard principle in their theoretical frameworks. Inclusion of the principle aids entire frameworks in maintaining Afrocentric integrity; because it is possible for a theoretical framework to have gaps, to lack integrity, in some part(s) of its structure.

The possibility of Afrocentric theoretical frameworks having gaps becomes clearer when it is considered that a diametrically opposite perspective predominates in the minds of many people, and occupies small bits of space in the minds of some, including some African people, all over the world. Among one group of non-African people, European people, a predominant perspective is that a person's being and her/his actions are two separate and distinct realities; or, they are realities that can be isolated, experienced, and assessed apart from each other.[60] Such a perspective may be tenable on paper, and a person may hold such a perspective as she or he lives life and experiences people. Depending on the tenor and content of those experiences, however, the person may become confused and dislocated psychologically and emotionally. So, *by including the* Nzuri *as Invitation and Standard principle in their various theoretical frameworks, Afrocentric thinkers aid themselves, Afrocencentric writers and practitioners, and African people generally in avoiding the aforementioned confusion—confusion that comes into our minds as a result of attempting to process as two unconnected realities that which is actually a unified reality.*

Consider an Afrocentric thinker building a theory. She or he builds into the theory the obvious yet profound truth of Nzuri. The Afrocentric thinker explains that notions of beauty and notions of goodness, aesthetics and ethics, are bound together. That which is truly beautiful (aesthetics) is thoroughly good (ethics); and that which is thoroughly good is truly beautiful.

The Afrocentric thinker explains that African people do not consider a person truly "beautiful," simply because a person has a melodic voice, or nice legs, or a sharp mind. Rather, centered African people consider a person beautiful, with or without traits like the aforementioned, when and as that person demonstrates good behavior consistently. If a person possesses "beautiful" traits like the aforementioned, but behaves in a destructive or negative manner, that person may be said to possess "a beautiful voice," "beautiful legs," "a beautiful mind," and so forth; but that person will never be said to be "a beautiful person"—unless and until the person learns or chooses to behave in a good manner. So, the Afrocentric thinker builds into her or his theoretical frameworks the understanding that aesthetics and ethics are intertwined; and the Afrocentric thinker also notes that ethics precedes aesthetics.

The Afrocentric thinker explicates that in the area of relationships, a most important area for African people, ethics *precedes* aesthetics. This is a pivotal point; and it can be reiterated repeatedly. After and as a person first respects and assists elders, children, and others consistently, then that person is known as "beautiful." After and as a person first speaks edifying words and lives making the community stronger consistently, then that person is classified as "beautiful." In relationships, the Afrocentric thinker explains to us, *first* a person demonstrates good, constructive actions regularly, *then* that person is known as beautiful. Aesthetics and ethics are linked together, and ethics leads aesthetics. They are like twins. Ethics is born first, and beauty follows thereafter. This is some of the truth of Nzuri.

An Afrocentric thinker builds into her/his theoretical framework that Nzuri consists of—includes—spirit, rhythm, and creativity, respectively.[61] She or he explains that when a person acknowledges and honors Spirit as the source of all things, that person is in a right relationship with—is in rhythm with—herself/himself and life. Being in rhythm with herself/ himself and with life means that person is able to navigate life circumstances without being obliterated by the various challenges that come along the way. The Afrocentric thinker tells us, when a person is in rhythm with herself/himself and life, that person is able to express constructive creativity in her/his work—whatever that work may be. And for the person whose creativity involves contributing seriously to the Afrocentric project, her or his work is that which serves a constructive *function* for African people, has edifying *meaning* for African people, possesses a *motif* which can be identified as "African," and holds and transmits the *ethos* of African people.[62]

The Afrocentric thinker, then—aware of the intricacy, the strength, and the sanity of Nzuri—includes the Nzuri as Invitation and Standard principle in her/his theoretical frame work. She/he invites African people, and others, to understand and hold the principle as an attainable standard worth practicing.

Afrocentric writers utilize the Nzuri as Invitation and Standard principle. They understand Nzuri to be a truth. They, therefore, share the truth of Nzuri, casting it in various implicit and explicit forms through their writing. This does not mean that Afrocentric artists write books and poems wherein the exclusive focus is Nzuri. It does mean, however, that in some of their books, poems, and plays substantive emphasis is given to the truth that a person is truly beautiful when that person manifests constructive behavior. It means that some of their writings teach us to value and look for unchanging beauty in people—such as the beauty embodied in a person protecting her/his community consistently, or the beauty personified by a person affirming teenagers consistently. When the Nzuri as Invitation and Standard principle is present in an Afrocentric writer's work, that work invites us to look for and value more than mere transitory beauty—the beauty of developed muscles or a shapely body, beauty which will one day change or fade.

Consider an Afrocentric writer writing a book wherein African women continually resist white racist, male sexist, wealthy classist, and other forms of oppression. Further, consider the book's story unfolding wherein other female and male characters refer to those indomitable, unbreakable, principled, resisting women as "beautiful." When an Afrocentric writer includes such or similar images and conversation in her or his writing, the truth of Nzuri is being transmitted to readers. Consider, similarly, an Afrocentric short story wherein groups of African men and African women work together and overcome exploitation, and then proceed to build a world wherein African people are treated in a just fashion. Consider also the story's characters calling "beautiful" those African people who live their lives overcoming anti-African traps and building a human African world. Again, when dialogue and interplay of that sort are written into an Afrocentric story, the Nzuri as Invitation and Standard principle is present.

Consider an Afrocentric writer committed to writing biographies of African people. She/He looks for and writes biographies of those people who give us beautiful and courageous demonstrations of what it means to be and stay human, especially when people and forces war and work steadily to liquidate people's humanity. An Afrocentric biographer does not write exclusively, and maybe not even frequently, of those who are "rich and famous," or even "popular." Rather, an Afrocentric biographer is most interested in writing the biographies of people whose lives are testaments of Nzuri.

Of course, an Afrocentric writer can write of intimate, personal, private matters, yet matters such as who slept with whom, and when, and how many times—such matters are never the focus, the core, or the majority content of Afrocentric writers' efforts. Afrocentric writers are not concerned with publicizing facts about lingerie, people's private sex lives, and so forth. All of that is the way of other people in other communities. It is also important to note that *Afrocentric* writing does not include "horror" novels or any writing which aims to scare, or frighten, or imprint readers' minds with *warped, anti-sanity, destabilizing, destructive words and images.*

Finally, any African person, and any non-African person, is free to write whatever she/he wishes. Writing of the sort outlined in the preceding paragraph, however, can never be classified as Afrocentric. It is anti-Nzuri. Specifically, centered African culture has no fascination with writing, or anything else that which serves as a vehicle for destructive excitation, which serves to frighten people nonsensically and unnecessarily. So, if a person's writing consists predominantly of a negative perspective—in contrast to a critical or a positive perspective—that person cannot be viewed as a positive person. Indeed, that person's writing, and that person, are contrary to the truth of Nzuri: beauty is as beauty does; good acts come from a person who is good; aesthetics and ethics are inseparably intertwined.

The Nzuri as Invitation and Standard principle ensures that a truly beautiful person does not produce writing which is predominantly and consistently negative-centered or fear-centered. If a person does produce such writing regularly, and if that person thinks she or he is a beautiful, positive person, then that person is dislocated and confused. She/He may possess incredible, proficient writing skills; nonetheless, that person is out of rhythm with the truth of the Nzuri as Invitation and Standard principle in particular and Afrocentric thought and praxis in general.

While the critical comments of the three preceding paragraphs may seem elementary, it is possible that they may be of significant value. It is quite probable that there will soon be highly touted "blood and gore" writings written by African people, replete with distorted and improper utilization of African culture and symbols, claiming to be Afrocentric. Whenever such dislocated, misoriented, confused, and confusing writings emerge, the preceding critical comments can serve as a ready Afrocentric response.[63]

Centered African culture affirms and propagates Nzuri—the oneness of right action and righteous being, the oneness of healthy ethics and wholesome aesthetics. An Afrocentric writer, then, being a conscious part of centered African culture—in the midst of setting forth a variety of writings—is careful to make substantive use of the Nzuri as Invitation and Standard principle. She/He is so careful, because the Afrocencentric writer knows that writing does influence how people live; and when people are invited to live up to the attainable standard of Nzuri, the world moves closer to being a truly human place.

Kariamu Welsh-Asante tells us that her "*Nzuri* model *locates* [and] *defines*"[64]; that is, it explicates "where" an Afrocentric work should emanate from and where it should be. It describes "what" the work should comprise and "how" the work should look, function, and feel. In short, *Nzuri functions to ensure that Afrocentric efforts are centered comprehensively.* Similarly, Nzuri as Invitation and Standard is a relatively subtle, yet important, focusing, centering principle in Afrocentric thought and praxis. When this principle is active in the work of Afrocentric practitioners, thinkers, or writers, their work is firmly within the Afrocentric universe.

The thirteen preceding principles can be utilized as a guide in the creation of theoretical, literary, and practical Afrocentric works. Further, because the principles are extracted from and anchored in the work of leading proponents of Afrocentric thought, the thirteen principles can be held as a standard template or grid against which extant and future contributions are evaluated.

In the next chapter, select contributions antecedent to Afrocentric thought and praxis will be discussed and assessed relative to *the Gray Template*.[65]

NOTES

1. See Henry Louis Gates Jr., "Beware of the New Pharaohs," *Newsweek*, 23 September 1991, p. 47; see Diane Ravitch, cited in Thomas Toch, "The Happening Department: Bush's Stellar Education Team," *U.S. News & World Report*, 22 April 1991, p. 22; and see John Leo, "A Fringe History of the World," *U.S. News & World Report,* 12 November 1990, p. 25.

2. Asante, *Afrocentricity*, revised ed., pp. 104, 6; Asante, *Idea*, pp. 35, 65-69, 72, 78; Asante, *Kemet*, pp. 192, 82-96, 7.

3. See Karenga, *The Husia*; Karenga, *Coming Forth by Day*.

4. See Asante, *Afrocentricity*, revised ed., pp. 104, 6; Asante, *Idea*, pp. 35, 65, 66, 67, 68, 69, 72, 78; Asante, *Kemet*, pp. 192, 82-96, 7.

5. See Drusilla Dunjee Houston, *Wonderful Ethiopians of the Ancient Cushite Empire* (Baltimore: Black Classic Press, 1985); George Wells Parker, *Children of the Sun* (Baltimore: Black Classic Press, 1981); J.A. Rogers, *The Real Facts About Ethiopia* (Baltimore: Black Classic Press, 1936); John G. Jackson, *Ethiopia and the Origin of Civilization* (Baltimore: Black Classic Press, 1985)—also see his *Introduction to African Civilizations* (Secaucus, N.J.: The Citadel Press, 1970), his *Christianity Before Christ* (Austin, Tex. American Atheist Press, 1938, 1985), and his *Man, God, and Civilization* (Secaucus, N.J.: The Citadel Press, 1972); also see The Rev. Sterling M. Means, *Ethiopia and the Missing Link in African History* (Harrisburg, Pa.: By the Author and The Atlantis Publishing Company, 1945; reprint ed., Dawud Hakim, 1980); also see William Edward Burghardt DuBois, *The World and Africa: An* Inquiry into the Part Which Africa Has Played in World *History* (New York: International Publishers, 1965); also see Rudolph R. Windsor, *From Babylon to* Timbuktu: A History of the Ancient Black Races Including the *Hebrews* (Smithtown,

N.Y.: Exposition Press, 1983); also see Chancellor Williams, *The Destruction of Black* Civilization: Great Issues of a Race from 4500 B.C. to 2000 *A.D.* (Chicago: Third World Press, 1987); also see Yosef ben-Jochannan, *Black Man of the Nile and His Family* (Baltimore: Black Classic Press, 1989); and see John Henrik Clarke, "Ancient Civilizations of Africa: The Missing Pages of World History," in *Egypt Revisited* (New Brunswick, N.J.: *Journal of African Civilizations*, 1982), pp. 113-121. Of course, it is absolutely essential that the work of Cheikh Anta Diop be cited; see especially C.A. Diop, *African Origin of Civilization: Myth or Reality* (Westport, Conn.: Lawrence Hill & Co., Publishers, Inc., 1974); see C.A. Diop, "Africa: Cradle of Humanity," in *Nile Valley Civilizations (Proceedings of the Nile Valley Conference, Atlanta [Ga.], September 26-30, 1984)*, ed. Ivan Van Sertima (New Brunswick, N.J.: Transactions Books, Journal of African Civilizations, November 1986), pp. 23-28; and see C.A. Diop, *Civilization or Barbarism: An Authentic Anthropology* (Brooklyn: Lawrence Hill Books, 1991), pp. 9, 11-68; also see Runoko Rashidi, "African Goddesses: Mothers of Civilization," in *Black Women in Antiquity*, ed. Ivan Van Sertima (New Brunswick, NJ: Journal of African Civilizations, 1984, 1988). Also see Gerald Massey, *A Book of the Beginnings* (London: Williams and Norgate, 1881); and see his *Ancient Egypt the Light of the World* (Baltimore: Black Classic Press, 1992); also see Anna Melissa Graves, *Africa—The Wonder and the Glory* (Baltimore: Black Classic Press, 1942); Richard Leakey, "The Origins of Mankind," *Anthroquest* no. 35 (Fall 1986): 3-4; see Bruce Williams, "The Lost Pharaohs of Nubia" and "Latest Research on Nubia: A Letter to the Editor," respectively, in the book cited above *Nile Valley Civilizations*, ed. I. Van Sertima, pp. 29-46. Also see John Tierney, Linda Wright, and Karen Springen, "The Search for Adam and Eve: Scientists Explore a Controversial New Theory About Man's Origins," *Newsweek*, January 11, 1988; and see the cover story written by William F. Allman, "The First Humans," *U.S. News & World Report,* February 27, 1989, pp. 52-59; and see "Earliest Ancestor of the Human Race Found in Africa [Awash, Ethiopia]," *Philadelphia New Observer*, 5 October 1994, p. 2.

6.   Ibid. Also, I am familiar with the name "Dinqnesh" through the writings of Dr. Ayele Bekerie, a professor in Africana Studies at Cornel University. He says he learned the designation from Dr. Elleni Telda, formerly of Colgate University. See Ayele Bekerie, "An Original Is Older Than Its Copy: The African Origin of Ethiopian Orthodox Christianity," *Imhotep: An Afrocentric Review* vol. 2, no. 1 (January 1990): 7, 18. Since the finds are in Africa, simple sanity

calls for African—Afrocentric—designations: "Dinqnesh" makes utter sense; "Lucy" makes no sense at all.

7. Ibid.; see Jean-Pierre Hallet and Alex Pelle, *Pygmy Kitabu* (New York: Random House, 1972); also see works by Yosef ben-Jochannan and Ivan Van Sertima; also see Albert Churchward, *Signs and Symbols of Primordial Man (Being an Explanation of the Evolution of Religious Doctrines from the Eschatology of the Ancient Egyptians)* (Chesapeake, Va.: ECA Associates, 1910, 1990), pp. 133-167, especially. Also see Theophile Obenga, *Ancient Egypt and Black Africa: A* Student's Handbook for the Study of Ancient Egypt in *Philosophy, Linguistics, and Gender Relations* (London: Karnak House, 1992); and others. Also see Cecil Conteen Gray, "The Influence of African Myth and Religion on Western Civilization," *Imhotep: An Afrocentric Review* vol. 3, no. 1 (Spring 1991): 31-50.

8. Ibid.; also see Asa Hilliard, III, Larry Williams, and Nia Damali, eds., *The Teachings of Ptahhotep (The Oldest Book in the World)* (Atlanta: Blackwood Press, 1987), p. 8; and see Asa G. Hilliard, *The Maroon Within Us (Selected Essays on African American Community Socialization* (Baltimore: Black Classic Press, 1995), pp. 207, 207-218. Also see C.A. Diop, *African Origin,* pp. 169, 179-181; George Wells Parker, *Children of the Sun;* John G. Jackson, *Christianity Before Christ*, pp. 27, 173-174, and see his *Ethiopia and the Origin of Civilization*; also see W.E.B. DuBois, *The World and Africa*; Sterling Means, *Ethiopia Missing Link*; Rudolph Windsor, *From Babylon to Timbuktu;* Gerald Massey, *A Book of the Beginnings*; Anna Melissa Graves, *Africa—The Wonder*.

9. "Chaosization" is a term and concept that I created and developed—in 1994—while contemplating current and past approaches to ordering society.

10. See the aforementioned work of Asante, Karenga, Welsh-Asante, and Ani.

11. Such progression—from clear to de-centered and dislocated, back to clear again—is evident in some of the work of James H. Cone. In his first book, *Black Theology and Black Power* (Minneapolis: Seabury Press, 1969), Cone wrote in a clear African voice, on behalf of and relevant to African people. In a few works that followed, Cone wrote in a peculiar voice—a voice relevant primarily to a European audience. Eventually, as a result of input from his brother, Cecil Cone, and other Africans, James Cone collected himself and began writing again in a clear African voice for African people. Once he regained clarity, he looked back and acknowledged his journey into irrelevance. In James H. Cone, *For My People*

(Maryknoll, N.Y.: Orbis Books, 1984), pp. 26-27, 1-30, Cone said that he and a number of other Black theologians had drifted into a place of "scholarship for the sake of scholarship"; he said they   ran into the problem of "*accountability*" [emphasis his]; they quit asking themselves "for *what purpose*, and for *whom*" [emphasis his] were they doing theology. He said, finally, Black theology degenerated "into an academic discipline cut off from the life of the [B]lack church and community"[;] and the internal debates of Black theologians "were useful in sharpening our critical tools for the intellectual development of [B]lack theology; and all of that "may have helped [Black] theology get academic respectability in white academia, but I cannot say that [activity was] useful in assisting the survival and liberation of [B]lacks during the Richard Nixon and Gerald Ford era of the 1970s." Clearly, Cone, and a number of other Black theologians, neglected being vigilant about holding an African audience as their priority audience. They lapsed for a number of years; once they finished with their wandering, it seems Cone and other Africans writing theology from a Black perspective came to themselves and began—again—holding Black people as their priority audience.

12.   Jacob Carruthers, "Outside Academia: Bernal's Critique of Black Champions of Ancient Egypt," *Journal of Black Studies* vol. 22, number 4 (June 1992): 474, 461.

13.   See Asante, *Afrocentricity*, pp.ix, 1, 21-30, 52, 109-120. Also see C.A. Diop, *Cultural Unity*, pp. 195-197 especially.

14.   *"Maafa"* is a Kiswahili term meaning "massive death" "catastrophic disaster," "great misfortune," "immeasurable catastrophe." Among Afrocentric scholars, Maafa refers most explicitly to the period from 1500s-1800s, when Europeans hunted, captured, transported away from Africa, enslaved, dehumanized, objectified, sold, and traded African people. See Dona Richards, *Let the Circle be Unbroken*, p. 12.

15.   See this kind of victorious consciousness explicated in Asante's *Afrocentricity*, pp. 21-24. Also, the writer of this paper has observed members of The Rites Of Passage Shule speak such words, December 1992 and June 1993; The Rites Of Passage Shule is a Philadelphia-based group of university students, local and professional people who practice and train others in the practice of Afrocentric thought and praxis.

16.   See *Afrocentricity*, pp. 31-34, 45-47, 50-65, 71-84. Actually, Asante's entire document reflects and demonstrates the Way of Heru as Theme.

17.   Some of the positions articulated here are suggested in Asante's

Afrocentricity and in his *Afrocentric Idea.*

18. Ibid.

19. Ibid.

20. This assertion is supported by Diop, *Cultural Unity of Black Africa* (Chicago: Third World Press, 1959, 1963, 1987), pp. 165, 164-165. Also see Ani's *Yurugu.*

21. Again, "Harmosis" is a word and concept cast by the writer of this paper; and it is being explicated thoroughly here. Also see Asante, *Afrocentricity*, pp. 38, 43, 52-58, 65-71, 85, 100-101, 103, 104. Examples of harmosis are also evident in the aforementioned work of Karenga, Asante, Welsh-Asante, and Ani.

22. See Malidoma Patrice Some, *Of Water and the Spirit: Ritual, Magic, and Initiation in the Life of an AfricanShaman* (New York: Jeremy P. Tarcher/Putnam Book, 1994), pp. 37-73.

23. James T. Stewart, "The Development of the Black Revolutionary Artist," in *Black Fire: An Anthology of Afro-American Writing,* eds. LeRoi Jones and Larry Neal (New York: William Morrow and Company, 1976), pp. 8, 9.

24. See the aforementioned work of Asante, Welsh-Asante, Ani, Asa Hilliard, and other Afrocentric Scholars. Also see Na'im Akbar, *Visions for Black Men* (Nashville: Winston-Derek Publishers, 1991); Linda James Myers, Understanding an Afrocentric Worldview: Introduction to an *Optimal Psychology* (Dubuque, Iowa: Kendall/Hunt Publishers, 1988); Wade Nobles, *African Psychology: Toward its Reclamation, Reascension and Revitalization* (Oakland, Ca.: The Institute for the Advanced Study of Black Life and Culture, 1986); and see other Afrocentric scholars.

25. Carter Godwin Woodson, *The Miseducation of the Negro* (Washington, DC: Associated Publishers, 1933; reprint ed., New York: AMS Press, 1977), p. xiii.

26. Ibid.

27. See Asante's *Afrocentricity*, pp. 107, 103-107, 85-107.

28. See *Afrocentricity*, pp. 2, 85. 86, 101, 105, 106-107.

29. Ibid., pp. 4, 6, 7-21, 40-42.

30. Consider Jacques Derrida and the Deconstructionists. They are often understood as writing often from a "contextless," ahistorical location. Such is an illusion—or a delusion. In fact, Deconstructionists are located inside of and work from a particular history. Their desire to deconstruct and oscillate meaning—really, to destabilize and scatter meaning, maybe even obliterate meaning—locates them primarily within European history, given that history's predominant proclivity toward deconstruction and

destabilization of other histories and peoples.

31. For example, drawing upon the wisdom and models of the people and movements noted in the text, Norman Harris, former chairperson of the Department of African American Studies at the University of Cincinnati, shared with this author that he inaugurated an independent, African-centered school in Ohio in the spring of 1995.

32. See, for example, *Afrocentricity*, pp. 31, 32, 33, 35, 36, 37.

33. Sonia Sanchez and her work are legend—yet, she is frequently unappreciated for the genius that she is. See her work—through 1980—examined and explicated with precision and appropriate appreciation in Mari Evans, ed., *Black Women Writers (1950-1980); A Critical Evaluation* (New York: Anchor Books, 1984), pp. 413-450. Note especially Haki Madubuti's essay, "Sonia Sanchez: The Bringer of Memories," pp. 419-432. Sanchez and her work are more than proficient relative to the "Nommoic Creativity" principle.

34. Sonia Sanchez, *Under a Soprano Sky* (Trenton, NJ: Africa World Press, 1993), pp. 12-14. Also see Sonia Sanchez, *I've Been a Woman (New and Selected Poems)* (Chicago: Third World Press, 1990); Sonia Sanchez, *Homegirls and Handgrenades* (New York: Thunder's Mouth Press. 1984), pp. 65-68, especially; and see selections from some of her earlier work—through 1971—in Dudley Randall, ed., *The Black Poets* (New York: Bantam Books, 1981), pp. 231-242. Also see Sanchez Sanchez, *Wounded in the House of a Friend* (Boston: Beacon Press, 1995); the entire work is a "wordwaterfall" of powerful, prophetic, freeing nommo. Also see Sanchez's *Like the Singing Coming off the Drums: Love Poems* (Boston: Beacon Press, 1998) and her *Shake Loose My Skin: New and Selected Poems* (Boston: Beacon Press, 1999).

35. "Newspells" is a term that the writer of this book utilizes to describe one small part of what Sanchez does with words on paper, on the printed page. "Newspells"also describes part of some other writers' technique.

36. Sonia Sanchez, *I've Been a Woman (New and Selected Poems)* (Chicago: Third World Press, 1990), pp. 21-22.

37. See especially the aforementioned work of Marimba Ani (Dona Marimba Richards), Kariamu Welsh-Asante, and Molefi Kete Asante.

38. See *Afrocentricity*.

39. See *Yurugu*; note Ani's concepts of asili, utamaroho, and utamawazo; they are some of the first, recent, highly creative tools which will help immensely in analyzing and critiquing Europeans and Eurocentric reality, from beyond the bounds and parameters of Eu-

ropeans' language and conceptual possibilities!

40. Interview with The Rev. Dana Moore, The Rites Of Passage Shule, Inc., Philadelphia, Pennsylvania, June 1993 and December 1993. This kind of "Nommoic Creativity" is expressed by Dana Moore and other Afrocentric practitioners who work with, serve as facilitators of, The Rites Of Passage Shule (ROPS), Inc. ROPS is committed to serving African people via teaching, demonstrating, and training others in the way of Afrocentric thought and praxis.

41. *Afrocentricity*, p. 37.

42. See Karenga and Carruthers, *Kemet African Worldview*, pp. 89, 90-94; and see Karenga's *Introduction*, pp. 162-163, 164-197, 322-349. The preceding sources deal with the multiple meanings of Maat. At this point in this study, however, I am delimiting the definitional possibilities and centering upon the particular meaning of Maat as "justice."

43. See, for example, Vivian V. Gordon, *Black Women, Feminism and Black Liberation: Which Way?* (Chicago: Third World Press, 1987, 1990); she is concerned about justice between African women and men, *and* she is concerned with African people achieving justice in our encounters with non-Africans.

44. See Welsh-Asante, *"Nzuri," African Keeper Traditions*, pp. 1, 3, 4, 6, 8, 9, 11, 13, 16, 17. Also see, Asante, *Kemet*, p. 5 and *Malcolm as Hero*, p. 100.

45. See Buchi Emecheta, *The Joys of Motherhood* (New York: George Braziller, 1988); Toni Cade Bambara, *The Salt Eaters* (New York: Vintage Books, 1981); Chinua Achebe, *Things Fall Apart* (New York: Fawcett Crest, 1991); Ngugi, *Weep Not, Child* (Oxford: Heinemann Educational Books, 1987).

46. See Asa Hilliard, *Ptahhotep, p. 2;* and see Yosef A. A. ben-Jochannan, *Black Man of the Nile*, and see his *Africa: Mother of Western Civilization* (Baltimore: Black Classic Press, 1988), and see his *Our Black Seminarians and Black Clergy Without a Black Theology* (New York: Alkebu-lan Books and Education Materials Association, 1978), and see his *Ta-Merry/"Egypt" and Her Religious Persecutors: From Judaism-Christianity-Islam to Marxian Humanism; or The Origins of Western Civilization—From Israel-Sumeria-Greece or Ta-Merry/"Egypt"* (New York: By the author, 1988).

47. See Obenga, *Ancient Egypt Black Africa*, pp. 169, 30-39; see Malidoma Patrice Some, *Of Water and the Spirit: Ritual, Magic, and Initiation in the Life of an African Shaman* (New York: Jeremy P. Tarcher/Putnam Book, 1994); see Migene Gonzalez, *Power of the Orishas: Santeria and the Worship of Saints* (New York: Original

Publications, 1992), and see his *Santeria: African Magic in Latin America* (New York: Original Publications, 1990); see Dona Richards, *Let the Circle Be*; see Karenga, *The Husia*; see J.E. Manchip White, *Ancient Egypt: Its Culture and History* (New York: Dover Publications, Inc., 1970); see E.A. Wallis Budge, *Egyptian Religion* (New York: Carol Publishing Group, 1959, 1987); see Isha Schwaller DeLubicz, *The Opening of the Way* (Rochester, Vt.: Inner Traditions International, Ltd., 1981); and for other Kemet-specific references see Vivian Verdell Gordon, *Kemet and Other Ancient African Civilizations: Selected References* (Chicago: Third World Press, 1991).

48.   Ibid. Also see Willis R. Harman and Howard Rheingold, *Higher Creativity* (Los Angeles: Jeremy P. Tarcher, 1984).

49.   While each Afrocentric thinker will set forth her or his theory in her or his own unique way, all Afrocentric theories share a common tenor and tone. All Afrocentric theories are affirming and encouraging, because one of the core elements of Afrocentric ontology is that being is essentially good; so, life is good and/or is always potentially good. Also, the various Afrocentric theories are relatively open-ended; because one aspect of Afrocentric epistemology is that knowledge comes via a variety of channels. Such being so, each Afrocentric theory addresses as much as the thinker wishes to or is able to—with the thinker understanding that the theory is never totally closed or complete; because other African people come along periodically and extend the theory, adding knowledge and insight to the theory. Consider Diop's theories, they affirm and encourage African people; Asante's theory affirms and encourages African people; Wade Nobles' theoretical constructs affirm African people; Vivian Gordon's theoretical efforts encourage African people; Welsh-Asante's theory affirms African people; Linda James Myers' and Marimba Ani's theoretical work encourages African people. Further, whatever the focus of the thinker's particular theory, the Afrocentric thinker's theory affirms African people clearly and encourages African people overtly. Her/His theory is not ambivalent, ambiguous, fatalistic, or built upon irrelevant-inaccessible-personal-oscillating, cerebral mysticism. If the tenor of a thinker's theory is pessimistic, if its tone is that of trepidation or timidity, that theory is not located [properly]; it is not utilizing the "Explicit Locational Indicators Intentionality" principle; and, most importantly, the theory cannot be considered or classified as Afrocentric.

50.   See George G. M. James, *Stolen Legacy* (New York: Philosophical Society, 1954; reprint ed., San Francisco: Julian Richardson Associates, 1985); also see Chukwunyere Kamalu, *Foundations of African*

Thought: A Worldview Grounded in the African Heritage of Religion, Philosophy, Science and Art (London: Karnak House, 1990); also see Obenga, *Ancient Egypt Black Africa*. Also, see related works cited earlier in this paper.

51. Many African families in the United States and beyond the United States are explicit and intentional in utilizing locational indicators of a non-African sort when they gather. I have observed African families in Bangkok, Thailand behaving in such manner, during random as well as special celebratory gatherings, 1969-1972; and I have observed African families in the United States behave in such manner, during family reunions as well as during other noteworthy celebratory gatherings, 1972-2000.

52. I have observed Afrocentric practice of this sort occurring at some ASCAC gatherings, 1989-1994; at Circle of DAWN-MAAT gatherings in Washington, D.C., 1994-1995; at The Rites Of Passage Shule gatherings in Philadelphia, Pa. and Gettysburg, Pa., 1991-2000; and at Haki Madhubuti's Institute of Positive Education gatherings in Chicago, Ill., 1982.

53. See Na'im Akbar, *Visions for Black Men* (Nashville: Winston-Derek Publishers, 1991). It is an African-centered effort, relative to its essential spirit; yet it offers few new words, posits no new concepts; the book is scant relative to the "Explicit Locational Indicators Intentionality" principle.

54. See Kariamu Welsh-Asante, "Dance Aesthetic Foundation," *African Culture*, pp. 71, 78, 79-80. Also see Wade Nobles discussion of "deep structure" and Larry Neal's "race memory" designation.

55. See Asante's *Malcolm X as Cultural Hero and Other Essays.*

56. Maya Angelou, *And Still I Rise* (New York: Bantam Books, 1980), pp. 41-42.

57. Ibid., pp. 41, 42.

58. See Welsh-Asante's *"Nzuri," African Keeper Traditions.*

59. This is a description of the Afrocentric practice, of Nzuri as Invitation and Standard, of Rasheedah Farid, an Afrocentric dance teacher affiliated with Virginia State University. She shared this in formal conversation, and I observed Farid evidencing and exemplifying this, in late spring 1991. Also, as a result of taking classes under Kariamu Welsh-Asante, professor and Afrocentric aesthetics and dance expert in the Department of African American Studies at Temple University, and believing that her classroom teaching informs some part of her dance teaching practice, I believe this kind of Afrocentric practice might also be part of Welsh-Asante's way.

60. See Marimba Ani's *Yurugu*; it dissects and labels this and other

aspects of Europeans thought and behaviour.

61. Welsh-Asante, *"Nzuri,"* pp. 9-13.

62. Ibid., pp. 9-11.

63. Back in the early 1990s, some young rappers were dealing confusedly and in an extremely non-African, uncivilized, disrespectful, and dangerous manner with "death." The themes—graveyards, digging up corpses, "devil" worship—and the young rappers' convoluted fascination with such themes, suggested the young rappers had essentially no ethical-aesthetic framework. The young rappers seemed to be unable to differentiate between good, cool, less than good, other than cool, and so forth. None of those rappers are famous yet. Nonetheless, undoubtedly, there are non-African people and misoriented African people who are eager to popularize such unhealthy movement—and call it "Afrocentric."

64. Welsh-Asante, *"Nzuri,"* p. 18.

65. "The Gray Template" of Afrocentric Thought and Praxis is the name I have given to the analytical tool constructed during the course of this chapter.

Chapter 5

ANTECEDENTS TO AFROCENTRIC THOUGHT AND PRAXIS

There are antecedents to Afrocentric theory and praxis; and while some of the antecedents may bear no resemblance to Afrocentric thought and praxis, some of the antecedents may be understood as incipient Afrocentric offerings. This paper will consider academic-intellectual antecedents, political-activist antecedents, and literary antecedents to Afrocentric theory and praxis. Specifically, this chapter will assess select works by Aime Cesaire, Malcolm X, and Ayi Kwei Armah, respectively.

In each instance, the person's work(s) will be introduced briefly. The work(s) will then be discussed and assessed relative to The Thirteen Principles of Afrocentric Thought and Praxis Gray Template. The work(s) will be evaluated by noting how and why they satisfy, if they satisfy, the Thirteen Principles. For convenience, a listing of the principles is set forth again:

1. The Meta-Constants: Humanizing and Harmonizing
2. The Primacy of African People and African Civilization
3. An African Audience as the Primary Audience
4. Njia as Theme
5. The Way of Heru as Theme
6. Harmosis as Mode
7. Wholistic Afrocentric Action as Goal
8. Sankofan Approach
9. Nommoic Creativity
10. Maatic Argumentation
11. Explicit Locational Indicators Intentionality
12. African Collective Memory-Perception Competence
13. Nzuri as Invitation and Standard

Relative to an academic-intellectual antecedent to Afrocentric thought and praxis, work of Aime Cesaire will be discussed. Cesaire, a diasporan African, born in 1913 on the island of Martinique in the Caribbean, is an accomplished poet, essayist, and playwright, a local Martiniquan politician and mayor, a conscientious member of the French parliament, a profound and practical thinker, and more. Indeed, he is a legendary African intellectual; and it seems fitting that his work be considered. While there are numerous writings that can be discussed, three representative works will be considered. Specifically, his 1939 effort, *Cahier d'un retour au pays natal (Notebook of a Return to the Native Land)*; his 1955 work, *Discours sur le colonialisme (Discourse On Colonialism)*; and a 1967 interview with Haitian poet Renee Depestre will be assessed.

Notebook, the work wherein the historic term "Negritude" was introduced to the world, is an extended, prose poem appealing passionately to African people to affirm and assert our Black personhood. *Discourse On Colonialism* is a brilliant, scathing yet humane essay critiquing European colonialism, people, and policies without apology or euphemism. The interview with Depestre is an instance wherein Cesaire shares explicitly some of his perspectives on Negritude, the term and the Movement.

Cesaire's work seems to satisfy five of the Template's Thirteen Principles of Afrocentric Thought and Praxis. Specifically, his work satisfies Principle 1, the Meta-Constants: Humanizing and Harmonizing; Principle 2, the Primacy of African People and African Civilization; Principle 4, Njia as Theme; Principle 9, Nommoic Creativity; and Principle 8, Sankofan Approach.

Principles 1 and 2, the Meta-Constants: Humanizing and Harmonizing and The Primacy of African People and African Civilization, are prevalent in *Discourse on Colonialism*. Cesaire's *Discourse* can be understood as an incipient Afrocentric critique of Europe's and Europeans' predominant perspective and practice toward African people and other people of color—a perspective characterized by barbaric disrespect and a practice consisting of comprehensive decimation. *Discourse*, however, is not a critique for the sake of critique. It is a piercing, painful, constructive critique, with two essential goals: (1)to invite the white people of Europe and the West in general to manifest humanity and harmony within themselves and toward African people and other people of color on the Earth, and (2)to aprise the white people of Europe and the rest of the West that African people and African civilization existed in advanced states of humanness and harmony before Europeans came to brutalize and colonize, in fact, before "Europe" itself existed. Consider Cesaire's words:

> *Europe is indefensible.*
> ... "Europe" is morally, spiritually indefensible. ... between *colonization* and *civilization* there is an infinite distance; that out of all the colonial expeditions that have undertaken, out of all the colonial statutes that have been drawn up, out of all the memoranda that have despatched by all the ministries, there could not come [and has not come] a single human value.[1]

Cesaire supports his position by dissecting and explicating the pseudo-humanism of bourgeois Europeans. He remembers Hitler and notes that bourgeois Europeans are gross contradictions, are immeasurably non-humanistic; because they have only one real problem with Hitler. They do not approve of Hitler because Hitler humiliated and committed crimes against "the white man," and utilized "colonialist procedures" that were to be perpetrated only upon Africans, Asian Indians, Arabs, and other people of color. Cesaire reiterates his indictment of bourgeois Europeans by citing the self-indicting, extremely anti-African words of numerous and various European spokespeople. Then, Cesaire states the following:

> No one.
> I mean not one established writer, not one academician, not one preacher, not one crusader for the right or for religion, not one "defender of the human person [can be found among the major voices of Europe]."[2]

In the excerpts above, Cesaire tells Europeans who they are and how warped and wicked they are in the eyes of African people and in the eyes of other people of color. Utilizing undeniable examples from Europeans' own history and verbatim quotations from multifarious of their "great men," Cesaire holds Europeans up and parades Europeans in front of their own eyes, in all of their moral nakedness, in all of their ethical shamelessness. He leaves no stone unturned; he closes all escape routes; he makes no allowances for Europeans' brazen yet calculated inhumanity.

Cesaire's intention, however, is not to do to them what they have done to others. His goal is not to leave the contemporary landscape strewn with millions of gashed or broken European hearts, and bashed or battered European minds. Rather, Cesaire hopes to evoke, even provoke, a response from Europeans that is diametrically opposite the anti-reality which their bourgeois leaders have mis-created. By framing, naming and relentlessly dismembering Europeans' pseudo-humanness, he hopes to catalyze them into creating and living an authentic humanness and harmony. Where Europeans have initiated and presently maintain hideous, antihuman policies, Cesaire's goal is to catalyze and call forth within them the implementation of sane, profoundly human policies. Consider words with which he closes *Discourse*:

> So . . . in Africa, in the South Sea Islands, in Madagascar [and South Africa], in the West Indies [and the United States], Western Europe [needs to undertake] on its own initiative a policy of *nationalities*, a new policy founded on respect for peoples and cultures . . . .[3] (emphasis his)

Cesaire's work, in a bold, uncompromising manner, attempts to humanize and harmonize Africans, other people of color, and Europeans; and it satisfies Principle 1, the Meta-Constants: Humanizing and Harmonizing.

In *Discourse*, relative to Principle 2, the Primacy of African People and African Civilization, Cesaire says that the civilizations of African people and other people of color were in existence before the capitalist societies of Europe. Further, they were "communal," "democratic," "cooperative" civilizations; they were collectives of civilized people. Cesaire emphasizes:

> They were the fact, they did not pretend to be the idea; despite their faults, they were neither to be hated nor condemned. They were content to be.[4]

Cesaire continues on and remarks that ancient African civilizations were "courteous civilizations." The task, adds Cesaire, is not to "return to" the past; rather, the work is to "go beyond," to create "a new society," "a society [with the] productive power of modern times, warm with all the fraternity of olden [ancient African] days." Cesaire notes that long before the French and other Europeans invaded Africa, Sudanese empires existed. Sophisticated, beautiful African music existed. The highly refined bronzes of Benin existed, and magnificent Shango sculpture existed—in contrast to "the sensationally bad art that adorns so many European capitals." Indeed, when the "first" European "explorers" entered Africa, says Cesaire, they saw Black people who were—in the words of the German anthropologist, Leo Frobenius—" "Civilized to the marrow of their bones. The idea of a barbaric Negro is a European invention.'"[5]

In one of his most explicit statements on the primacy of African civilizations, Cesaire notes "the invention of arithmetic and geometry by the Egyptians." He also notes that the ancient Egyptians were Black people [Nubians; Ethiopians], who migrated down the Nile River from farther inland out to the lower, northeastern part of Africa. In fact, Cesaire undergirds his position by citing Cheikh Anta Diop's work. Cesaire asserts simply and confidently:

> Sheikh Anta Diop [has definitively deconstructed he machinations of European Egyptologists, who, serving as some of the watchdogs of colonialism, falsify facts and delude readers. Indeed, Sheikh Diop's 1955] book, *Nations negres et culture* [*Black Nations and Culture*], [is] the most daring
> book yet written by a Negro and one which will without question play an important part in the awakening of Africa.[6]

Considering the evidence in the three preceding paragraphs, it seems apparent that Cesaire is clear relative to the primacy of African people and civilization; and thereby, his work satisfies Principle 2 of Afrocentric thought and praxis. Much of the evidence in the three preceding paragraphs also reinforces Cesaire's aforementioned satisfaction of Principle 1, the Meta-Constants: Humanizing and Harmonizing. It is also noteworthy that the current Afrocentric movement and its frequent reliance upon the work of Diop prove Cesaire's astute 1955 anticipatory assertion to be correct on the—

then future—major impact of Diop's work.

Njia as Theme, Principle 4, and Nommoic Creativity, Principle 9, are prevalent in *Notebook.* Cesaire's *Notebook,* in all of its controlled meandering complexity, is an autobiographical poem. It is also a brilliant and cathartic work written on behalf of the African people of Martinique. *Notebook* is a work that rails against the politics of unrestrained assimilation, that is, the almost absolute psychological domination that French and other European people perpetrated upon the African people of Martinique—and upon many millions of other African people. And *Notebook* is also a work that faces and speaks transformatively and valiantly to the 1939 socio-psycho-historical circumstances of the African people of Martinique—and to other Africans—whose collective psyche consisted of an almost insatiable self-alienation and docility, "an incompleteness of self-identification," and whose collective feelings included feelings "of being somehow 'abnormal.'"[7]

In the midst of the poem recounting the horrible European-created reality lived by the Africans in Martinique, and the grotesque European-created reality forced upon Africans around the world, in the midst of tremendous empirical socio-economical mountains and stupendous less empirical psychological mountains, Cesaire launches an audacious, victory-seeking, African voice:

> I would go to this land of mine and I would say to it: "Embrace me without fear . . . And if all I can do is speak, it is for you I shall speak.". . . "My mouth shall be the mouth of those calamities that have no mouth, my voice the freedom of those who break down in the solitary confinement of despair.". . . behold here I am![8]

Thereafter, *Notebook* proceeds again with listing the swirling European-initiated brokenness shouldered by Africans, the madness spewed forth by Europeans. It notes, the "hatred[, the] weight of the insult and a hundred years of whip lashes. . . . [the] venomous flowers . . . the epileptic mornings; the white blaze of abyssal sands . . . ."[9] As the list unfurls and unravels, periodically, momentarily, Europeans' anti-African sentiments are unsheathed and explicit. Hear Cesaire set forth some of the words and feelings that Europeans share with each other privately, and that they sometimes speak publicly to African people:

> (niggers-are-all-alike, I-tell-you vices-all-the-believe-you-
> me nigger-smell, that's-what-makes-cane-grow remember-
> the-old-saying: beat-a-nigger, and you feed him)[10]

Then, immediately following the preceding notation of European's raw, anti-African sentiments, Cesaire releases two more energetic, unfolding, victory-conscious African voices:

> I circle about, an *unappeased* filly.[11] (emphasis mine)
> By a sudden and beneficent *inner revolution*, I now ignore
> my repugnant ugliness [an ugliness fabricated and thrust
> upon me by Europeans].[12] (emphasis mine)

Finally, near the middle of *Notebook*, Cesaire makes a definite commitment to Principle 4, Njia as Theme, that is, the theme of victorious consciousness. Throughout the first half of the poem, there is substantial oscillation and alternation. The theme of Njia is relatively subterranean, indefinite, too intermittent. The consciousness of victory in the poem is not convincing. Near the middle of the poem, however, and forever thereafter, Njia as Theme—the consciousness of victory, the optimistic consciousness of the attainability of victory—is a decisive reality. Consider the following excerpts. Hear the strength of the voice, the undaunted determined tone, the clarity, the certainty:

> . . . what strange pride suddenly illuminates me!
> . . . grant me the savage faith of the sorcerer
> grant my hands power to mold
> grant my soul the sword's temper
> I won't flinch. Make my head into a figurehead
> and as for me, my heart, . . . *make me* into . . .
> the father, the brother, the son,
> . . . *the lover of this unique people*
> . . . Make me a steward of its blood
> make me trustee of its resentment
> make me into a man for the ending
> make me into a man for the beginning
> make me into a man of meditation but also

make me into *a man of germination*
make me into the executor of these lofty works the time has
come to gird one's loins like a
brave man—
. . . I accept, I accept it all
. . . rise
rise
rise
I follow you who are imprinted on
my ancestral . . . cornea[13] (emphasis mine)

There is no trepidation in the preceding voice. It is solid and centered, victorious. Cesaire's work satisfies Principle 4 of Afrocentric thought and praxis, Njia as Theme.

Nommoic Creativity, the creative empowered use of words and the strategic creation of concepts, Principle 9, is also prevalent in *Notebook*. The poem often shifts focus and changes direction without warning. Sometimes, it consists of sentences and paragraphs; then, suddenly, it consists of lines containing short or long phrases, or simply one word. The poem refuses to be straitjacketed; it refuses to fit into any preconceived or pre-existing literary boxes. Such refusal, at least in some part, fuels the enormous energy of the poem; and such refusal, in *Notebook*, makes for Nommoic Creativity. Additionally, the poem contains numerous instances of regular, rhythmic, almost hypnotic, repetitions of lines or parts of lines; and that is a form of Nommoic Creativity. Further, that rhythmic repetition—still felt in a poem written in French, then translated into English!—gives the poem a powerful pulse and makes for a distinct African beat, traceable to Cesaire's surface- and deep-structure African origins. That, too, is Nommoic Creativity.

An example of this recurring rhythmic phrasing can be seen in the excerpt in the paragraph preceding the last two paragraphs. Note the pulsing beat and energy emanated by the repetitive phrasing: "grant me . . . grant my . . . grant my . . . make my . . . make me . . . make me . . . make me . . . make me . . . make me . . . make me . . . make me . . .make me . . . rise rise rise."

Notebook's most pronounced and celebrated manifestation of Nommoic Creativity, however, is Cesaire's creation and introduction of the term "Negritude." Taking the French word *negre*,

Cesaire creates his own word. This is so significant because the French word *negre* translates, essentially, as "nigger." In creating the term "negritude," then, Cesaire takes the word that disrespects-cuts-injures him and his people most and transforms it into a tool to heal and free himself and his people. Hear him:

> my negritude is not a stone, its deafness hurled
> against the clamor of the day
> my negritude is not a leukoma of dead liquid over
> the earth's dead eye
> my negritude is neither tower nor cathedral
> [my negritude] takes root in the red flesh of the
> the soil
> it takes root in the ardent flesh of the sky
> it breaks through the opaque prostration with its
> upright patience
> . . . I say right on! the old negritude
> progressively cadavers itself.
> . . . I say right on! The old negritude
> progressively cadavers itself.[14]

To a significant degree, Cesaire's altering, inverting, and redefining of an anti-African word, so that it becomes a positive pro-African word and concept—his asserting of his negritude in Martinique and beyond—is an act of defiance and liberation. Indeed, his creation of the Negritude concept—and the Negritude movement which followed—anticipates the pro-African attitude and the Black Power and Black Arts Movement that burst forth in the United States in the 1960s, replete with the even more explicit, more bold, yet, Negritude-like proclamations, "Black is Beautiful," "Say it Loud, I'm Black and I'm Proud!" Additionally, Cesaire's Negritude concept can also be understood as an incipient groping toward the more sophisticated concept and philosophy of "Afrocentricity," which Asante set forth in 1980.

In using the French language creatively, intentionally, and unrestrainedly, and in creating Negritude—the word and the concept, Cesaire moves on his own terms. He does not allow Europeans—French folk in particular—to be the only people wielding word and conceptual power. Cesaire gives words meaning which suit and benefit him and other African people; he creates fresh liberating concepts. Cesaire's work satisfies Principle 9, Nommoic Creativity.

Cesaire's work also satisfies Principle 8, Sankofan Approach. In *Notebook*, in 1939, he does not have volumes of African historical information to reference, due to France's policy of assimilation and absorption, that is, "Frenchcentricism." Nonetheless, Cesaire references and draws upon what he is aware of. In the course of *Notebook*, he references "(TOUSSAINT, TOUSSAINT L'OUVERTURE)...[a] king of Dahomey... princes of Ghana... Askia the Great... and my Bambara ancestors."[15] Almost thirty years later, in the aforementioned 1967 interview with Haitian poet Renee Depestre—perhaps benefitting from the years of his own history-changing work and growth, as well as from the work and growth of other Africans around the world—Cesaire's Afrocentric historical references are more numerous. He cites "the Marcus Garvey movement," "Langston Hughes and Claude McKay," "McKay's novel, *Banjo*," "the Negro Renaissance Movement in the United States," "the Haitian movement and [Jean] Price-Mars' important book, *Ainsi parla l'oncle* [*So Spoke the Uncle*]," "Henri Christophe, Jean-Jacques Dessalines . . . ."[16]

Cesaire's work satisfies the Sankofan Approach principle, Principle 8. He utilizes African history to anchor and strengthen his work. It is noteworthy that Cesaire is particularly learned relative to Europe's—especially France's—history, that he is quite adept relative to particular moments and personalities in that history. It is also noteworthy that he is not trapped by that history. Relative to African history, Cesaire seems to possess a combination of a good grasp of some of the particulars of the history and an excellent hazy-yet-correct-deep-structure-intuition of the broad particulars of the history. Given Cesaire's birth fairly early in the twentieth century, and his extensive formal training within French institutions, his European historical knowledge base is to be expected. His positive African historical knowledge base, and his real commitment to African people, is perhaps a miracle.

Aime Cesaire's work can be understood as incipient Afrocentric academic-intellectual work. It is similar to Afrocentric thought and praxis, but it is not the same. It satisfies some of, but not all of, the Thirteen Principles of the Afrocentric Thought and Praxis Gray Template. Cesaire's work and the Negritude movement that he helped to launch appear earlier in history than the Afrocentric movement. As a consequence perhaps, and especially considering the smaller volume of information available to Cesaire, Cesaire's work is not as comprehensive, not as centered, not as clear as Afrocentric thought and praxis.

Finally, and understandably, much of Cesaire's work emerges, in great part, from a mindset that needs to speak and scream *to and against* Europe and Europeans. In contrast, Afrocentric thought and praxis moves forth from a mindset that determines to speak *to and for* Africa and Africans. Further, the relationship between Cesaire's work and Afrocentric thought and praxis is not antagonistic; the relationship is complementary. Appearing almost forty years after Cesaire's first major efforts, Afrocentric thought and praxis are supposed to be broader, more refined, more sophisticated. Indeed, Afrocentric thought and praxis are here now, because Cesaire's work prepared part of the way.

As a Political-Activist antecedent to Afrocentric thought and praxis, the words and practice of Malcolm X—El Hajj Malik El Shabazz—will be discussed. Named Malcolm Little by his parents, given a Yoruba name "Omawale" ["the son who has come home"] by Nigerian college students, and carrying a number of different nicknames at various points in his life, Malcolm X—the son of an African couple who supported and adhered to the program set forth and led by Marcus Garvey, a man who eventually experiences and lives the most exploited and decadent aspects of a European-dominated African life, a man who joins the Nation of Islam (NOI) and makes it exceedingly relevant and significant, a man who so quests after real truth and practical answers for African people that he leaves the NOI when the quest necessitates, a man who risks and gives his life with his eyes wide open for African people—is an African whose words and work warrant consideration.

Malcolm's legacy makes it clear that he is to be classified as other than a great writer. He does not have a list of books to his credit. Indeed, there is only one book that bears his name as author. So, Malcolm's legacy is not one of sitting, thinking, and writing eloquent books. Rather, it is one of thinking-and-acting, of formulating-and-practicing a pro-African life-giving politicized consciousness. Malcolm's legacy suggests that he is to be understood as a brilliant and extraordinary African thinker, speaker, teacher, and practitioner. Always, his essential legacy shows him speaking-teaching, applying-practicing, and trying to speak and teach, trying to apply and practice his thoughts, words, teachings.

Consequently, Malcolm's autobiography and select books containing speeches he made during the 1963-1965 years of his life will be considered. Specifically, we will assess his 1964-1965 effort *The Autobiography of Malcolm X*, the 1965 collection of speeches *Malcolm X Speaks*, the 1967 collection *Malcolm X on Afro-American History*, the 1969 collection *Malcolm X: The Man and His Times*, the 1970 collection *Malcolm X: By Any Means Necessary,* and the 1991 collection *Malcolm X Talks to Young People.*

The Autobiography of Malcolm X is an autobiographical sharing, covering important aspects of Malcolm's life from childhood through a few months before his assassination. *Malcolm X: The Man and His Times*, edited by John Henrik Clarke, consists essentially of essays on Malcolm, dialogues between Malcolm and others, an Organization of Afro-American Unity (OAAU) organizational statement, and an outline of the petition Malcolm planned to present at the United Nations. The remaining books, set forth by their titles in the preceding paragraph, all contain various speeches that Malcolm made to various audiences.

Malcolm's work seems to satisfy ten of the Template's Thirteen Principles of Afrocentric Theory and Praxis. It is appropriate to note how his efforts satisfy Principles 1, 2, 4, and 8—that is, the Meta-Constants: Humanizing and Harmonizing, the Primacy of African People and African Civilization, Njia as Theme, and Sankofan Approach, respectively. Thereafter, it is important to highlight how Malcolm's work satisfies Principles 3, 5, 7, 10, 12, and 13, An African Audience as the Priority Audience, the Way of Heru as Theme, Wholistic Afrocentric Action as Goal, Maatic Argumentation, African Collective Memory-Perception Competence, and Nzuri as Invitation and Standard, respectively.

Relative to Principle 1, the Meta-Constants: Humanizing and Harmonizing, the matter is clear. Once he begins in the 1950s journeying away from a life of insanity-decadence-and-unconscious-victimization, Malcolm X works the rest of his life humanizing and harmonizing himself and other African people.[17]

While with the NOI and while on his own, he is constant in his efforts to restore sanity and harmony to African people's minds, bodies—even souls—and communities. By overcoming his years as a person lost from himself, a hustler, womanizer, pimp, thief, drug-dealer, drug-abuser, non-stop-party-man, and incarcerated African, and by subsequently living his life—with few contradictions and high integrity—as an African dedicated and committed to teaching African people to move in a similar fashion, Malcolm X manifests and propogates profound humanness and much harmony. Convincing and persuading thousands of Black people to know our Black selves for our Black selves, he helps us to humanness and harmony within our African selves.[18]

By challenging and helping us to love ourselves and our people, and by teaching and showing us how to teach and depend on ourselves and our people, and by modelling for us that one can overcome drugs for ourselves and our people, and by training us to serve and defend ourselves and our people—Malcolm helps us find humanness, sanity, and harmony within ourselves. He helps us create harmony within our families and communities. By shedding seasons of pyschological blindness, general ignorance, and anchorless-purposeless, anti-African living, and then rising up lucid, learned, full of purpose, and thankful-to-be-an-African—and by encouraging African people to do likewise—Malcolm X satisfies Principle 1.[19]

Malcolm's work also satisfies Princple 2, the Primacy of African People and African Civilization. In a number of different instances, Malcolm notes that the oldest and first people and civilizations on the Earth are African; and he supports his assertions with noteworthy African, and some non-African, references. In asserting African people's primacy, Malcolm cites the work of the European—Austrian—monk, Gregor Mendel; and he also references the work of British anthropologist Louis S. B. Leakey. [20]

Relative to the primacy of African civilization, Malcolm cites—among others—Carter G. Woodson's *Negro History* and J.A. Rogers' *Sex and Race*. Also, his enlightenment is undoubtedly enhanced and expanded by his contact in New York with John Henrik Clarke and Yosef Ben-Jochannan. Malcolm notes that the civilizations of ancient Egypt, Ethiopia, Sumeria, and India, as well as the less ancient civilizations of Carthage, Ghana, Mali, Songhai, and of the Moors were all civilizations of Black people. He also notes the ancient Africans' building of *Hr M Akht* (known most popularly as "the Sphinx"), and their mastery of mathematics, architecture, engineering, astronomy, geology, pyramid building, and chemistry—especially color creation.[21] Malcolm's work and words satisfy Principle 2.

Principle 4, Njia as Theme, is quite apparent in Malcolm's practice and words. Indeed, Njia—victorious consciousness, a commitment to the idea of the attainability of victory—is one of the essential themes of his life. It is Njia that compels and propels Malcolm to travel to many of the United States' major urban cities and plant local NOI mosques, building the NOI into a formidable organization. A pessimistic person or one with limited vision shrinks from such work. It is Njia that sustains Malcolm when he must move away from the NOI. It is a belief in the attainability of victory that enables him to initiate the Muslim Mosque, Inc. and the OAAU, so that he and others can serve African people with even greater integrity and authenticity.[22]

Additionally, Njia as Theme is prevalent when Malcolm speaks truthfully to African people and other people all over the world. Njia as Theme is operative when he explains in multifarious ways— almost redundantly—that *people* with optimism and courage can make the world into something better than a nightmare. Hear Malcolm, as strong and as victory-conscious in 1965 as in 1963 and earlier:

> I'm the man you think you are. . . . If you want to know what I'll do, figure out what you'll do. I'll do the same thing—only more of it.[23]

In the aforementioned ways and instances, and in so many other small and large ways, Njia as Theme is a predominant theme in Malcolm's practice and words—in the totality of his life!

Malcolm's words overflow with the Sankofan Approach, Principle 8. In one well known November 1963 speech, "Message to the Grassroots," Malcolm makes it clear that he approaches matters primarily from a historical angle, using knowledge of past and recent history to shape present and future reality, in effective, pro-African ways. Hear Malcolm explain, in his characteristic straightforward manner:

> Of all our studies, history is best qualified to reward our research. And when you see that you've got problems, all you have to do is examine the [histories of] others who have problems similar to yours. Once you know how they got theirs straight, then you know how you can get yours straight. . . .[Look at] Africa[, in] Kenya, [look at] the Mau Mau . . . [look in] Algeria [at the] Algerians . . .[look in] Asia . . . in Latin America. [Look at the] Cuban Revolution . . . .[24]

On January 25, 1965, at the Audubon Ballroom in Harlem, at an OAAU meeting, Malcolm explicates the Sankofan Approach's intrinsic advantages:

> . . . If you start to talk to any one of them [to any kind of European person], I don't care where he [or she] is, if you know history, you can put him [or her] right in his [or her] place. In fact, he'll stay in his place, if he knows that you know your history.[25]

To facilitate optimum connection and communication with his audiences, and to extend almost irresistible persuasion to them, Malcolm's formal speeches, public dialogues, and even some private conversations pivot upon the concrete truths revealed in ancient and contemporary African history, as well as in the ancient and contemporary histories of non-African people.

Depending on his context, Malcolm cites the ancient Africans, and Hannibal, and Toussaint, Christophe and Dessalines, and Nat Turner, and Marcus Garvey and the Universal Negro Improvement Association (UNIA), the Mau Mau, the Civil Rights Movement and personalities within it, the years of the 1500s-1800s when Europeans held Africans in captivity, the European American Revolution in 1776, the Civil War of the 1800s in the United States, John Brown, the Russian Revolution the Chinese Revolution, the Bandung Conference of people of color from all over the globe, the Algerians battling the French in Algeria, and many other landmark occurrences and personalities in past and recent history.[26] He thinks in Sankofan terms, and his approach to matters is Sankofan. As one constantly trying to transform people, and working steadily to change a society and world bent upon manipulating and mystifying people, Malcolm understands the pure power of the Sankofan Approach. He employs it relentlessly, wonderfully.

Afrocentric theory and praxis Principle 3, An African Audience as the Priority Audience, is satisfied by the words and practice of Malcolm X. While anyone can read his work and his speeches, and while Malcolm speaks to non-African and integrated audiences as well as African audiences, his priority audience is African. Throughout his life as a voice for and organizer of African people, Malcolm is forever centered relative to speaking for and to African people. He *never* cowers, never hides himself in the language of noncommittal ambiguity, never speaks with a diluted tongue, never distances himself from nor becomes confused about his allegiance to African people, never sells us out.

With the NOI until 1964, at Oxford University in England at the end of 1964, interviewing with the Young Socialist Alliance (YSA) in January 1965, at the London school of Economics in February 1965, with the Muslim Mosque, Inc. and the OAAU in 1964-1965, in Saudi Arabia, in Africa—wherever he is, whoever he is addressing, there is no wavering, ambivalence, or abnegation. Malcolm speaks accessibly, boldly, for African people, for the concerns of African people, from the perspective of African people. Consider two brief examples, at an OAAU rally in Harlem in 1964 and in an interview with two YSA representatives in 1965, respectively:

> . . . I was in Paris Monday [with] Alioune Diop's, group, Presence Africaine. . . . [and they] are organizing . . . [and are as] concerned with what is going on here as you and I are. You and I have to link up with our people who are in Paris— when I say our people, you know, *us* [Black people]—we have to link up with our people in London, . . . in the Caribbean, in Trinidad, in Jamaica, in all the islands, and we've got to link up with our people who are in Central . . . and South America. Everywhere we see someone who looks like us, we've got to get together. . . . [then], we can get some action, because we'll find we are not the underdog.
>
> Whites who are sincere should organize among themselves and figure out some strategy to break down the prejudice that exists in white communities. This is where they

can function intelligently and more effectively, in the white community itself [rather than in African organizations], and this has never been done.[27]

Unmistakably, the speaker of the preceding words holds African people—their needs, their aspirations, and their view of the world—as his primary audience, explicitly and implicitly. Malcolm's words, then, and Malcolm's exemplary local-, national-, and pan-African practice satisfy Principle 3.

The Way of Heru as Theme, Principle 5, involves the confident resurrection and restoration of African people to lives of order, balance, and strength—by employing a comprehensive critical cultural method, and by wielding conceptual power intentionally. This theme is apparent in Malcolm's words and—once he leaves the NOI—in his practice.

In May of 1964, while traveling in Africa—and probably before that time—Malcolm determines to initiate the OAAU, an organization committed to studying-analyzing-and-acting to secure fully functioning freedom for African people, especially the "22 million Afro-Americans" and other African people in the Western Hemisphere, "by any means necessary."[28] At this point, the Way of Heru is a prevalent theme in Malcolm's words; and it continues being so. Consider that the essential program of the OAAU consists of African self- and community-defense, African community-controlled Afro-American-centered education, African community-centered politics and economics, social responsibility for and accountability to African people and African communities, and an African history-based cultural revolution. This is a comprehensive program, dedicated to resurrecting and restoring African people.[29] In Harlem, at the June 28, 1964 founding rally of the OAAU, hear Malcolm emphasizing the necessity of a sophisticated understanding of culture, the necessity of a comprehensive critical cultural method:

> Armed with the knowledge of our past, we can with confidence charter a course for our future. Culture is an indispensable weapon in the freedom struggle. We must take hold of it and forge the future with the past.[30]

Additionally, relative to the intentional wielding of conceptual power to facilitate the resurrecting and reestablishing of African people, naming the organization the "Organization of Afro-American Unity" after the Organization of African Unity (OAU) is a most intentional and timely wielding of conceptual power. Then, by patterning the OAAU after the OAU and linking it in tangible ways to the OAU— by visiting and strategizing with supportive continental African citizens, leaders, and heads of state—Malcolm demonstrates additional instances of brilliant, practical wielding of conceptual power. This kind of thinking and moving hastens the resurrection and restoration of African people. It contains and carries within it the theme of the Way of Heru. It satisfies Principle 5.

Wholistic Afrocentric Action as Goal, Principle 7, is quite apparent in the words of Malcolm X. Malcolm's goal in his speaking and teaching is to inspire and catalyze African people to *act* in *every* sphere of life, to act in ways that reflect the best of African culture and to act in every righteous way that elevates African *women*, men, and children,[31] in the United States and in every other part of the world. Consider some of his local-African and pan-African words:

> [December 3, 1964, at Oxford University in England, Malcolm states he believes] in extremism [that is, wholistic Afrocentric action by and for African people], intelligently directed extremism, extremism in defense of liberty, extremism in quest of liberty, [indeed, 22 million African people in the United States are within their rights as human
> beings to] use any means necessary to [achieve their wholistic] freedom [and halt every injustice being perpetrated upon them].
> [February 9, 1965, speaking by phone from London to Carlos Moore in Paris, Malcolm says, the African] community in France and other parts of Europe *must unite with the African community* [in Africa and in other parts of the world].
> [This] unity will . . . enable us to make some real, concrete [wholistic] progress whether we be in Europe, America, or on the African continent. I [want us to form] a *working* community[with] our brothers [and sisters on the African continent.[32] (emphasis his)

Malcolm's words make clear that his goal is not for African people to simply talk about doing for African people, or to simply feel closer to Africa and Africans around the world. His words make clear that his goal for African people is nothing less than wholistic Afrocentric action. His words, then—and his actions too, from 1964-1965—satisfy Princple 7, Wholistic Afrocentric Action as Goal.

Maatic Argumentation, Principle 10, is concerned with justice for and between human beings. It is prevalent in Malcolm's practice and words. Malcolm is passionate about justice existing between and among African people;[33] and he is equally or more passionate about African people securing justice in the United States and throughout the Earth. Indeed, he desires that justice exist in all places for all people. Consider his pointed, passionate words:

> All 22 million Afro-Americans have . . . the same basic objective. We want freedom, *justice*, and equality . . . . (emphasis mine). . . Our common goal is to obtain the *human rights* that America has been denying us.[34] (emphasis his) . . . when one[—any person of any color or culture—] is moderate in the pursuit of justice for human beings, I say he's [and she's] a sinner.[35]

Further, when it is considered that Malcolm is working closely with Fannie Lou Hamer and the Mississippi Freedom Democratic Party (MFDP)—and beginning to connect with similar though less well known people and organizations in the South—from 1964-1965, then it is understood that Maatic Argumentation is necessarily part of his words and work. This is so, because the MFDP in the 1960s is a kind of personification of plain, simple, serious, uncompromising Maat—justice.[36] Malcolm's practice and work meet the requirements of Maatic Argumentation, and so, satisfy Principle 10.

As noted briefly in the previous chapter of this text, Principle 12, African Collective Memory-Perception Competence, is quite apparent in the words of Malcolm X. Indeed, Malcolm's words, and the affirmative response to his words by African people, evidence an extraordinary ability to articulate African people's collective memory, and an equally extraordinary ability to activate our collective perception and response. He articulates so clearly our past and present external historical-experiential journey, that, when we hear him, our internal collective memory and perception jump up and run to meet him, to embrace him, to thank him. He knows us, and he feels us; and we feel him. Consider the following words, spoken in Harlem, January 1, 1965, to African high school students—freedom workers—from Mississippi:

> For a long time they accused me of not getting involved in politics. They should've been glad I didn't get involved in politics, because anything I get in, I'm in it all the way. Now if they say that we don't take part in the Mississippi struggle, we will organize brothers here in New York who know how to handle these kinds of affairs, and they'll slip into Mississippi like Jesus slipped into Jerusalem.[Laughter and applause]. [As far as working for freedom and nonviolence being his sole mode of moving, Malcolm says:] No, I don't go along with any kind of action that ties up my hands and then puts me in the ring with Sonny Liston or Cassius Clay.[Laughter] No, don't tie my hands, unless you're going to tie up their hands too. Then it's fair.[37]

In paralleling New York brothers slipping into Mississippi with Jesus slipping into Jerusalem, Malcolm does three things: (1) He connects his primary context (New York) with his audience's primary context (Mississippi), making for a horizontal and united relationship rather than a hierarchical, partitioned, or no relationship; (2) he validates present (1965) efforts by connecting them with past (Biblical) "already validated" events; and (3) by citing "Jesus" and not attacking "Jesus," he accesses and achieves total positive touch with the collective memory of the young "Christianized-Biblicized" Africans from the South, and they subsequently perceive and respond to Malcolm in the positive manner that he deserves. When being nonviolent eternally and dogmatically with an often-violent opponent is paralleled with one having tied hands while fighting Liston or Ali with their hands untied—Malcolm again demonstrates proficient employment of Principle 12, African Collective Memory-Perception Competence. He employs and demonstrates mastery of this principle in speech, after speech, after speech.

Afrocentric theory and practice Principle 13, Nzuri as Invitation and Standard, is evident in Malcolm's words and practice. The beautiful committed, disciplined Africans of integrity whom Malcolm encourages, inspires, and invites us to be—he himself is. His aesthetics and his ethics are one; they are not contradictory. He speaks about and lives life in a manner that is beautiful, strong, pro-African, pan-African; so he is one who earns the honor of being called beautiful, good, strong, pro-African, and pan-African. His aesthetics and his ethics are one. His teaching and his practice demonstrate an effulgent yet attainable consistency. Consider some of his words:

> [Speaking during his earlier days in the NOI, Malcolm shares earnestly:] I own nothing, except a record player. The house where I am living is owned by the Temple. The clothes I wear are made by the Muslim women. When I came into the Temple I made a vow that I was never going to own anything, because frequently a very sincere leader becomes trapped by material possessions and consequently he [or she] becomes alienated from the aspirations of his [or her] followers.[38]

Malcolm is ever a man in touch with, identified with, and loved by his followers and supporters—local, grassroots African people, and sincere, sane African people of all strata.

Additionally, in the midst of manifesting Nzuri—beauty in his being and goodness in his actions—far more than most people, he is still a person of exemplary humility. Indeed, his humility adds to his manifestation of Nzuri:

> [While in Cairo, in an August 29, 1964 letter to the OAAU, Malcolm writes:] I hope my position is clear: I am not interested in fighting Elijah Muhammad or any other Afro-American. . . . *If our own program produces results then our work will speak for itself.* If we don't produce results then we have no argument anyway. Brother Benjamin is the best teacher I left behind: he has many faults and weaknesses, but then so have I and so have many of the rest of you. (emphasis mine). . . I have so much faith in *Allah*, and in *right*, and in my people, that I believe I can come back and start from scratch if it is necessary[;] and as long as I mean right *Allah* will bless me with success and our people

will help me in this fight.[39] (emphasis his)

His elders and peers, people who know him from a distance and those who know him intimately, Africans from the United States and from other parts of the globe—and even some non-Africans, all speak in one voice relative to Malcolm demonstrating for us that beauty is as beauty does.[40] They say he lives beautifully, and so he is indeed beautiful; and he invites us—gently, yet passionately, and urgently—to attain to a similar standard, and an even higher standard than he. Malcolm's words and practice satisfy Nzuri as Invitation and Standard, Principle 13.

Malcolm X's words and practice can be understood as incipient Afrocentric political/activist contributions. It is almost Afrocentric work. Malcolm's work is incipient as a result of its lack of explicit system, clear codification, explicit-intentional locational indicators. Consider Molefi Asante and how he works to codify Afrocentric thought. Malcolm does not work clearly to align African people's deep structure and surface structure; indeed, he does not even have the deep structure and surface structure map. Consider Wade Nobles and how he works to chart African people's deep and surface structures. Perhaps Malcolm's being a driven doer, a man of action—and so much more—does not lend itself to his taking the time to be a professional Afrocentric thinker and practitioner.

As a nonetheless astounding, exceedingly brilliant, and necessary antecedent to Afrocentric thought and praxis, Malcolm's cumulative work—his inimitable words and his singular practice—in 1965 gives us a practical visionary's outline of what is happening and what is called for in the new millennium. Asante and others are placing—and for about twenty years have been putting—fortified substance on the skeletal-yet-quite-substantive framework that Malcolm offers. As Malcolm plants an incipient Afrocentric thought and practice seed, engineer it and create a true seed; and others cultivate it into a tree, and extend its roots, give it more height, and girth, and branches—and give African people and the world sophisticated Afrocentric fruit.

Finally, while Malcolm's work can be understood as an incipient contribution to Afrocentric thought and praxis; it can also be understood as the work of an incipient-prototypical-almost-Afrocentric exemplar. Further, his love for African people is not incipient. It is fully formed, quite advanced, and superior in its sophistication. Indeed, it is because Malcolm loves us so and wants so much for us—he is such an urgent spirit—that he does his best in 1965 to make a space for us, so that we can walk, and be, and do the work of Afrocentric thought and praxis now.

As a literary antecedent to Afrocentric thought and praxis, work of Ayi Kwei Armah—a continental African—will be discussed and assessed. Specifically, his *Two Thousand Seasons* will be assessed.

Published in 1979, *Two Thousand Seasons* is a novel that reads in many ways like a historical narrative;[41] but it is much more than that. Essentially, the creative, powerful, provocative work recounts the story of African people's demise over one thousand years ago and posits the path to our reascension over the next one thousand years.[42]

Two Thousand Seasons seems to satisfy all of the Template's Thirteen Principles of Afrocentric Thought and Praxis. It is most convincing, however, in how it satisfies Principles 1-3 and 6-13, the Meta-Constants: Humanizing and Harmonizing, the Primacy of African People and African Civilization, An African Audience as the Primary Audience, Harmosis as Mode, Wholistic Afrocentric Action as Goal, Sankofan Approach, Nommoic Creativity, Maatic Argumentation, Explicit Locational Indicators Intentionality, African Collective Memory-Perception Competence, and Nzuri as Invitation and Standard, respectively. Consideration will be given to how Armah's work satisfies Principle 3, An African Audience as the Primary Audience, and Principle 11, Explicit Locational Indicators Intentionality, respectively.

An African Audience as the Priority Audience, Principle 3, is exceedingly prevalent in *Two Thousand Seasons*. Right at its outset, beginning with the poetic, prophetic, lucid, haunting voice of the book's "Prologue," it is clear that the novel is written *for* and *to* other African people from the perspective of a centered African person. Challenges to African people's existence are exposed; some of the errors, weaknesses, and strengths of African people are noted; mention is made of those who exploited and continue to exploit African people mercilessly; and Armah speaks of the way to African people's return to collective equilibrium and self-determination.[43] Such clarity, honesty, and concern are evidence that the narrator is writing primarily for and to African people—to affirm and reinforce Africans who are centered, and to awaken and beckon home Africans who are dislocated and/or misoriented.

Additionally, the narrator speaks consistently of "truths of *our* origins . . . *our* own survival,"[44] "find *our* audience . . . open *our* mouths,"[45] ". . . *we* whisper *our* news of the way,"[46] ". . . of *our own blackness* they have yet to learn."[47] (all emphases mine) Clearly, the narrator's voice is a centered African voice; and the narrator's primary audience and core concern, clearly and explicitly, is African people. There is no pretense that anything else is the case. As further evidence, consider the following excerpt from Armah's "Prologue":

> Remember this: against all that destruction some yet remain among us unforgetful of origins . . .hearing secret voices of our purpose. . . .Not all our souls are aware of a nature to answer the call to death, however sweetened.[48]

Throughout the novel, beyond the tone-creating "Prologue," the narrator is centered, concerned passionately about African people, writing to and on behalf of a pan-African audience. As a final example of Armah's satisfying Principle 3, An African Audience as the Primary Audience, consider the following words from Chapter One, "The Way":

> We are not a people of yesterday. . . . . . . What has been cast abroad is not a thousandth of our history, even if its quality were truth. . . .
> We were not always outcasts from ourselves. . . .
> That we the black people are one people we know. Destroyers will travel long distances in their minds and out to deny you this truth. We do not argue with them, the fools. Let them presume to instruct us about ourselves. . . . That too is in the flow of their two thousand seasons against us.[49]

Principle 11, Explicit Locational Indicators Intentionality, permeates *Two Thousand Seasons*. Armah is intentional in filling the novel with metaphors and symbols derived (a)from the physical environment of Africa, and (b)from the experiences of African people and the way African people choose to name and label those experiences. *Two Thousand Seasons'* symbols include springwater, the desert, headwater, setting sun, falling fire, falling sun, the predators, the destroyers, the dance, and others.

The alternating metaphors of springwater, headwater, spring(s), stream(s)[50] all symbolize, essentially, African people, our lives, our life-giving nature, our future. Hear *Two Thousand Seasons'* omnipresent narrator explicate:

> It is for the spring to give. It is for springwater to flow. But if the spring would continue to give and the springwater continue flowing, the desert is no direction. . . .
>
> No spring changes the desert. . . . [Only] the waters of the universe in unison, flowing not to coax the desert but to overwhelm it, ending its regime of death, that, not a single perishable spring, is the necessity.[51]

The metaphor of the desert—a metaphor possessing at least two layers of meaning—is most apparent in the novel's "Prologue" and its first chapter.[52] The desert symbolizes the white dry sand that is the desert; and it symbolizes white people—white Europeans and white western Asians. It symbolizes especially those who moved— and who move—upon the African continent and its people, devouring the land and the people, making both barren, draining life from them, killing them. Note this explicit, revealing statement:

> It was not always so. The desert was made the desert, turned barren by a people whose spirit is itself the seed of destruction. Each . . . of them is a carrier of destruction. . . . An insatiable urge drives them. Wherever there is life . . .the harbingers of death must go—to destroy it. . . . They have wiped the surface barren with their greed. They have dug deep to take what the earth needed for itself to stay fertile earth. . . . the destroyers have already voided [some Africans] of their spirits, like the earth of its fertility.[53]

The predators[54] and the destroyers[55] are metaphors representing white people, western Asians who came via the desert and Europeans who came via the sea, respectively. The terms derive from African people's experience with western Asians and Europeans; and the terms are centered metaphors in that they derive from an astute African person's—Armah's—naming of African people's collective experiential journey.

Consider that it is improbable—and rare—that conquering, pillaging western Asians and Europeans speak of themselves as predators or destroyers. It is equally improbable—and equally or even more rare—that mentally conquered and cerebrally pillaged African authors label western Asians and Europeans so precisely, so honestly. From a centered, properly located, African perspective, however, considering the reality of centuries of being preyed upon and destroyed by the aforementioned peoples, such terms, such metaphors, are quite logical, quite appropriate.

Principle 11, Explicit Locational Indicators Intentionality, is also very apparent in *Two Thousand Seasons'* utilization of African names. Almost every name in the novel is an African name. In fact, generally, the only names that are not African are those few attached to predators, destroyers, and some of the Africans who work against the African community.

Anoa, the prophetess, is referred to with great admiration.[56] The names of those ignoble, anti-African Africans who used and abused the community when the white killers came are listed: Oduntun, Bentum, Oko, Krobo, Jebi, Jonto, Sumui, Oburum, Ituri, Dube, Mununkum, Esibir, Bonto, Peturi, Topre, Tutu, Bonsu, and Koranche.[57] The young women and men who made it their life's work to care for and reconstruct the community are referenced, Pili, Ndelela, Suma, Kwesi, Manda, Ude, Tawia, Dovi, Ankoanda, Sobo, Liamba, Mokili, Kenia, Limi, Makaa, Ashale, Ona, Kamara, Naita, Abena, and the teacher of all the young women and men—Isanusi.[58] Juma is also referenced, the one who taught Isanusi and his students how to use guns.[59] Finally, the foolish and pitiful African prince Bentum is referenced again, the one who eagerly took on the European name "Bradford George."[60]

A pool of water and a river carry the names Baka and Kwarra, respectively. A spring named after the righteous women Noliwe and Ningome is also referenced.[61] Of course, there are additional Afrocentric names and references in *Two Thousand Seasons* other than the ones cited above.

Finally, relative to the Principle 11, it is very important to note that *Two Thousand Seasons'* ontological and epistemological assumptions are apparent and clearly Afrocentric; and its teleological stance is equally apparent and Afrocentric. Armah makes known his ontological, epistemological, and teleological location via *Two Thousand Seasons'* core, galvanizing metaphor, "the way."[62]

In various, ever recurring references to the way, Armah communicates the novel's ontological assumption: African people hold that visible physical life and material experience is preceded, and ultimately superseded, and permeated by an Invisible Metaphysical Positive Ultimate Reality. That is, physical existence is undergirded and permeated by Spirit; Spirit is predominantly good; so, physical existence is essentially good—and when it is not, people are to work in concert with Spirit, with "the way," and make it so. Hear Armah:

> . . . we have been a people fleeing our true destiny.
> . . . It is our destiny not to flee . . . not to seek hiding places [forever]; but to turn against the predators [and] destroyers, and bending all our soul against their thrust, turning every stratagem of the destroyers against themselves, destroy them. That is our destiny: to end destruction—utterly;   to begin the highest, the profoundest work of creation, the work that is inseparable from *our way*, inseparable from *the way*.
> . . . *the way* is a call to [a difficult, patient, urgent, relatively lonely, often unpraised call to every African to contribute fully to the work of] creation.[63] (emphases mine)

Similarly, Armah communicates the novel's epistemological assumption: African people "know" what is true and what we need to know via empirical experiments, via life experiences, and via non-empirical avenues such as dreams, trance or spirit possession, "vibes," and so forth. Consider the knowing we obtain through the lessons of history. And consider the knowing we obtain from various ones connected profoundly to Spirit. Consider the prophetess Anoa and her often profound, yet often involuntary utterances, that is, the ancestors using her body to speak truth—"utterances"—of the future, as the future arrived and before the future arrived.[64] *Two Thousand Seasons'* narrator explains:

> [Anoa] spoke in two voices—twin, but clearly discernible
> one from the other. . . . The first. . . harassed . . . fiery . . . . .
> . . the second [was] calmer, so calm. . . For every shrieking
> horror the first voice had given sound to, this other voice
> gave calm causes, indicated effects, and never tired of iter-
> ating the hope at the issue of all disasters; the rediscovery
> and the following again of *our way, the way.*[65] (emphasis
> mine)

Through the aforementioned teacher, Isanusi, Armah sets forth the
novel's teleological stance: African people's lives have purpose,
and that constant purpose is to become and be wholistic, positive
exemplars for other Africans, and finally, for all people. Chapter
Five, "The Dance of Love,"[66] describes the way as the voca-
tion—as the consuming life purpose—of a few, atypical, strong
members of the community. Hear the narrator speak of one who is
passionate about preserving the way—the indigenous teleology of
all African people:

> [There was] Isanusi . . . a fundi whose art went beyond any
> skill of the body, whose mastery reached the conscious-
> ness itself of our people; he whose greatest desire, whose
> vocation it was to keep the knowledge of *our way, the way*,
> from destruction, to bring it back to an oblivious people . .
> . he whose highest hope it was to live *the way* as purpose,
> the
> purpose of our people.[67] (emphases mine)

"The way," then, is Armah's central and pivotal locational metaphor. He uses it as a broad multidimensional, multifunctional designation and appellation for the ancient-and-ever-relevant guiding,
constructive, personal-and-community maintaining mundane-meta-
physical practices and principles of African people. The way transcends and absorbs various political, economic, and religio-spiritual
differences.

In innumerable ways, Armah's *Two Thousand Seasons* is overwhelming in its satisfaction of Principle 11, Explicit Locational Indicators Intentionality.

Ayi Kwei Armah's *Two Thousand Seasons* may—or may not—

be understood as Afrocentric literary work. It is published just one year before Asante's *Afrocentricity*. The novel demonstrates magnificent clarity relative to understanding African people's culture and history; it conveys the said understanding with great competence; and Armah has a solid understanding of his subject—as Asante requires.[68] Additionally, *Two Thousand Seasons* is convincing in its handling of the Meta-Constants: Humanizing and Harmonizing; and it is clear about the Primacy of African People and African Civilization. In short, the novel satisfies the *essence*—but not necessarily the entire requirement—of each of the remaining Thirteen Principles of Afrocentric Theory and Praxis.

If there are deficiencies in *Two Thousand Seasons*, they are qualitative technical deficiencies, not utter deficiencies. In the midst of all of the novel's lyrical beauty and quiet power, it is noteworthy that The Way of Heru as Theme and Njia as Theme do not shine through convincingly. The themes of restoration and victory are visible in the novel, but they are not vigorous. They are set forth subtlely, gracefully—but not absolutely, decisively. The reader can assume that a comprehensive restoration will occur—at some point. It can be surmised that African people in sufficiently large numbers will attain and maintain a victorious consciousness, and victory will be won and sustained—someday.

Two Thousand Seasons culminates with something of a sad, almost melancholic tone.[69] While it is not a defeated tone, it is not a bold one. The novel does not culminate surging, driving, pronouncing, and pointing toward certain African resurrection, restoration, and victory. It should, however, because Afrocentric thought and praxis are vociferous about victory. Njia and the Way of Heru are not themes of timidity; they are bold about the certainty of African victory.

Perhaps that which appears in *Two Thousand Seasons* as deficient satisfaction of Principles 4 and 5, is in fact simply Armah's chosen way of expressing the aforementioned themes. Perhaps he chooses to impress rather than impact. Perhaps Armah himself is a gentle soul and chooses to impress the reader in a manner which is gentle, and lingering. Perhaps he does not choose to impact the reader in a forceful, overpowering manner. Maybe he wishes us to depart from the novel in a serious, reflective state of mind, rather than an inspired and ecstatic one. Perhaps his chosen way is to let

Two Thousand Seasons close like *mosi oh tunya* (like "smoke that thunders"), rather than like fire-and-storm, with the spirits of Nzingah and Shaka.

Two Thousand Seasons, then, is a creative, relatively simple, yet disarmingly profound African literary work. Assessed stringently by The Thirteen Principles of Afrocentric Thought and Praxis Gray Template, the novel qualifies as incipient Afrocentric literary work. If it is assessed relative to its significant awakening influence within the African community over the last twenty-one years, it is more than an incipient contribution to Afrocentric thought and praxis.

Consideration and evaluation of academic-intellectual, political-activist, and literary antecedents to Afrocentric theory and praxis is concluded.

NOTES

1.   Aime Cesaire, *Discourse on Colonialism*, trans. Joan Pinkham (New York: Monthly Review Press, 1972), p. 9, 10, 11-12.
2.   Ibid., pp. 17, 13-25.
3.   Ibid., pp. 60-61.
4.   Ibid., p. 24.
5.   Ibid., pp. 31-32.
6.   Ibid., pp. 35-36, 52.
7.   F. Abiola Irele, *Literature and Ideology in Martinique: Rene Maran, Aime Cesaire, Frantz Fanon* (Buffalo, NY: State University of New York at Buffalo, Special Studies Council on International Studies, F.A. Irele, 1972), p. 6.
8.   Aime Cesaire, *Aime Cesaire, The Collected Poetry,* trans. with an Introduction and Notes by Clayton Eshleman and Annette Smith (Berkeley: University of California Press, 1983), p. 45.
9.   Ibid., p. 55.
10.   Ibid., p. 59.
11.   Ibid.
12.   Ibid., p. 61.
13.   Ibid., pp. 67, 70-71, 77, 85.
14.   Ibid., pp. 67-68, 79.
15.   Ibid., pp. 47, 61, 77.
16.   "Cesaire Interviewed by Haitian Poet Renee Depestre, at the Cul-

tural Congress, Havana, Cuba, 1967," in *Discourse on Colonialism*, pp. 70-72, 74.

17. See Malcolm X with the assistance of Alex Haley, *The Autobiography of Malcolm X* (New York: Grove Press, 1966), pp. 151, 153-382. Also see Malcolm X, "How to Organize the People," *Malcolm X Speaks (Selected   Speeches and Statements)*, ed. with prefatory notes by George Breitman (New York: Grove Press, 1966), p. 198. Also see Malcolm X, "Outline for Petition to the United Nations Charging Genocide Against 22 Million Black Americans," in *Malcolm X: The Man and His Times*, ed. John Henrik Clarke (Trenton, N.J.: Africa World Press, Inc., 1990), pp. 343-351; this is the essential framework of a presentation that Malcolm intended to deliver on behalf of all African people living in the United States of America— and ultimately on behalf of all humanity-and harmony-loving people everywhere. Malcolm satisfies Principle 1, "The Meta-Constants: Humanizing and Harmonizing."

18. Ibid.

19. Ibid. Also see Malcolm X, *Malcolm X Talks to Young People: Speeches in the U.S., Britain, and Africa*, ed. Steve Clark (New York: Pathfinder Press, 1991), pp. 85-86.

20. *Autobiography*, pp. 175, 181. It also important to note his later, clarifying comments at a meeting with Alioune Diop and other members of the African cultural organization Presence Africaine, in Paris, France, November 23, 1964 in Malcolm X, *Malcolm X: By Any Means Necessary (Speeches, Interviews, and a Letter by Malcolm X)*, ed. George Breitman (New York: Pathfinder Press, 1989), p. 121.

21. Malcolm X, *Malcolm X on Afro-American History*, 2nd ed. (New York: Pathfinder Press, 1992), pp. 65, 27-31, 33-36.

22. See *Autobiography*, pp. 211-382. Also see *The Man*, pp. xiii-41, 125-127, 132-143.

23. *Malcolm Speaks*, pp. 197-198.

24. Ibid., pp. 8-9.

25. *Afro-American History*, p. 33.

26. *Speaks*, pp. 5-17, 18-226. Also see *Autobiography* and *Afro-American* in their entirety. See, really, any of Malcolm's speeches; the Sankofan Approach principle is always prevalent. It is apparent that he is an extraordinary student of African history—and global history.

27. *By Any Means*, pp. 155-156, 164, *Talks to Young People*, p. 90, respectively.

28. *By Any Means*, pp. 35-38.

29. Ibid., pp. 40-56. And see *The Man*, pp. 343-351.

30. *By Any Means*, p. 56.

31. Ibid., p. 179. On that page, Malcolm notes that a people's progress is reflected in the status of the people's women. He goes on to say that as African people struggle for freedom, African women must be granted "all the leeway possible because they've made a greater contribution than many of us men."
32. Ibid., pp. 177, 171, respectively. Also see *The Man*, pp. 210, 312-313.
33. C. Eric Lincoln, *The Black Muslims in America* (Boston: Beacon Press, 1961), pp. 157-158. As one example, Malcolm pleads with Black Christian clergy in Los Angeles to do justice to their church members, pointing out to the clergy that there is a greater need for them to build factories and supermarkets rather than spend almost all of the parishioners' financial contributions to build more churches.
34. *The Man*, p. 304. This comes from an article Malcolm wrote for the *Egyptian Gazette*, 25 August 1964.
35. *Speaks*, p. 182. Malcolm made this remark during an Oxford Union Society Debate, in London, December 3, 1964.
36. See two speeches made on December 20, 1964, in Harlem, with Mrs. Fannie Lou Hamer, in *Speaks*, pp. 105-136. Also see *Talks to Young People*, pp. 48-82; in this speech, January 1, 1965, Malcolm is speaking with African youth—from Mississippi—who are visiting Harlem. Also, it is noteworthy that in formal conversations from 1983-1994 with Victoria Gray [Adams]—founding member of MFDP, MFDP candidate for the U.S. Senate, Director of MFDP's National Office in Washington, DC, 1964-1967; suppporter, Student Non-Violent Coordinating Committee; elected to two terms on the National Executive Board of the Southern Christian Leadership Conference, serving from 1963-1968—who shared that Malcolm was scheduled to speak at an MFDP meeting on the day he was assassinated. She called his contact people on February 20, 1965, telling them MFDP needed to reschedule; they said that was fine, as that would actually allow Malcolm to get some other things done before going to Mississippi; the next day, Malcolm was assassinated in Harlem. Today, MFDP is studied as one of the best models—if not the best model—of serious local organizing, as it consisted of local people organizing local people for tangible change and justice. MFDP did not depend on a "superstar," and that was one of its greatest strengths. At its most critical moments during the 1960s, MFDP *never* compromised on getting Maat (justice) for the African people of Mississippi. Depending greatly on the strength and integrity of the African women in its membership, MFDP *never* sold African people out. Malcolm's association with MFDP and Mrs. Hamer amplifies his commitment to getting Maat for African people.

37. *Talks to Young People*, pp. 65, 73-74, respectively.
38. E. U. Essien-Udom, *Black Nationalism: A Search for Identity in America* (New York and Chicago: Dell Publishing and University of Chicago Press, 1962), p. 116.
39. *By Any Means*, p. 112.
40. See *The Man*; in it, scholars, friends, and his wife Betty Shabazz all share perspectives and feelings about Malcolm; and there is a consistent theme throughout the sharing that he was a person of unusual integrity. He was hardly a perfect person, but his words and actions were quite consistent, publicly and privately. Also see *Talks to Young People*, pp. 93-100. Also see *Autobiography*. Also see Eugene Victor Wolfenstein, *The Victims of Democracy: Malcolm X and the Black Revolution* (Berkeley: University of California Press, 1981); on page 195, Wolfenstein says, "Malcolm was, perhaps above all else, an honest man. . . His conversion to Islam had been realized through that honesty . . . [ultimately], he had been saved and the Truth had become a living force in his character. Subsequently, his whole life had been dedicated to telling that Truth to others, [B]lack and white alike." On January 22, 1990, in a Department of African American Studies seminar at Temple University, Pulitzer Prize (playwright) winner Charles Fuller says, "Malcolm was one of our very greatest individuals . . . he was probably the most honest leader we've ever had." Also see Henry Hampton and Steve Fayer, eds., *Voices of Freedom* (New York: Bantam Books, 1990); on pages 251-252, Ruby Dee and Ossie Davis recount their experience of Malcolm, "We knew there was an honest, earnest, dedicated young brother. And we had seen leaders, white and [B]lack . . . and we loved all the leaders and we worked for all the leaders, Malcolm was by far morally the most pure person that we had ever run across"; on page 255, Sonia Sanchez says, "What he said out loud is what African American people had been saying out loud forever behind closed doors. . . . That's why we loved him so much. Because he made us feel holy. He made us feel whole. He made us feel loved. And he made us feel that we were worth something finally on this planet Earth." Also see *Malcolm X: Make it Plain*, text by William Strickland, oral histories selected and edited by Cheryll Y. Greene (New York: Viking Penguin, Penguin Books USA Inc., 1994). Also, a most peculiar, essentially *anti-Malcolm* collection—including many relatively amorphous writings from the deconstructionist school—is Joe Wood, ed., *Malcolm X: In Our Own Image* (New York: Anchor Books, 1994).
41. See Ayi Kwei Armah, *Two Thousand Seasons* (Chicago: Third World

Press, 1979, 1984). And see Chancellor Williams, *The Destruction of Black Civilization* (Chicago: Third World Press, 1987); Armah's novel—*Seasons*—in some ways, runs relatively parallel to Williams' work and other historical accounts.

42. See Armah, *Seasons.*
43. Ibid., pp. ix, xviii.
44. Ibid., p. ix.
45. Ibid., p. x.
46. Ibid.
47. Ibid., p. xvii.
48. Ibid., p. xv.
49. Ibid., pp. 1, 2, 3, 4, respectively.
50. Ibid., pp. ix-xi.
51. Ibid., p. xi.
52. Ibid., pp. ix-xi, 6-11.
53. Ibid., p. 10.
54. Ibid., pp. 53-116.
55. Ibid., pp. 117-132, 212.
56. Ibid., pp. xv, 19-21, 23-25, 28.
57. Ibid., p. 100.
58. Ibid., p. 147.
59. Ibid., p. 230.
60. Ibid., p. 308.
61. Ibid., p. 69.
62. Ibid., pp. 1-29, xiii, xv, xvii, xviii, 134-135, 138-140, 209, 310, 314, 316-317, 320-321.
63. Ibid., pp. 245-246, 317, 318.
64. Ibid., pp, 9-29.
65. Ibid., pp. 24-25.
66. Ibid., pp. 138-139, 131-141.
67. Ibid., p. 139.
68. Asante, *Afrocentricity*, p. 60.
69. Armah, *Seasons*, pp. 313-321.

Chapter 6

CULMINATION AND COMMENCEMENT: IN THE WAY

This work has attempted to set forth an intellectual history of Afrocentric thought and praxis, defining Afrocentricity and considering works antecedent to Afrocentricity in the continuum of African intellectual- socio-political-literary efforts. This work has also attempted to demonstrate that Afrocentric thought and praxis are not separate from the continuum of African thought and praxis, rather Afrocentric thought and praxis are part of the continuum.

This work has attempted to discuss the history, context, content, and intent of Afrocentric theory and praxis, as well as noteworthy antecedents to Afrocentric theory and praxis. Beginning with the work of Molefi K. Asante, the idea and meta-concept of "Afrocentricity" was located and anchored historically. Thereafter, the philosophical, defining core of Afrocentric thought and praxis—the work of Asante, Maulana Karenga, and Kariamu Welsh-Asante, respectively—was discussed and examined. When appropriate, the work of other scholars and organizations committed to the Afrocentric project were cited and discussed. From the work of Asante, Karenga, and Welsh-Asante, Afrocentricity's major distinguishing characteristics were determined and extracted. Of those characteristics, thirteen were most prominent. Those thirteen, most salient, characteristics were then grouped and held as an evaluative tool—as a template, *The Gray Template*—to be used in examining multifarious efforts, but especially theoretical, practical, and literary efforts. Efforts antecedent to Afrocentricity were then excavated and examined. Utilizing the evaluative template, works of Aime Cesaire, Malcolm X, and Ayi Kwei Armah were assessed and classified.

Generally, the assessment of the antecedent efforts indicated they were incipient Afrocentric efforts moving toward Afrocentricity. It is quite significant, for example, that not only did Cesaire cite Cheikh Anta Diop and evince great respect for Diop's work—Cesaire helped publish and circulate Diop's work. In 1955-1956 and later, utilizing *Presence Africaine*, a periodical—and a publishing house and a cultural organization all carrying that same name—which Alioune Diop, Cesaire and other intellectuals founded, Cesaire helped Diop's work reach increasingly greater numbers of African people.[1] Of course, today, Diop's work is one of the critical pillars fortifying important aspects of the Afrocentric project. So, Cesaire's assistance in gaining a wider audience for Diop's work is a kind of Afrocentricity in action; it is Afrocentric praxis.

Cesaire's considerable appreciation of Diop's work indicates that Cesaire had vision enough to recognize substantive and important pro-African, pan-African work. Additionally, his foster-ing and endorsing of Diop demonstrates that he practiced humanness and harmony toward other African scholars, even when their work was not quite the same as his. It is conceivable that Cesaire could have left Diop adrift, could have delayed the African world community's receiving the gift of Diop's contribution. Then, too, Cesaire could have missed or ignored the tremendous import of Diop's work. To Cesaire's credit and to the benefit of the African world, Cesaire did not. Instead, Cesaire practiced one of the great Afrocentric principles held in his own work. Even with the emerging work of Diop available to him, Cesaire's work and his conception of Negritude consisted greatly of Cesaire struggling with himself and within himself to speak a new Black picture into being, yet having to lean mostly on old white images. He was working to create a new African reality, yet possessing mostly old white tools. In his praxis, in his intellectual work generally, and in his conception of Negritude particularly—probably consciously and subconsciously—Cesaire moved toward, reached for, and anticipated that which is today called "Afrocentricity."

Similarly, it can be said that Malcolm was moving toward Afrocentricity. Surely Malcolm's work birthed—or influenced, or lent direction or focus to—at least some of the work of Asante, Karenga, and Welsh-Asante. Inarguably and undeniably, Malcolm's efforts set the stage and the standard for the work of people like

Baraka—when he is at his most centered, and Sonia Sanchez, Nathan Hare, Mari Evans, Larry Neal, Haki Madhubuti, and Na'im Akbar—some of whom claim to be Afrocentric proponents outright, and some of whom epitomize much of the best of Afrocentric thought and praxis but choose to place no labels on themselves. (Malcolm said it is often best not to label oneself;[2] as being label-free can give one mobility and longevity.) Admittedly, Malcolm was a pulsing whirlwind; he was not a placid lake. So, he did not take the time—or have the time—to get to Afrocentricity. Nevertheless, his words and his praxis indicate he was headed there; he was trying to get there.

Ayi Kwei Armah's work anticipated and perhaps even ventured foggily into the literary realm of Asante's Afrocentricity. His work was well-centered, pan-African, and leaning toward an uncompromising optimism. Being a continental African, however, might Armah's nearness to the historic and visionary yet difficult struggles of Nkrumah and the principled yet protracted struggles of Neyerere, and the brilliant yet CIA-truncated efforts of Lumumba and Cabral have blunted Armah's ability to hold a soaring unceasing vision of the way—the way of which he speaks consistently yet with the tiniest unsettling glint of hesitation? So, Armah alternated, entering and exiting the literary region of Afrocentricity. Perhaps wrestling in his own mind, he did not lay swift, unyeilding, and full claim to the way. In 1979, he tasted and anticipated, but did not savor and fully appreciate, the sweet Njia—the Way, the ever optimistic and victorious consciousness–that Asante would proclaim one year later.

In looking closely at the concept of Afrocentricity and the Afrocentric movement that has emerged since 1980, it seems *codification* is the matter that should be appreciated most and that should be handled most carefully.

Essentially, *at its best, codification protects knowledge. It enables the relatively facile—and sure, precise—transfer of Afrocentric thought and praxis from person to person, generation to generation. Simultaneously, codification of African knowledge makes it difficult for non-African people and all anti-African people—including anti-African Africans—to access, enervate, and destroy the knowledge. Proper, sophisticated codification is intrinsically self-protecting. Additionally, codification, depending greatly upon thought, ensures that*

African "feeling" does not exploit, oppress, or run off and leave African thought. It puts a check upon the often unchecked sway of feeling. Further, because codification depends upon at least the momentary freezing of ideas in time and space— that is, making ideas relatively static for some bit of time— Afrocentric thought and praxis can be studied, assessed, and refined as often as necessary, so that the same is ever relevant to the human needs of African people.

This research has made clear that *while codification is a great gift, it is important that we not straightjacket ourselves. While codifying and systematizing, it is essential that we not kill the vibrant, victorious, aforementioned African "feeling" or spirit that is an undeniable part of African people and the African community. It is important that African scholars not move unwittingly into the European rhythm of labeling and codifying to such an extent that we halt our own movement. African "feeling" must be allowed its part in our codifying; that is, space must be guarded and kept for the ancestors to speak and work through us and our best efforts. While codifying, vigilance must prevail so that our people are not manipulated, so that we do not violate and imprison ourselves. With such vigilance, our efforts will produce our best wishes—and better wishes than that!*

The intent of this study is to add to the clarity and definition of the history of and to the external and internal anatomy of Afrocentric thought and praxis. It is desired that it proves a bridge, assisting African people in our historical-intellectual and wholistic movement from where we are to where we need to be, from current realms of humaness and harmony to ever higher and deeper realms of humanness and harmony. It is hoped, too, that this work will inspire others to continue the work—to pick it up, shine it, refine it, purify it, and contribute to moving the intellectual history of Afrocentric thought and praxis to its next necessary place. This work is a small beginning; much more work is needed. There are other antecedents to Afrocentricity. The antecedent work of African women needs to be studied closely; and there are new aspects of Afrocentricity emerging even as this particular piece of research culminates. All of this needs to be researched, addressed, and located properly.

Finally, this research reveals that the intellectual tradition of African people consists of a great and high standard. It invites and enjoins scholars to merge thought and praxis; make them complementary, and make them one. Do not separate that which is not to be separated. This is the message of Afrocentricity: let the Afrocentric Way mark every possible facet of our thinking, our speaking, our being, and our behavior. This is the example of Cesaire—an African with a brilliant mind *and* an African who chooses to serve as a local civil servant for grassroots African people. And this was/is the example of Malcolm—an African who is constantly reading-thinking-critiquing-and-analyzing his environment *and* organizing grassroots African people so that we could/can have more justice and joy in our lives. This, then, is the requirement also of Afrocentric thought and praxis.

As African students, scholars, and community practitioners honor the best of the African intellectual tradition, our scholarship will be like the scholarship of the legendary Ahmed Baba. We will make the earlier pioneering-courageous-legendary African Centered ones proud of us, our indomitable foreparents, our prolific-and-practical predecesors: Queen Tiye, Governor Ptahhotep, Queen Makeda, Queen Nzingah, Yaa Asante Waa, Nehunda, all of the Unnamed Africans from the entire eastern side of Africa (Libya-Egypt-the Horn-South Africa) and the rest of Africa (Namibia-Angola-Congo-Ghana-and beyond) who fought and resisted oppression, the eighteenth century Pan-Africanist Paul Cuffe, the unheralded yet effective John Rock, the unyielding Maria Stewart, the uncompromising and profoundly focused David Walker, the holy warrior The Rev. Nat Turner, the freedom-loving Rev. Henry Highland Garnett, the nineteenth century Pan-Africanist Martin Delany, the thoughtful and far-seeing Rev. Edward Wilmot Blyden and his Ghanian student Joseph Casely-Hayford, the relentless Bishop Henry McNeal Turner, and the more recent intellectual-and-practical warriors Dr. W.E.B. DuBois, Sylvester Williams, William Monroe Trotter, Ms. Ida B. Wells, Dr. Julia Cooper, the thoughtful pioneer Dr. Carter G. Woodson, Ms. Mary McCloud Bethune, Ms. Drusilla Dunjee Houston, Conteen and Frozene Jackson, the forward-moving Rev. Vernon Johns (who was vindicated by the one who followed him, The Rev. Dr. Martin Luther King, Jr.), the historic master writer-warrior Richard Wright, the insightful George Padmore, the brilliant genius and giant President Dr. Kwame Nkrumah (whose vision of a United States of Africa will be fulfilled because it must be fulfilled), the master strategist and beloved legendary President Gamel Nasser, the insightful and incisive Frantz Fanon, the incomparable wholistic warrior-builder Amilcar Cabral, the master teacher and exemplar Ms. Ella Baker, the great lover of African people Ms. Septima Clarke, teh African lamb Dr. Martin Luther King, Jr., the historic human trinity of Ms. Fannie Lou Hamer, Ms. Victoria Gray Adams, and Ms. Annie Devine, the gentle giants Dr. Vincent and Ms. Rosemarie Freeney Harding, the quiet guarded giant Bob Moses, and other Africans known and unknown.

We are working and we will continue working to make them proud of us—all of them. We will dance the sacred dances again, like the Twa. We will build pyramids again—theoretical ones, literary ones, and even empirical ones. We will master ourselves—again. Wielding the tool of Afrocentricity, giving our best efforts to the principles and standards of Afrocentric thought and praxis—we will be in The Way; we will be in our Way. We will exemplify, personify, and multiply Njia. The Neters and our Ancestors will smile and dance; and the Amon—the Hidden one—will be satisfied adn well pleased.

NOTES

1.   Cesaire, *The Collected Poetry*, p. 7.
2.   *Malcolm X Speaks*, pp. 203-204.

BIBLIOGRAPHY

Abarry, Abu Shardow, ed. *Journal of Black Studies.* Vol 21, No. 2 (December 1990).

Achebe, Chinua. *Things Fall Apart.* New York: Fawcett Crest, 1991.

Adams, Ann Josephine. "Sisters of the Light: The Importance of Spirituality in the Afra-American Novel." Ph.D. dissertation, Indiana State University, 1989.

Adams, Victoria Jackson Gray. Founding member of Mississippi Freedom Democratic Party (MFDP), MFDP candidate for the United States Senate, Director of MFDP's National Office in Washington, DC, 1962-1967; supporter, Student Non-Violent Coordinating Committee; National Board member, Southern Christian Leadership Conference, 1963-1968/1969. Petersburg, Virginia. Formal conversations, 1983-1994.

Addae, Erriel Kofi (Roberson, Erriel D.), ed. *To Heal a People: Afrikan Scholars Defining a New Reality.* Columbia, Md.: Kujichagulia Press, 1996.

Akbar, Na'im. *Chains and Images of Psychological Slavery.* Jersey City, N.J.: New Mind Publishers, 1986.

—————. *Visions for Black Men.* Nashville: Winston- Derek Publishers, 1987.

"African Dreams." *Newsweek,* 23 September 1991, pp. 42-45.

"A is for Ashanti, B is for Black . . ." *Newsweek,* 23 September 1991, pp. 45-48.

Allman, William F. "The First Humans." *U.S. News and World Report,* 27 February 1989, pp. 52-59.

Ampim, Manu. *Towards Black Community Development: Moving Beyond the Limitations of the Lecture Model* (Critical *Issues in the Current Africentric Movement, Volume II).* Oakland: Advancing the Research, 1993.

Angelou, Maya. *And Still I Rise.* New York: Bantam Books, 1980.

Ani, Marimba (Richards, Dona). *Yurugu: An African-Centered Critique of European Cultural Thought and Political Behavior.* Trenton: Africa World Press, 1994.

Armah, Ayi Kwei. *Two Thousand Seasons.* Chicago: Third World Press, 1984.

Asante, Molefi Kete. *The Afrocentric Idea.* Philadelphia: Temple University Press, 1987.

———————. *Afrocentricity.* Revised ed. Trenton: Africa World Press, 1988.

———————. *Afrocentricity: The Theory of Social Change.* Washington, D.C. and Buffalo, N.Y.: FAS Printing and Amulefi Publishing, 1980.

———————. "Guilty as Charged: I am a Cultural Nationalist." *City Sun*, 25-31 March 1992, pp. 30-31.

———————. *Kemet, Afrocentricity and Knowledge.* Trenton: Africa World Press, 1990.

———————. *Malcolm X as Cultural Hero and Other Afrocentric Essays.* Trenton: Africa World Press, 1993.

———————. "Markings of an African Concept of Rhetoric." *Today's Speech* (March 1971).

———————. "The Painful Demise of Eurocentrism." *The World & I* (April 1992): 305-317.

———————. "Putting Africa at the Center." *Newsweek*, 23 September 1991, p. 46.

———————. "Socio-Historical Perspectives of Black Rhetoric." *Quarterly Journal of Speech* (October 1970).

———————. "Systematic Nationalism." *Journal of Black Studies* (September 1978):115-128.

———————. "Toward a Revolutionary Rhetoric." In *A Return to Vision.* Edited by Richard L. Cherry. New York: Houghton Mifflin, 1974.

Asante, Molefi, and Mattson, Mark T. *The Historical and Cultural Atlas of African Americans.* New York: Macmillan Publishing, 1991.

Asante, Molefi, and Welsh-Asante, Kariamu, eds. *African Culture: The Rhythms of Unity.* Westport, Conn.: Greenwood Press, 1985.

Association for the Study of Classical African Civilizations. ". . . Building for Eternity: ASCAC Association for the Study of Classical African Civilizations." (official organizational tri-fold brochure). Philadelphia: ASCAC, P.O. Box 42511, 19101, 1995.

Association for the Study of Classical AfricanCivilizations. "Fourth Annual ASCAC Conference, July 8-10, 1987 (6227 A.F.K. - After the Founding of KEMET), Aswan, Egypt, Conference Packet." Aswan, Egypt: n.p., 1987.

Association of African Historians. "Prefatory Remarks to Our Readers." T*he Afrocentric World Review* 1, 1 (1973): 1-2.

Azibo, Daudi Ajani ya. "Advances in African Personality Theory." *Imhotep: An Afrocentric Review* Vol. 2, No. 1 (January 1990): 22-47.

_____. "Articulating the Distinction Between Black Studies and the Study of Blacks: The Fundamental Role of Culture and the African-Centered Worldview." *The Afrocentric Scholar: The Journal of the National Council for Black Studies* Vol. 1, No. 1 (May 1992): 64-97.

_____. "Pitfalls and Some Ameliorative Strategies in African Personality Theory." *Journal of Black Studies* Vol. 19, No. 3 (March 1989): 306-319.

Azibo, Daudi Ajani ya, ed. *African Psychology in Historical Perspective and Related Commentary*. Trenton, N.J.: Africa World Press, 1996.

Babbie, Earl. *The Practice of Social Research*. 4th ed. Belmont, Calif.: Wadsworth Publishing, 1986.

Bailey, Chauncey; Crittendon, D; Hayes, J.; Hernandez, R; Marchetti, D,; Russell, R.; and Tobin, J. "Afrocentrism: Teaching Pride or Prejudice?" *Detroit News*, 31 January 1991, pp. 1F-8F.

Bailey, Stanley. "Afro-doctoral Program a Dream Come True." *Philadelphia Tribune*, 16 September 1988.

Baldwin, Joseph A. *Afrikan (Black) Personality: From an Africentric Framework*. Tallahassee, Fla.: By the Author, Department of Psychology, Florida A & M University, 1980.

Baldwin, Joseph A., and Bell, Yvonne R. "The African Self-Consciousness Scale: An Africentric Questionnaire." *The Western Journal of Black Studies* Vol. 9, No. 2 (1985): 61-68.

Begley, Adam. "Henry Louis Gates Jr., Black Studies' New Star." *New York Times Magazine*, 1 April 1990, p.24.

Bekerie, Ayele. "An Original Is Older Than Its Copy: The African Origin of Ethiopian Orthodox Christianity." *Imhotep: An Afrocentric Review* Vol. 2, No. 1 (January 1990): 7, 18.

_____. *Ethiopic, An African Writing System: Its History and Principles*. Lawrenceville, N.J. and Asmara, Eritrea: Red Sea Press, 1997.

Bell, Derrick. *Faces at the Bottom of the Well: The Permanence of Racism*. New York: Basic Books, HarperCollins Publishers, 1992.

Ben-Jochannan, Yosef A.A. *Abu Simbel to Ghizeh: A Guide Book and Manual*. Baltimore: Black Classic Press, 1989.

_____. *African Origins of the Major "Western Religions"*, New York: Alkebu-lan Books, 1973.

_____. *Africa: Mother of Western Civilization*. Baltimore: Black Classic Press, 1988.

_____. *Black Man of the Nile and His Family*. Baltimore: Black Classic Press, 1989.

_____. *Our Black Seminarians and Black Clergy Without a Black Theology*. New York: Alkebu-lan: Books and Educational Materials Association, 1978.

_____. *Ta-Merry/"Egypt" and Her Religious Persecutors: From Judaism-Christianity-Islam to Marxian Humanism; or The Origins of Western Civilization—From Israel-Sumeria-Greece or Ta-Merry/"Egypt"*. New York: By the author, 1988.

Berger, Joseph. "Ibn Batuta and Sitar Challenging Columbus and Piano in Schools." *New York Times*, 12 April 1989.

Biko, Steve. *Steve Biko—I Write What I Like (A Selection of His Writings)*. San Francisco: Harper and Row, 1978.

Bishop, Maurice. *Maurice Bishop Speaks (The Grenada Revolution 1979-83)*. New York: Pathfinder Press, 1983.

Blyden, Edward Wilmot. *Black Spokesman: Selected Published Writings of Edward Wilmot Blyden*. Edited by Hollis R. Lynch. London: Frank Cass, 1971.

_____. *Christianity, Islam and the Negro Race*. Black Classic Press, 1887, 1888, 1994.

_____. *Selected Letters of Edward Wilmot Blyden*. Edited by Hollis R. Lynch. Millwood, NY: KTO Press, A Division of Kraus-Thomson Organization, 1978.

_____. *West Africa Before Europe*. [Place and publisher unavailable.] 1915.

Bradford, Phillips Verner, and Blume, Harvey. *Ota Benga: The Pygmy in the Zoo*. New York: St. Martin's Press, 1992.

Bradley, Michael. *The Iceman Inheritance (Prehistoric Sources of Western Man's Racism, Sexism, and Aggression)*. New York: Kayode Publications, 1978.

Braxton, Joanne M., and McLaughlin, Andree Nicola, eds. *Wild Women in the Whirlwind: Afra-American Culture and the Contemporary Literary Renaissance*. New Brunswick, N.J.: Rutgers University Press, 1990.

Brent, Linda. *Incidents in the Life of a Slave Girl*. Edited by L. Maria Child; New Introduction and Notes by Walter Teller. New York: Harcourt Brace Jovanovich, Publishers, 1983.

Browder, Anthony T. *From the Browder File: 22 Essays on the African American Experience*. Washington, D.C.: The Institute of Karmic Guidance, 1989.

_____. *Nile Valley Contributions to Civilization (Exploding the Myths - Volume 1)*. Washington, D.C.: The Institute of Karmic Guidance, 1993.

Brown, William Wells. *The Rising Son; or, The Antecedents and Advancement of the Colored Race.* New York: Negro Universities Press, Greenwood Press, 1970.

Budge, E.A. Wallis. *The Book of the Dead (The Papyrus of Ani).* Interlinear Transliteration and Translation of the Egyptian text by E.A. Wallis Budge. New York: Dover Publications, Inc., 1967.

_____. *Egyptian Religion.* New York: Carol Publishing Group, 1987.

Cabral, Amilcar. *Unity and Struggle (Speeches and Writings).* New York and London: Monthly Review Press, 1979.

Cade Bambara, Toni. *The Salt Eaters.* New York: Vintage Books, Random House, 1981.

Cade [Bambara], Toni, ed. *The Black Woman: An Anthology.* New York: A Mentor Book, The New American Library, 1970.

Campbell, Joseph. *The Hero with a Thousand Faces.* Princeton and New York: Princeton University Press and The Bollinger Foundation, 1969.

Campbell, Joseph, with Moyers, Bill. *The Power of Myth.* New York: Doubleday, 1988.

Carmichael, Stokely [Toure, Kwame], and Hamilton, Charles V. *Black Power: The Politics of Liberation in America.* New York: Vintage Books, Random House, 1967.

Carruthers, Jacob. *African or American: A Question of Intellectual Allegiance.* Chicago: Kemetic Institute, 1994.

_____. "Carruthers on Schlesinger." In *Critical Commentaries.* Los Angeles: ASCAC Foundation, 1992.

_____. *Essays in Ancient Egyptian Studies.* Los Angeles: Timbuktu Publishers, 1984.

_____. *Mdw Ntr: Divine Speech (A Historiographical Reflection of African Deep Thought From the Time of the Pharaohs to the Present).* London and Lawrenceville, N.J.: Karnak House and Red Sea Press, 1995.

_____. "Outside Academia: Bernal's Critique of Black Champions of Ancient Egypt." *Journal of Black Studies* Vol. 22, Number 4 (June 1992): 474, 461.

Carruthers, Jacob, ed. "Constitution of The Association for the Study of Classical African Civilizations, Article II (Purpose)." Los Angeles: n.p. 1985.

Cesaire, Aime. *Aime Cesaire, The Collected Poetry.* Translated with an Introduction and Notes by Clayton Eshleman and Annette Smith. Berkeley: University of California Press, 1983.

_____. "Cesaire Interviewed by Haitian Poet Renee Depestre, at the Cultural Congress, Havana, Cuba, 1967." Translated from the Spanish by Maro Riofrancos. In *Discourse on Colonialism*. By Aime Cesaire. New York: Monthly Review Press, 1972.

_____. *Discourse on Colonialism*. Translated from the French by Joan Pinkam. New York: Monthly Review Press, 1972.

Chinweizu. *The West and the Rest of Us: White Predators, Black Slavers and the African Elite*. Lagos, Nigeria: Pero Press, 1987.

Chiwengo, Ngwarsungu. "Peter Abrahams in Perspective (South Africa)." Ph.D. dissertation, State University of New York at Buffalo, 1986.

Churchward, Albert. *Signs and Symbols of Primordial Man (Being an Explanation of the Evolution of Religious Doctrines from the Eschatology of the Ancient Egyptians)*. Chesapeake, Va.: ECA Associates, 1990.

Circle of DAWN-MAAT. Afrocentric pan-African advocacy organization. Washington, District of Columbia. Observations, 1994-1995.

Clarke, John Henrik. "The African Heritage Studies Association (AHSA): Some Notes on the Conflict with the African Studies Association (ASA) and the Fight to Reclaim African History." *Issue: A Quarterly Journal of Africanist Opinion* Vol. VI, Number 2/3 (Summer/Fall 1976): 5-11.

_____. *Africans at the Crossroads: Notes for an African World Revolution*. Trenton, N.J.: Africa World Press, 1991.

_____. *The Boy Who Painted Christ Black*. [Place and publisher unavailable]. 1940.

_____. *Rebellion in Rhyme: The Early Poetry of John Henrik Clarke*. Trenton, N.J.: Africa World Press, Inc., 1991.

Clarke, John Henrik, ed.; assisted by Bailey, A. Peter, and Grant, Earl. *Malcolm X: The Man and His Times*. Trenton, NJ: Africa World Press, 1990.

Clarke, John Henrik, ed., with the assistance of Garvey, Amy Jacques. *Marcus Garvey and the Vision of Africa*. New York: Vintage Books, 1974,

Cleage, Albert B., Jr. *Black Christian Nationalism: New Directions for the Black Church*. New York and Detroit: Morrow Quill Paperbacks and Luxor Publishers of the Pan-African Orthodox Christian Church, 1972.

_____. *The Black Messiah*. Trenton, N.J.: Sheed and Ward, Africa World Press, 1989.

Cone, James H. *Black Theology and Black Power*. Minneapolis: Seabury Press, 1969.

_____. *For My People*. Maryknoll, N.Y.: Orbis Books, 1984.

_____. *Speaking the Truth: Ecumenism, Liberation, and Black Theology*. Grand Rapids, Mich.: William B. Eerdmans Publishing Company, 1986.

Coughlin, Ellen K. "Scholars Work to Refine Africa-Centered View of Life and History of Black Americans." *Chronicle of Higher Education*, 28 October 1987.

Cruse, Harold. *The Crisis of the Negro Intellectual: A Historical Analysis of the Failure of Black Leadership*. New York: William Morrow, 1984.

_____. *Plural but Equal (A Critical Study of Blacks and Minorities and America)*. New York: William Morrow, 1987.

Davis, Angela. *Angela Davis: An Autobiography*. New York: Random House, 1974.

_____. *Women, Race and Class*. New York: Vintage Books, Random House, 1983.

Davis, Angela, and Other Political Prisoners. *If They Come in the Morning: Voices of Resistance*. New York: Signet Classics, 1971.

DeGraft, Johnson, J.C. *African Glory: The Story of Vanished Negro Civilizations*. Baltimore: Black Classic Press, 1986.

De Lancey, Frenzella Elaine. "Intertextuality and Willful Transformation as Narrative Strategies in African-American Women's Writing: From Whence the Imperative? (Jacobs, Hurston, Asante)." Ph.D. dissertation, Temple University, 1989.

Delany, Martin R. *Blake, or, The Huts of America*. Edited and with an Introduction by Floyd J. Miller. Boston: Beacon Press, 1970.

Delany, Martin R., and Campbell, Robert. *Search for a Place: Black Separatism and Africa, 1860*. Edited by Howard R. Bell. Ann Arbor: University of Michigan Press, 1969.

Deloria, Vine, Jr. *God Is Red*. Maryknoll, NY: 1983.

DeLubicz, Isha Schwaller. *The Opening of the Way*. Rochester, Vt.: Inner Traditions International, 1981.

Diop, Cheikh Anta. "Africa Cradle of Humanity." In *Nile Valley Civilizations (Proceedings of the Nile Valley Conference, Atlanta [Ga.], September 26-30, 1984)*, pp. 23-28. New Brunswick, NJ: Transaction Books, Journal of African Civilizations, November 1986.

_____. "Africa's Contribution to World Civilization: The Exact Sciences." In *Nile Valley Civilizations (Proceedings of the Nile Valley Conference, Atlanta [GA], September 26-30, 1984)*, pp. 69-83. Edited by Ivan Van Sertima. New Brunswick, NJ: Transaction Books, Transaction Books, Journal of African Civilizations, Ltd., Inc., November 1984, 1985, November 1986.

_____. *The African Origin of Civilization: Myth or Reality?*. Translated from the French by Mercer Cook. Westport, Conn.: Lawrence Hill and Co., 1974.

_____. *Black Africa: The Economic and Cultural Basis for a Federate State*. Translated from the French by Harold J. Salemson. Revised ed. Westport, CT and Trenton, N.J.: Lawrence Hill and Co. and Africa World Press, 1987.

_____. *Civilization or Barbarism: An Authentic Anthropology*. Translated from the French by Yaa-Lengi Meema Ngemi. Edited by Harold J. Salemson and Marjolijn de Jager. Brooklyn, N.Y.: Lawrence Hill Books, 1991.

_____. *Cultural Unity of Black Africa*. Chicago: Third World Press, 1978.

_____. *Great African Thinkers, Vol. 1: Cheikh Anta Diop*. Edited by Ivan Van Sertima. New Brunswick, N.J.: Transaction Books, 1987.

_____. *Precolonial Black Africa (A Comparative Study of the Political and Social Systems of Europe and Black Africa, from Antiquity to the Formation of Modern States)*. Translated from the French by Harold Salemson. Westport, Conn.: Lawrence Hill and Co.,1987.

_____. *Towards the African Renaissance (Essays in African Culture and Development, 1946-1960)*. London and Lawrenceville, N.J.: Karnak House and Red Sea Press, 1996.

Dozier, P. Oare. "The Politics of Knowledge: Selected Critiques of Western Education." Ph.D. dissertation, University of Massachusetts, 1985.

Drake, St. Clair. *Black Folk Here and There (An Essay in History and Anthropology)*. Vol. 1. Los Angeles: Center for Afro-American Studies, University of California, Los Angeles, 1987.

DuBois, William Edward Burghardt. *Darkwater: Voices from Within the Veil*. New York: Harcourt Brace, 1921; reprint ed., Millwood, N.Y.: Kraus-Thomson Organizaton, 1975.

_____. *The Souls of Black Folk*. New York: Signet Classics, 1903, 1969.

_____. *The World and Africa: An Inquiry into the Part Which Africa Has Played in World History*. New York: International Publishers, 1965.

"Earliest Ancestor of the Human Race Found in Africa [Awash, Ethiopia]." *Philadelphia News Observer,* 5 October 1994, p. 2.

Eliade, Mircea. *The Myth of the Eternal Return or, Cosmos and History*. Translated from the French by Willard R. Trask. Princeton: Princeton University Press, 1974.

Emecheta, Buchi. *The Joys of Motherhood*. New York: George Braziller, Inc., 1988.

Erenrich, Susie, ed. *Freedom Is a Constant Struggle: An Anthology of the Mississippi Civil Rights Movement*. Montgomery: Black Belt Press, 1999.

Essien-Udom, E.U. *Black Nationalism: A Search for Identity in America*. New York and Chicago: Dell Publishing and University of Chicago Press, 1962.

Evans, Mari, ed. *Black Women Writers (1950-1980): A Critical Evaluation*. New York: Anchor Books, 1984.

Fanon, Frantz. *The Wretched of the Earth*. Translated from the French by Constance Farrington. New York: Grove Press, 1968.

Farid, Rasheedah. Afrocentric dance teacher, Virginia State University. Conversations and observation, Spring 1991.

Fine, Mark Allen. "The Effects of Worldview on Adaptation to Single Parenthood." Ph.D. dissertation, The Ohio State University, 1983.

Friere, Paulo. *Pedagogy of the Oppressed*. Translated from the Spanish by Myra Bergman Ramos. New Revised 20th Anniversary ed. New York: Continuum Publishing, 1993.

Gagnon. Alain. *Intellectuals in Liberal Democracies: Political Influence and Social Development*. New York: Praeger Publishers, 1987.

Garvey, Marcus. *Marcus Garvey and the Vision of Africa*. Edited, with an Introduction and Commentaries by John Henrik Clarke; with the Assistance of Amy Jacques Garvey. New York: Vintage Books, Random House, 1974.

_____. *Philosophy and Opinions of Marcus Garvey*. Edited by Amy Jacques-Garvey. New York: Atheneum, 1923, 1968.

Gates, Henry Louis. "Beware of the New Pharaohs." *Newsweek*, 23 September 1991, p. 47.

Giddings, Paula. *When and Where I Enter: The Impact of Black Women on Race and Sex in America*. New York: Bantam Books, 1985.

Gonzalez, Migene. *Power of the Orishas: Santeria and the Worship of Saints*. New York: Original Publications, 1992.

_____. *Santeria: African Magic in Latin America*. New York: Original Publications, 1990.

Gordon, Vivian V. *Black Women, Feminism and Black Liberation: Which Way?*. Chicago: Third World Press, 1991.

_____. *Kemet and Other Ancient African Civilizations: Selected References*. Chicago: Third World Press, 1991.

Gould, Stephen Jay. *The Mismeasure of Man*. New York: W.W. Norton and Company, 1981.

Gowan, Susan; Lakey, G.; Moyer, W.; and Taylor, R. *Moving Toward a New Society*. Philadelphia: New Society Press, 1976.

Graves, Anna Melissa. *Africa—The Wonder and the Glory*. Baltimore: Black Classic Press, 1942.

Gray, Cecil Conteen. "African Based/African Centered African Females and Males: Messengers and Manifestations of MA' AT." In *Testimony: Young African-Americans on Self-Discovery and Black Identity*, pp. 24-258. Edited by Natasha Tarpley. Boston: Beacon Press, 1995.

_____. "Afrocentricity: Definitions, Explication, Application, and the Future." Paper presented at Harvard University Graduate School of Education conference "Emerging Voices in Afrocentricity," Harvard University, Boston, Mass., 11 May 1992.

_____. "Afrocentric Thought and Praxis in the United States of America: A Brief Historical Survey of Major (Male) Contributions, A Projection of Future Directions and Promise." Paper submitted for Department of African American Studies' course "Pro-Seminar in Graduate Studies in African American Studies," Temple University, November-December 1988, 13 December 1988.

_____. "Authentic African Leadership for the 1990s and Beyond." *The Burning Torch: Our Culture, Our People, Our Future*, November 1989, pp. 3, 7.

_____. "Bobby Seale [From Seizing the Time to Seeding the Time]." In *Leaders from the 1960s: A Biographical Sourcebook of American Activism*, pp. 149-156. Edited by David DeLeon. Westport, Conn.:Greenwood Press, 1994.

_____. "Ontology and Ontological Oscillation in Carter G. Woodson's *The Miseducation of the Negro*." Paper submitted for Department of African American American Studies' course, "Pro-Seminar in Graduate Studies in African American Studies," Temple University, September 27, 1988.

_____. "The Influence of African Myth and Religion on Western Civilization." *Imhotep: An Afrocentric Review* Vol. 3, No. 1 (Spring 1991): 31-50.

_____. "The Rising Tide of Rites of Passage Programs: Deconstructing Faddish Tendencies, Constructing Serious Systems." Paper presented at An Agenda for the 21st Century of African American Education Conference, The University of Cincinnati, Cincinnati, Ohio, 5-7 November 1992.

_____, ed. *Bma: The Sonia Sanchez Literary Review*. Volume 3, Number 2 (Spring 1998).

Gray [Adams], Victoria Jackson. Founding member of Mississippi Freedom Democratic Party (MFDP), MFDP candidate for the United States Senate, Director of MFDP's National Office in Washington, DC, 1964-1967; supporter, Student Non-Violent Coordinating Committee; National Board member, Southern Christian Leadership Conference, 1963-1968/1969. Petersburg, Virginia. Formal conversations, 1983-1994.

Green, Richard L., ed. *Historic Black Women*. Chicago: Empak Enterprises, 1990.

_____. *A Salute to Black Civil Rights Leaders*. Chicago: Empak Enterprises, 1987.

_____. *A Salute to Blacks in the Arts*. Chicago: Empak Publishing Company, 1989.

Greenberg, Chery Lynn. *A Circle of Trust: Remembering SNCC*. New Brunswick, New Jersey, and London: Rutgers University Press, 1998.

Griaule, Marcel. *Conversations with Ogotemmeli: An Introduction to Dogon Religious Ideas*. London: Oxford University Press, 1980.

Gutierrez, Gustavo. *We Drink from Our Own Wells (The Spiritual Journey of a People)*. Translated from the Spanish by Matthew J. O'Connell. Maryknoll, NY: Orbis Books, 1985.

Hale-Benson, Janice E. *Black Children: Their Roots, Culture, and Learning Styles*. Revised edition. Baltimore and London: Johns Hopkins University Press, 1986.

Hallet, Jean-Pierre, and Pelle, Alex. *Pygmy Kitabu*. New York: Random House, 1972.

Hamlet, Janice Denise. "Religious Discourse as Cultural Narrative: A Critical Analysis of the Rhetoric of African American Sermons (Sermons)." Ph.D. dissertation, Ohio State University, 1982.

Hampton, Henry and Fayer, Steve., eds. *Voices of Freedom*. New York: Bantam Books, 1990.

Hancock, D. Rick. "African Studies Need to be Based on Afrocentric Viewpoints, Scholar Says to Black Studies Group." *Black Issues in Higher Education* (1 May 1988).

Hansberry, William Leo. *Pillars in Ethiopian History: The William Leo Hansberry African History Notebook, Volume 1*. Edited by Joseph E. Harris. Washington, DC: Howard University Press, 1974.

Harding, Vincent. *Hope and History: Why We Must Share the Story of the Movement*. Maryknoll, N.Y.: Blackside and Orbis Books, 1990.

_____. *Martin Luther King: The Inconvenient Hero*. Maryknoll, N.Y.: Orbis Books, 1999.

_____. *There Is a River*. New York: Vintage Books, Random House, 1983.

Hare, Nathan, and Hare, Julia. *Crisis in Black Sexual Politics.* San Francisco: Black Think Tank, 1989.

_____. *The Endangered Black Family:Coping with the Unisexualization and Coming Extinction of the Black Race.* San Francisco: Black Think Tank, 1986.

Harman, Willis R. *Global Mind Change: The Promise of the Last Years of the Twentieth Century.* Indianapolis: The Institute of Noetic Science with Knowledge Systems, Inc., 1987.

Harman, Willis R., and Rheingold, Howard. *Higher Creativity.* Los Angeles: Jeremy P. Tarcher, 1984.

Harris, Ethel Patricia. "An Afrocentric View of the Rhetoric of Dick Gregory." Ph.D. dissertation, Ohio State University, 1982.

Harris, Norman. [past] Chairperson, Department of African American Studies, University of Cincinnati. Communication, Spring 1995.

Herodotus. *The Histories.* Translated by Aubrey de Selincourt. Harmondsworth, Middlesex, United Kingdom: Penguin Books, 1983.

Heru, Nzingha Ratibisha. "From the President's Office." *Serekh: Promoting an African Worldview* Vol. 5, No. 1 (1994).

Hilliard, Asa G., III. *The Maroon Within Us (Selected Essays on African American Community Socialization).* Baltimore: Black Classic Press, 1995.

_____. "Psychological Factors Associated with Language in the Education of the African-American Child." *Journal of Negro Education* Vol. 52, No. 1 (1983): 24-34.

_____. *SBA: The Reawakening of the African Mind.* Gainesville, Fla.: Makare Publishing Company, 1998.

Hilliard, Asa G., III; Williams, Larry; and Damali, Nia. *The Teachings of Ptahhotep (The Oldest Book in the World).* Atlanta: Blackwood Press and Company, 1987.

Hine, Darlene Clark; Brown, Elsa Barkley; Terbourg-Penn, Rosalyn, eds. *Black Women in America: An Historical Encyclopedia* (Volumes 1 and 2). Bloomington and Indianapolis: Indiana University Press, 1994.

_____. *Black Women in United States History.* New York: Carlson Publishers, 1990.

Holmes, Oliver W. *Human Reality and the Social World: Ortega's Philosophy of History.* Amherst: University of Massachusetts Press, 1975.

Hord, Fred Lee, and Lee (Okpara, Mzee Lasana), Jonathan Scott, eds. *I Am Because We Are (Readings in Black Philosophy).* Amherst: University of Massachusetts Press, 1995.

Horner, Carol. "Out of Africa [An Interview with Molefi Kete Asante]." *Philadelphia Inquirer*, 19 January 1992.

Houston, Drusilla Dunjee. *Wonderful Ethiopians of the Ancient Cushite Empire.* Baltimore: Black Classic Press, 1926, 1985.

Hughes, Langston. *The Dream Keeper.* New York: Alfred Knopf, 1932, 1945.

——————. *Selected Poems of Langston Hughes.* Vintage Books, 1974.

——————. *Good Morning Revolution: Uncollected Writings of Social Protest.* Edited by Faith Berry. New York: Carol Publishing Group, 1992.

Huntsville, Ala. Alabama A & M University. Department of History and Political Science. James Wesley Johnson, "Kawaida and Kuminalism: Basis for a New Ecumenism," 1990.

Hurston, Zora Neale. *Moses, Man of the Mountain.* Urbana and Chicago: University of Illinois Press, 1984.

——————. *The Sanctified Church.* Berkeley: Turtle Island, 1981.

——————. *Their Eyes Were Watching God.* Urbana and Chicago: University of Illinois Press, 1978.

Hyman, Mark. *Blacks Before America.* Philadelphia: Bell of Pennsylvania, [1983?].

Idowu, E. Bolaji. *Olodumare: God in Yoruba Belief.* New York: Wazobia, 1994.

Institute of Positive Education. Chicago, Illinois. Observation, 1982.

Irele, F. Abiola. *Literature and Ideology in Martinique: Rene Maran, Aime Cesaire, Frantz Fanon.* Buffalo, NY: State University of New York at Buffalo, Special Studies Council on International Studies, F.A. Irele, 1972.

"*IS THE CURRICULUM BIASED?* A Statement by the National Association of Scholars." *Chronicle of Higher Education*, 8 November 1989, p. A23.

Jackson, George L. *Blood in My Eye.* Baltimore: Black Classic Press, 1990.

Jackson, John G. *Christianity Before Christ.* Austin, TX: American Atheist Press, 1985.

——————. *Ethiopia and the Origin of Civilization.* Baltimore: Black Classic Press, 1985.

——————. *Introduction to African Civilizations.* Secaucus, N.J.: The Citadel Press, 1970.

——————. *Man, God, and Civilization.* Secaucus, N.J.: The Citadel Press, 1972.

Jahn, Janheinz. *Muntu: An Outline of the New African Culture.* Translated from the German by Marjorie Grene. New York: Grove Press, Inc., 1961.

_____. *Neo-African Literature: A History of Black Writing.* Translated from the German by Oliver Coburn and Ursula Lehrburger. New York: Grove Press, 1969.

James, C.L.R. *The C.L.R. James Reader.* Edited by Anna Grimshaw. Oxford, UK and Cambridge, Mass.: Blackwell Publishers, 1993.

James, George G. M. *Stolen Legacy.* New York: Philosophical Society, 1954; reprint ed., San Francisco: Julian Richardson Associates, 1985.

Janos, Andrew C. *Politics and Paradigms: Changing Theories of Change.* Stanford: Stanford University Press, 1986.

Jeffries, Leonard. "Reclaiming Nile Valley Civilization." *Africa Commentary: A Journal of People of African Descent* Vol. II, Issues 1 & 2 (January/February 1990): 24.

Jenifer, Franklyn G. "Afrocentricity Is No Cause for Alarm." *Washington Post*, 19 November 1990.

Johnson, Julie. "Curriculum Seeks to Lift Blacks' Self-Image." *New York Times*, 8 March 1989.

Jones, Charles E., ed. *The Black Panter Party Reconsidered.* Baltimore: Black Classic Press, 1998.

Jones, Le Roi (Baraka, Amiri). *Black* Music. New York: Quill, 1967.

_____. *Blues People.* New York: Quill, 1963.

_____. *Home (Social Essays).* Hopewell, N.J.: The Ecco Press, 1966.

Jones, William R. *Is God a White Racist?: A Preamble to Black Theology.* Garden City, NY: Anchor Books, Anchor Press/Doubleday, 1973.

Joyce, Joyce Ann. *Ijala: Sonia Sanchez and the African Poetic Tradition.* Chicago: Third World Press, 1996.

Kamalu, Chukwunyere. *Foundations of African Thought: A Worldview Grounded in the African Heritage of Religion, Philosophy, Science and Art.* London: Karnak House, 1990.

Kambon, Kobi K.K.(Baldwin, Joseph A.) *Afrikan/Black Psychology in the American Context: An African-Centered Approach.* Tallahassee, Fla.: Nubian Nations Publications, 1998.

Karenga, Maulana. *The African American Holiday of Kwanzaa: A Celebration of Family, Community, and Culture.* Los Angeles: University of Sankore Press, 1988.

_____. *The Book of Coming Forth by Day: The Ethics of the Declaration of Virtues.* Translation and Commentary by Maulana Karenga. Los Angeles: University of Sankore Press, 1990.

_____. *Introduction to Black Studies.* Los Angeles: Kawaida Publications, Fourth Printing, April 1987.

_____. *Introduction to Black Studies.* 2nd ed. Los Angeles: University of Sankore Press, 1990.

_____. *Odu Ifa: The Ethical Teachings.* Translation and Commentary, A Kawaida Interpretation. Los Angeles: University of Sankore Press, 1999.

_____. *Selections from the Husia: Sacred Wisdom of Ancient Egypt.* Selected and Retranslated by Maulana Karenga. Los Angeles: University of Sankore Press, 1984, 1989.

Karenga, Maulana, ed. *Reconstructing Kemetic Culture: Papers, Perspectives, Projects [Selected Papers of the Proceedings of the Conferences of the Association for the Study of Classical African Civilizations, Including the Fourth Conference, Aswan Egypt, 1987 (6227 A.F.E.)].* Los Angeles: University of Sankore Press, 1990.

Karenga, Maulana, and Carruthers, Jacob, eds. *Kemet and the* African Worldview: Research, Rescue and Restoration [*Selected Papers of the First and Second Conferences of the Association for the Study of Classical African Civilizations, 24-26 February 1984 (6223 AFE), Los Angeles, and 1-3 March 1985 (6225 AFE), Chicago*]. Los Angeles: University of Sankore Press, 1986.

Keto, C. Tsehloane. *The Africa Centered Perspective of History: An Introduction.* Blackwood, N.J.: K.A. Publications, 1991.

_____. *Vision, Identity and Time: The Afrocentric Paradigm and the Study of the Past.* Dubuque, Iowa: Kendall/Hunt Publishing Company, 1995.

Kondo, Zak A. *The Black Student's Guide to Positive Education.* Washington, D.C.: Nubia Press, 1989.

_____. *Conspiracys: Unravelling the Assassination of Malcolm X.* Washington, D.C.: Nubia Press, 1993.

_____. *A Crash Course in Black History.* Washington, D.C.: Nubia Press, 1991.

_____. *Historical Lies and Myths that Miseducate Black People (Volume I: U.S. History).* Washington, D.C.: Nubia Press, 1989.

Leakey, Richard. "The Origins of Mankind." *Anthroquest* 35 (Fall 1986): 3-4.

Lemonick, Michael D., and Dorfman, Andrea. "How We Became Human." *Time,* 23 August 1999, pp. 50-58.

Leo, John. "A Fringe History of the World." *U.S. News & World Report,* 12 November 1990, pp. 25-26.

Leonard, Carolyn M, and Little, William A., eds. *National Council for Black Studies, Inc. Constitution and Bylaws.* Bloomington: National Council for Black Studies, Inc., Memorial Hall East 129, Indiana University, 1988.

_____. *National Council for Black Studies Organizational Handbook.* Bloomington: National Council for Black Studies, Inc., Memorial Hall East 129, Indiana University, 1988.

Lewis, Rupert. *Marcus Garvey: Anti-Colonial Champion.* Trenton: Africa World Press, 1988.

Lincoln, C. Eric. *The Black Muslims in America.* Boston: Beacon Press, 1961.

Locke, Alain, ed. *The New Negro.* New York and Don Mills, Canada: Atheneum and Maxwell Macmillan Canada, 1992.

Lomax, Louis E. *When the Word Is Given . . . (A Report on Elijah Muhammad, Malcolm X, and the Muslim World).* Cleveland: World Publishing, 1963.

Madhubuti, Haki. *Black Men: Obsolete, Single, Dangerous? Afrikan American Family in Transition: Essays in Discovery, Solution, and Hope).* Chicago: Third World Press, 1990.

_____. *Earthquakes and Sunrise Missions: Poetry and Essays of Black Renewal, 1973-1983.* Chicago: Third World Press, 1984.

_____. *Enemies: The Clash of Races.* Chicago: Third World Press, 1978.

_____. "Sonia Sanchez: The Bringer of Memories." In *Black Women Writers (1950-1980): A Critical Evaluation*, pp. 419-432. Edited by Mari Evans. New York: Anchor Books, 1984.

Madhubuti, Haki, ed. *Confusion by any Other Name: Essays Exploring the Negative Impact of the Blackman's Guide to Understanding the Blackwoman.* Chicago: Third World Press, 1990.

Maglanbayan, Shawna. *Garvey, Lumumba and Malcolm: Black National-Separatists.* Chicago: Third World Press, 1973.

Magubane, Bernard. "The American Negro's Conception of Africa: a Study in the Ideology of Pride and Prejudice." Ph.D. dissertation, University of California, Los Angeles, 1967.

Malveaux, Julianne. "Clash of Visions." *New Orleans Tribune*, June 1991.

Mandela, Nelson. *Long Walk to Freedom: The Autobiography of Nelson Mandela.* Boston and Canada: Black Bay Books and Little, Brown, and Company, 1995.

Marable, Manning. *How Capitalism Underdeveloped Black America (Problems in Race, Political Economy and Society).* Boston: South End Press, 1983.

_____. *Race, Reform and Rebellion: The Second Reconstruction in Black America, 1945-1982.* Jackson: University Press of Mississippi, 1989.

_____. *Race, Reform and Rebellion: The Second Recon-struction in Black America, 1945-1990.* Revised 2nd ed. Jackson and London: University Press of Mississippi, 1991.

Martin, Lorenzo. "Arab Imperialism." *The Afrocentric World Review* 1, 1 (1973): 43-46.

Martin, Tony. *Marcus Garvey, Hero: A First Biography.* Dover, Mass.: Majority Press, 1983.

Massey, Gerald. *Ancient Egypt the Light of the World.* Baltimore: Black Classic Press, 1992.

_____. *A Book of the Beginnings.* London: Williams and Norgate, 1881.

Mays, Benjamin E. *Born to Rebel.* New York: Charles Scribner's Sons, 1971.

_____. *The Negro's God.* New York: Atheneum Press, 1968, 1973.

McIntyre, Charshee. Professor, State University of New York, Old Westbury; former president, African Heritage Studies Association. Conversations, 1989-1991.

Means, Sterling M. *Ethiopia and the Missing Link in African History.* Harrisburg, Pa.: By the Author and The Atlantis Publishing Company, 1945; reprint ed., Dawud Hakim, 1980.

Mercer, Joye. "Nile Valley Scholars Bring New Light and Controversy to African Studies." *Black Issues in Higher Education* (28 February 1991): 1, 12-16.

Mills, Kay. *This Little Light of Mine: The Life of Fannie Lou Hamer.* New York: Plume, 1994.

Mokhtar, G., ed. *General History of Africa II: Ancient Civilizations of Africa.* Abridged edition. United Nations Educational, Scientific, and Cultural Organization (UNESCO) International Scientific Community for the Drafting of a General History of Africa. London; Berkeley, Ca.; Paris:James Currey, University of California Press, UNESCO, 1990.

Moore, Dana. Rites of Passage Shule, Inc., Philadelphia,Pennsylvania. Interviews, June 1993, December 1993.

Morrison, Roy D., II. "Black Enlightenment: The Issues of Pluralism, Priorities, and Empirical Correlation." *Journal of the American Academy of Religion* XLV/2 (June 1978): 218-240.

_____. *Science, Theology and the Transcendental Horizon: Einstein, Kant and Tillich.* Atlanta: Scholars Press, The American Academy of Religion, 1994.

Murphy, Joseph M. *Working the Spirit: Ceremonies of the African Diaspora.* Boston: Beacon Press, 1994.

Murungi, John Justo. "Two Views of History: A Study of the Relation of European and African Culture." Ph.D. dissertation, The Pennsylvania State University, 1970.

Myers, Linda James. *Understanding an Afrocentric Worldview: Introduction to an Optimal Psychology* Dubuque, Iowa: Kendall/Hunt Publishers, 1988.

Nasciemento, Abdias Do. *Brazil: Mixture or Massacre? (Essays in the Genocide of a Black People)*. 2nd ed. Translated from the Portuguese by Elisa Larkin Nasciemento. Dover, Mass.: Majority Press, 1989.

Neal, Larry. "The Black Arts Movement." *The Drama Review* Vol. 12, No. 2 (Summer 1968): 257-268.

_____. "Some Reflections on the Black Aesthetic." In *The Black Aesthetic*, pp. 12-15. Edited by Addison Gayle. Garden City, N.Y.: Anchor Books, 1972.

_____. *Visions of a Liberated Future: Black Arts Movement Writings*. New York: Thunder's Mouth Press, 1989.

Ngugi wa Thiong'o. *Weep Not, Child*. Oxford: Heinemann Educational Books, 1987.

Neumann, Holm Wolfram. "The American Negro—His Origins and His Present Status as a Hybrid or Secondary Race." Ph.D. dissertation, Indiana University, 1962.

Nichols, J.L. and Crogman, William H. *The Progress of a Race (or the Remarkable Advancement of the American Negro)*. Naperville, Ill.: J.L. Nichols and Company, 1920.

Nkrumah, Kwame. *Africa Must Unite*. London: Panaf Books, 1998.

_____. *Revolutionary Path*. London: Panaf Books, 1980.

Nobles, Wade. "African Philosophy: Foundations for Black Psychology." In *Black Psychology*, pp. 23-26. Edited by Reginald L. Jones. 2nd ed. New York: Harper and Row, 1980.

_____. *African Psychology: Toward Its Reclamation, Reascension and Revitalization*. Oakland: The Institute for the Advanced Study of Black Family Life and Culture, 1986.

_____. "Extended Self: Rethinking the So-Called Negro Self-Concept" In *Black Psychology*, pp. 99-105. Edited by Reginald L. Jones. 2nd ed. New York: Harper and Row, 1980.

_____. ""Toward an Empirical and Theoretical Framework for Defining Black Families." *Journal of Marriage and the Family* (November 1978): 679-688.

Nobles, Wade; Goddard, Lawford L.; and Cavill, William, III. *The KM Ebit Husia: Authoritative Utterances for the Black Family*. Oakland: The Institute for the Advanced Study of Black Family Life and Culture, 1986.

Nyerere, Julius K. *Man and Development/Binadamu Na Maendeleo.* London and New York: Oxford University Press, 1974.

Obenga, Theophile. *Ancient Egypt and Black Africa: A Student's Handbook for the Study of Ancient Egypt in Philosophy, Linguistics, and Gender Relations.* London: Karnak House, 1992.

Outlaw, Lucien Turner. "Language and the Transformation of Consciousness: Foundations for a Hermeneutics of Black Culture." Ph.D. dissertation, Boston College, 1972.

——————————. *On Race and Philosophy.* New York: Routledge, 1996.

Parker, George Wells. *Children of the Sun.* Baltimore:Black Classic Press, 1981.

Payne, Charles M. *I've Got the Light of Freedom: The Organizing Tradition and the Mississippi Freedom Struggle.* Berkeley: University of California Press, 1995.

Penick, Benson Ellsworth. "Knowledge of Black Culture as a Factor in Attitudes and Behaviours of Whites and Blacks." Ph.D. dissertation, Kansas State University, 1970.

Pennington, James W.C. *A Text Book of the Origin and History of the Colored People.* Hartford: L. Skinner, 1841.

Pinkney, Alphonso. *The Myth of Black Progress.* New York: Cambridge University Press, 1986.

Person-Lynn, Kwaku, ed. *First Word: Black Scholars, Thinkers, Warriors (Knowledge, Wisdom, Mental Liberation).* New York: Harlem River Press, 1996.

Preston, Frederick William. "Red, White, Black and Blue: The Concept of Race in American Sociology—An Exploration in the Sociology of Knowledge." Ph.D. dissertation, The Ohio State University, 1970.

Price, Richard, ed. *Maroon Societies: Rebel Slave Communities in the Americas.* Baltimore and London: The John Hopkins University Press, 1983.

Price-Mars, Jean. *So Spoke the Uncle.* Translated and with an Introduction by Magdaline W. Shannon. Washington, D.C.: Three Continents Press, 1928, 1990.

Raines, Howell. *My Soul Is Rested (The Story of the CivilRights Movement in the Deep South).* New York: Penguin Books, 1983.

Randall, Dudley, ed. *The Black Poets.* New York: Bantam Books, Inc., 1971, 1981.

Rashidi, Runoko. "African Goddesses: Mothers of Civilization." In *Black Women in Antiquity.* Edited by Ivan Van Sertima. New Brunswick, N.J.: Journal of African Civilizations, 1988.

Ravitch, Diane. "Multiculturalism, E Pluribus Plures." *The American Scholar* (Summer 1990): 341-343, 337-354.

Rescher, Nicholas. *Ethical Idealism: An Inquiry into the Nature and Function of Ideals.* Berkeley and Los Angeles: University of California Press, 1987.

Richards, Dona Marimba. *Let the Circle be Unbroken: The Implications of African Spirituality in the Diaspora.* Trenton: Red Sea Press, 1989.

Rites of Passage Shule, Inc Organization. Philadelphia, Pennsylvania. Observations, 1991-1995.

Robeson, Paul. *Here I Stand.* Boston: Beacon Free Press, 1958, 1971.

Rodney, Walter. *How Europe Underdeveloped Africa.* Washington, DC: Howard University Press, 1982.

Rogers, J.A. *The Real Facts About Ethiopia.* Baltimore: Black Classic Press, 1936.

_____. *World's Great Men of Color, Volume II.* New York, Macmillan, 1972.

Ross, Andrew. *No Respect: Intellectuals and Popular Culture.* New York and London: Routledge, Chapman and Hall, 1989.

Rowe, Cyprian Lamar. *Crisis in African Studies: The Birth of the African Heritage Studies Association.* Buffalo: Black Academy Press, 1970.

Sanchez, Sonia. *Homegirls and Handgrenades.* New York: Thunder's Mouth Press, 1984.

_____. *I've Been a Woman (New and Selected Poems).* Third World Press, 1990.

_____. *Like the Singing Coming off the Drums: Love Poems.* Boston: Beacon Press, 1998.

_____. *Shake Loose My Skin: New and Selected Poems.* Boston: Beacon Press, 1999.

_____. *Under a Soprano Sky.* Trenton, N.J.: Africa World Press, 1993.

_____. *Wounded in the House of a Friend.* Boston: Beacon Press, 1995.

Scott-Heron, Gil. *So Far, So Good.* Chicago: Third World Press, 1990.

Seale, Bobby. *A Lonely Rage: The Autobiography of Bobby Seale.* New York: Bantam Books, 1979.

_____. *Seize the Time: The Story of the Black Panther Party and Huey P. Newton.* New York: Random House, 1968.

Shabazz, Wilfred [Little]. Blood brother of Malcolm X [El Hajj Malik El Shabazz]. Detroit, Michigan. Interview with Charles Fuller, November 1989.

Shakur, Assata. *Assata: An Autobiography.* Westport, Conn.: Lawrence Hill and Co., 1987.

Shujaa, Mwalimu J., ed. *Too Much Schooling, Too Little Education: A Paradox of Black Life in White Societies.* Trenton: Africa World Press, 1994.

Sillen, Samuel. *Women Against Slavery.* New York: Masses and Mainstream, 1955.

Sims, Nathaniel. "Strategy for Teaching Afro-American Cultural Studies in the Humanities." Ph.D. dissertation, University of Massachusetts, 1971.

Smith, Pamela Joan. "The Forest of the Almighty: Being a Translation of D.O. Fagunwa's 'Igbo Olodumare' from Yoruba into English." Ph.D. dissertation, University of Washington, 1986.

Smitherman, Geneva. *Talkin and Testifyin: The Language of Black America.* Detroit: Wayne State University Press, 1977, 1986.

Some, Malidoma Patrice. *Of Water and the Spirit: Ritual, Magic, and Initiation in the Life of an African Shaman.* New York: Tarcher/Putnam Book, 1994.

Stewart, James B. "The Field and Function of Black Studies." Paper prepared for the William Trotter Institute for the Study of Black Culture at the University of Massachusetts, July 1987.

Stewart, James B., "Reaching For Higher Ground: Black/Africana Studies." *The Afrocentric Scholar* 1 (1) (1992): 1-63.

Stewart, James B., and Cheatham, Harold E., eds. *Black Families: Interdisciplinary Perspectives.* New Brunswick, N.J. and London, U.K.: Transaction Publishers, 1990.

Stewart, James T. "The Development of the Black Revolutionary Artist." In *Black Fire: An Anthology of Afro-American Writing,* pp. 3-10. Edited by LeRoi Jonesand Larry Neal. New York: William Morrow, 1968.

Stewart, Maria W. *Maria W. Stewart, America's First Black Woman Political Writer (Essays and Speeches).* Edited and Introduced by Marilyn Richardson. Bloomington and Indianapolis: Indiana University Press, 1987.

Strenski, Ivan. *Four Theories of Myth in the Twentieth Century: Cassirer, Eliade, Levi-Strauss and Malinowski.* Iowa City: University of Iowa Press, 1987.

Sutton, William Stanley. "The Evolution of the Black Studies Movement: With Specific Reference to the Establishment of the Black Studies Institute at The Ohio State University." Ph.D. dissertation, Ohio University, 1972.

Tarpley, Natasha, ed. *Testimony: Young African Americans on Self-Discovery and Black Identity.* Boston, Beacon Press, 1995.

Tate, Claudia, ed. *Black Women Writers at Work*. New York: Continuum Publishing, 1985.

Thomas, Greg. "The Black Studies War: Multiculturalism Versus Afrocentricity." *Village Voice*, 17 January 1995, pp. 23-24, 26-29.

Thorpe, Earl Endris. *Negro Historians in the United States*. Baton Rouge, La.: Fraternal Press, March 1958.

Tierny, John; Wright, Linda; and Springen, Karen. "The Search for Adam and Eve: Scientists Explore a Controversial New Theory About Man's Origins." *Newsweek*, 11 January 1988.

Toch, Thomas. "The Happening Department: Bush's Stellar Education Team." *U.S. News & World Report*, 22 April 1991, p. 22.

The Toronto Arts Group for Human Rights, eds. *The Writer and Human Rights*. Toronto: Lester and Orphen Dennys Publishers, 1983.

Toynbee, Arnold. *Experiences*. London: Oxford University Press, 1969.

Turke, Garrett Laughton. "Traditional African Psychological Styles in Middle Income African-Americans: An Africentric View of the Normal Black Personality as Measured by Rorschach Indices." Ph.D. dissertation, University of Detroit, 1983.

Turnbull, Colin M. *The Forest People: A Study of the Pygmies of the Congo*. New York: Touchstone, 1962.

Turner, Henry McNeal. *Respect Black: The Writings and Speeches of Henry McNeal Turner*. Edited by Edwin S. Redkey. New York: Arno Press, 1971.

Van Cubie, Michael. "The Missing Link in the Afrocentric Model: Employment and the Role of the Black Father." Ph.D. dissertation, The Wright Institute, 1988.

Van Sertima, Ivan. *They Came Before Columbus*. New York: Random House, 1976.

Van Sertima, Ivan, ed. *Black Women in Antiquity*. New Brunswick, N.J.: Journal of African Civilizations, 1984, 1988.

_____. *Egypt: Child of Africa*. New Brunswick, N.J. and London: Transaction Publishers, 1995.

_____. *Nile Valley Civilizations Proceedings of the Nile Valley Conference, Atlanta [Ga.],September 26-30, 1984)*. New Brunswick, N.J.: Transaction Books, Journal of African Civilizations, November 1986.

Vargus, Ione Dugger. "Revival of the Afro-American Society Movement." Ph.D. dissertation, Brandeis University, Florence Heller Graduate School, 1971.

Walker, Alice. *In Search of Our Mothers' Gardens*. San Diego: Harcourt Brace Jovanovich, 1983.

Walker, Margaret. *How I Wrote Jubilee and Other Essays on Life and Literature*. Edited by Maryemma Graham. New York: Feminist Press at the City University of New York, 1990.

——————. *Jubilee*. New York: Bantam Books, 1966, 1967.

Welsh-Asante, Kariamu. "Philosophy and Dance in Africa: The Views of Cabral and Fanon." *Journal of Black Studies*. Vol. 21, No. 2 (December 1990): 224-233.

Welsh-Asante, Kariamu, ed. *The African Aesthetic: Keeper of the Traditions*. Westport, Conn.: Greenwood Press, 1993.

Welsh-Asante, Kariamu, and Asante, Molefi, eds. *African Culture: The Rhythms of Unity*. Westport, Conn.: Greenwood Press, 1985.

Welsing, Frances Cress. *The Isis (Yssis) Papers: The Keys to the Colors*. Chicago: Third World Press, 1991.

West, Cornell. *Prophesy Deliverance! (An Afro-American Revolutionary Christianity)*. Philadelphia: Westminster Press, 1982.

——————. *Prophetic Fragments*. Grand Rapids and Trenton: Wm. B. Eerdmans Publishing and Africa World Press, 1988.

White, J.E. Manchip. *Ancient Egypt: Its Culture and History*. New York: Dover Publications, 1970.

Williams, Bruce. "Latest Research on Nubia: A Letter to the Editor." In *Nile Valley Civilizations (Proceedings of the Nile Valley Conference, Atlanta [Ga.], September 26-30, 1994*. New Brunswick, N.J.: Transaction Books, Journal of African Civilizations, Ltd., Inc., November 986.

——————. "The Lost Pharaohs of Nubia." In *Nile* Valley Civilizations (*Proceedings of the Nile Valley Conference, Atlanta [Ga.], September 26-30, 1984*. Edited by Ivan Van Sertima. New Brunswick, N.J.: Transaction Books, Journal of African Civilizations, November 1986.

Williams, Chancellor. *The Destruction of Black Civilization (Great Issues of a Race from 4500 B.C. to 2000 A.D.)*. Chicago: Third World Press, 1987.

Williams, Lorraine A., ed. *Africa and the Afro-American Experience: Eight Essays*. Washington, DC: Howard University Press, 1981.

Williamson, Dorothy Kaye. "Rhetorical Analysis of Selected Modern Black American Spokespersons on the Women's Liberation Movement." Ph.D. dissertation, The Ohio State University, 1980.

Wilmore, Gayraud. *Black Religion and Black Radicalism: An Interpretation of the Religious History of Afro-American People*. 2nd ed. Maryknoll, N.Y.: Orbis Books, 1984.

Wilmore, Gayraud, and Cone, James H., eds. *Black Theology: A Documentary History, 1966-1979.* Maryknoll, N.Y.: Orbis Books, 1990.

Wilson, Amos N. *The Developmental Psychology of the Black Child.* New York: Africana Research Publications, 1978.

Wimberly, Anne Streaty, ed. *Honoring African American Elders: A Ministry in the Soul Community.* San Fransisco: Jossey-Bass Publishers, 1997.

Windsor, Rudolph R. *From Babylon to Timbuktu: A History of the Ancient Black Races Including the Hebrews.* Smithtown, N.Y.: Exposition Press, 1983.

Wolfenstein, Eugene Victor. *The Victims of Democracy: Malcolm X and the Black Revolution.* Berkeley and Los Angeles: University of California Press, 1981.

Wolf-Wasserman, Miriam, and Hutchinson, Linda. *Teaching Human Dignity: Social Change Lessons for Everyteacher.*Minneapolis: Education Exploration Center, 1978.

Wood, Joe, ed. *Malcolm X: In Our Own Image.* New York: Anchor Books, 1994.

Woodson. Carter G. *The African Background Outlined; or, Handbook for the Study of the Negro.* New York: Negro Universities Press, 1968.

_____. *African Heroes and Heroines.* 3rd ed. Washington, D.C.: Associated Publishers, 1969.

_____. *African Myths, Together with Proverbs A Supplemental Reader Composed of Folk Tales from Various Parts of Africa, Adapted to the Use of Children in the Public Schools).* Washington, D.C.: Associated Publishers, 1945.

_____. *The History of the Negro Church.* Washington, D.C.: Associated Publishers, 1945.

_____. *The Journal of Negro History.* New York: United Publishing, January 1916-1995.

_____. *The Miseducation of the Negro.* Washington, D.C.: Associated Publishers, 1933; reprinted., New York: AMS Press, 1977.

_____. *The Negro in Our History.* 4th ed. Washington, D.C.: Associated Publishers, 1927.

_____. *Negro Makers of History.* Washington, D.C.: Associated Publishers, 1928.

_____. *Negro Orators and Their Orations.* Washington, D.C.: Associated Publishers, 1925.

_____. *The Story of the Negro Re-Told.* 2nd. ed. Washington, D.C.: Associated Publishers, 1935.

Wright, Richard. *American Hunger*. New York: Perrenial Library and Harper and Row, 1997.

_____. *Black Boy*. New York: Perennial Library and Harper and Row, 1989.

_____. *Eight Men*. New York: Avon Books, 1961.

_____. *Haiku: This Other World*. New York: Arcade Publishing, 1998.

_____. *Native Son*. New York: Perrenial Classics, 1966.

_____. *12 Million Black Voices*. New York: Thunder's Mouth Press, 1941.

X, Malcolm. *Malcolm X: By Any Means Necessary (Speeches, Interviews, and a Letter by Malcolm X*. Edited by George Breitman. New York: Pathfinder Press, 1989.

_____. *Malcolm X: The Last Speeches*. Edited by Bruce Perry. New York: Pathfinder Press, 1989.

_____. *Malcolm X: Make It Plain*. Text by William Strickland, Oral Histories Selected and Edited by Cheryll Y. Greene. New York: Viking Penguin, 1994.

_____. *Malcolm X on Afro-American History*. 2nd ed. New York: Pathfinder Press, 1992.

_____. *Malcolm X Speaks (Selected Speeches and Statements)*. Edited and with Prefatory Notes by George Breitman. New York: Grove Press, 1966.

_____. *Malcolm X: The Man and His Times*. Edited by John Henrik Clarke; Assisted by A. Peter Bailey and Earl Grant. Trenton, N.J.: Africa World Press, 1990.

X, Malcolm, with the assistance of Haley, Alex. *The Autobiography of Malcolm X*. New York: Grove Press, 1966.

Young, Josiah U., III. *Black and African Theologies: Siblings or Distant Cousins?* Maryknoll, N.Y.: Orbis Books, 1986.

_____. *A Pan-African Theology: Providence and the Legacies of the Ancestors*. Trenton, N.J.: Africa World Press, 1992.

Index

Harmosis 23, 26, 27, 81, 89,
98-100, 127, 133, 155
Harmosis as Mode 89, 98,
100, 133, 155
Harris, Ethel Patricia 7, 13
Harris, Norman 128
Heru, Nzingha Ratibisha 75, 88
Hilliard, Asa G. 10, 47, 79,
125, 127, 129
Hirsch, E. D. 1, 10
Hitler 135
Horn of Africa 171
Houston, Drusilla Dunjee 17,
92, 123, 171
Hr M Akht 145
Huggins, Nathan I. 10
Hughes, Langston 29-30
Human Rights ix, 151

I

Incipient ix, x, xi, 2, 4, 12,
15-16, 33, 100, 116, 133-4,
141-142, 154, 162, 168
India 145
Indonesia 92
Institute of Positive Education
131
Intellectual history 1, 2, 4, 5,
15, 89, 167, 170
Irele, F. Abiola 162
Israel 129

J

Jackson, Frozene 171
Jackson, Conteen 171
Jackson, Jesse 31
Jackson, John G. 92, 123, 125
Jackson, Michael 48
Jacobs 8, 14
Jamaica 148
James, George G. M. 32, 47, 130
James, William 61

Jehuty 33
Jenifer, Franklyn G. 10
Jerusalem 152
Jesus 152
Johns, Vernon Rev. 171
Johnson, James Wesley 87
Johnson, Julie 10
Jones, Laurence C. 102
Jones, LeRoi 127

K

Kamalu, Chukwunyere 130
Kambon, Kobi K. K. 13, 79
Karenga, Maulana ix, x, xi, 10,
12, 17, 25, 28-29, 33-46,
75-76, 82-84, 87-89, 102,
123, 125, 127, 129-130,
167-168
Kawaida 36, 42, 43, 44, 45,
82, 88
Keats 61
Kemet x, 4, 15, 18, 24, 31-
34, 38, 76-78, 82-85, 87-
88, 92, 123, 129, 130
Kenya 147
Keto, C.T. 79
King 102
King, Martin Luther 29, 38,
71, 171-172
Kunjufu, Jawanza 10

L

Latin America 130, 147
Leakey, Richard 92, 124
Lewis, Robert Benjamin 47, 76
Leo, John 11, 90, 123
Leonard, Carolyn M. 87
Libya 171
Lincoln, C. Eric 164
Liston, Sonny 152
Little, William A. 87

V

Van Sertima, Ivan 124, 125
Vargus, Ione Dugger 12
Vesey, Denmark 102

W

Waa, Yaa Asante 171
Walker, Alice 8
Walker, David 29, 32, 95, 171
Walters, Ronald 9
Washington , Booker T. 29
Washington, D.C. 9, 13, 110, 131
Wells, Ida B. 32, 171
Welsh-Asante, Kariamu ix, x, xi, 12, 17,22- 23, 28, 47, 50-63, 84-85, 89, 113-122, 125, 127-129, 131-132, 167-168
Welsing 102
West Indies 136
Western Asia 92
western Asians 157, 158
White, J.E. Manchip 130
Wholistic Afrocentric Action as Goal 89, 100-101, 133, 144, 150-151, 155

Williams, Bruce 92, 124
Williams, Chancellor 43, 79, 124, 166
Williams, Larry 125
Williams, Sylvester 171
Williamson, Dorothy K. 7
Wilson, Julius 40
Windsor, Rudolph R. 123
Wolfenstein, Eugene Victor 165
Wood, Joe 165
Woodson, Carter G. 9, 100, 127, 145, 171
Wright, Linda 92, 124
Wright, Richard 172

X

X, Malcolm ix, x, xi, 16, 18, 29, 60, 71, 85, 102, 116, 129, 131, 133, 143-155, 163-165, 167-172

Y

Yoruba 7, 13, 143

Z

Zimbabwe 61, 95, 102
Zulu 96